Soldiering

Sergeant Rice C. Bull
123rd New York Volunteer Infantry

(Courtesy of Miss Helen L. Bull)

Soldiering

The Civil War Diary of
Rice C. Bull,
123rd New York Volunteer Infantry

Edited by K. Jack Bauer

PRESIDIO PRESS
SAN RAFAEL · CALIFORNIA

CONTENTS

MAPS

EDITOR'S PREFACE

The Civil War holds a special attraction for Americans, even in the years of national bicentennial, for it is both a pivotal point in the history of the nation and the only major war fought wholly within the borders of the United States. The participants, with very rare exceptions, were Americans and the sites are usually accessible to tourists. Perhaps more important, the participants, northern or southern, sprang from a cultural background immediately intelligible to most mid-twentieth-century Americans.

Unlike the American Revolution, whose rhetoric often appears stilted and whose philosophies seem archaic, the Civil War is comprehensible to most students. This should not surprise. The American Civil War was the first major conflict of the industrial era; the first to see extensive use of railroads, telegraphic communications, fast-firing weapons, armored warships, and machine-made uniforms, boots, and horseshoes. The fratricidal clash of 1861-65 witnessed the shift from the war of movement of Napoleon and Winfield Scott to the war of attrition of Grant, Sherman, and the western front. Perhaps even more important, the struggle

was waged by men and women who thought much like pres-
ent-day Americans and who spoke and wrote a language
with which we are still comfortable.

Rice C. Bull's account of his service during the Civil War
has several distinctions. It is one of the few surviving enlisted
men's accounts which is both coherent and readable. Not
only does Bull write well but he has a farmer's eye for land-
form and weather and an uncommon sensitivity for the feelings of his companions. Throughout, however, he maintains
a sufficient detachment to view his experiences with a balance uncommon in first-hand accounts. In part, Bull's detachment results from the manner in which the account was
written. During the war Bull kept a diary and wrote letters
home, which became the basis of a memoir he wrote in 1913,
following his retirement from business. Writing fifty years
after the events he detailed allowed him to soften his views
and lengthen his perspective.

Rice Bull was born June 9, 1842, on a farm near Hartford
in the grain-growing area of northeastern New York's Washington County. His family had emigrated from Connecticut
and he harbored vain hopes of returning there to enter Yale
College. Although, like most farm boys, he received only a
common school education, Bull grew into an intelligent and
articulate youth. Unlike many, if not most, of the other New
York State farm youth he maintained a keen interest in the
events of the day and in the progress of the war. He had
apparently thought of enlisting in 1861, when President
Abraham Lincoln issued his first calls for men to put down
the Southern insurrection. The opportunity to enlist finally
came late in the spring of 1862 when a regiment was recruited in Washington County. Why did he volunteer? His answer was:

> Certainly a meager thirteen dollars a month was no induce-
> ment, neither could it have been ambitious desire for promo-
> tion or honor, for a man in the ranks had small chance of
> either. Surely it was no worldly consideration; for those who

stayed home had all the opportunities for success. I believe
with most of us it was our sense of duty; that we felt that if our
country was to endure as a way of life as planned by our
fathers, it rested with us children to finish the work they had
begun.

Bull's account catches the subtle change of a green recruit
into a seasoned veteran as well as sharp-etched glimpses of
the pleasures and horrors of service. Bull was not a romantic;
like Stephen Crane and Ambrose Bierce he described war as
it was: mud, blood, and blunder as well as humor, heroism,
and compassion. Nor does he attempt to describe events or
explain decisions to which he was not a party. So, the account
remains an enlisted man's view, but an intelligent and interested view from the ranks.

After the Civil War, Bull returned home and in 1866 made
his way forty miles south to the booming industrial center of
Troy, New York. He joined the Mutual National Bank, ulti-
mately becoming its cashier. He was also one of the founders
and secretary-treasurer of the Troy and New England Railroad. He was a respected civic leader and for thirty years
served as treasurer of the Ninth Presbyterian Church. He
died on May 19, 1930, a scant three weeks before his eighty-
eighth birthday.

The diaries, letters, and the longhand copy of the memoirs
passed into the hands of Bull's children. In 1948 his son
George had the memoirs transcribed. This edition of the
memoirs was prepared from one of the typescript copies
which was retained by Miss Helen L. Bull, Sergeant Bull's
surviving child. The editor has tried as far as possible to keep
from intruding into the account. He has limited himself to
correcting lapses in grammar, eliminating a scattering of
redundant or unimportant passages, and occasionally at-
tempting to make Bull's meaning clearer. In a few instances,
a paragraph or two have been added to summarize matters
not appearing in the text. These are set in italics.

The student who wishes to consult the original manuscript

copy will find it on deposit at the Rensselaer County Historical Society in Troy.

I cannot close without a word of appreciation to Miss Helen Bull whose ambition has been to see her father's work in print; to Mr. George B. Leckonby, who first brought the account to my attention; and to Mrs. Frederick R. Walsh and Miss Christina Shaver of the Rensselaer County Historical Society for their assistance far beyond the call of duty.

K. Jack Bauer

Haynersville, N.Y.
June 30, 1976

Rice C. Bull
banker, railroader, civic leader

(Courtesy of Miss Helen L. Bull)

Soldiering

CHAPTER ONE

Volunteer Soldiering

September 4th-October 4th, 1862

Before beginning the story of my experience as a Union Soldier during the Civil War, it might be well to tell of the conditions in our part of the country previous to my enlistment, as a boy of nineteen noted them in the spring of 1862. The war had started a year before and the period had been one of excitement and anxious waiting. We who lived on farms had no daily papers, only the weekly editions, so everyone who passed our house was questioned as to war news. At times we heard the distant sound of cannon at Whitehall or Glens Falls but the news, when details came, told either of a drawn battle or a defeat. Victories were few. We had met with so many military reverses that many feared that it would be impossible to reunite the country by force of arms. Thousands of boys like me felt a sense of duty to aid the Union cause for service in the Army.

The 500,000 man army recruited under President Lincoln's calls for volunteers in 1861 proved insufficient to stem the course of Southern independence. When the failure of Major General George B. McClellan's Peninsular Campaign became clear during later June 1862, Lincoln prepared a new request for volunteers. It took the form of a call for 300,000 men to serve for three years. The New York quota was 59,705 men, which was apportioned among the individual counties of the state. One regiment, later designated the 123rd New York State Volunteer Regiment, was allotted to Washington County. It was the only regiment raised solely from that county during the war.

One of our most prominent citizens, Archibald L. McDougall of Salem, was commissioned Colonel.[1] During July enlistment stations were opened in every town. I had often thought of enlisting, believing it to be my duty, but until then no opportunity had come for me to do so. Before this time, most of the recruiting had been from the large towns far from the country districts. Now a regiment was to be raised in our own county, and it would consist mostly of farmers and farm boys.

A neighbor and school friend, Phineas Spencer,[2] and I had agreed that we would go together and stand by one another. Spencer took action first by going to Fort Ann,[3] where he enlisted; after that he came to me to go with him, as we had planned. My parents were at first loath to give their consent, but they realized that it was a call to duty that could not be disregarded. After grave and prayerful consideration,

[1]   Archibald L. McDougall (1817-1864) came from Salem, N.Y. Commissioned Colonel of the 123rd New York on August 22, 1862, he served until June 23, 1864 when he died of wounds received May 25 in the Battle of Dallas, Ga.
[2]   Phineas M. Spencer enlisted from Fort Ann as a private in Company D. He was discharged for disability in 1863.
[3]   Fort Ann was a trading and manufacturing village in the farming country of northeastern New York. It was a station on the railroad from Troy to Whitehall and a waypoint on the Champlain Canal. It is about forty miles north of Troy, N.Y., and forty-five miles southwest of Rutland, Vt.

they tearfully consented to my going. I know now how hard it must have been for them to give their approval.

On August 13th, 1862 I worked with my father in the oat field until noon gathering the grain; that afternoon I went to Fort Ann and signed the papers that bound me to army service for three years, unless sooner discharged. I became a member of Company D, 123rd Regiment, New York Volunteer Infantry. That night I stopped at the Battle Hill Hotel in Fort Ann. The next morning, in company with several others who were to be my comrades, I took wagon for Salem where the Regiment was being organized and would camp until it was ordered to some place for preliminary training. We arrived in Salem on the afternoon of the 14th and found a large number of men already there. They were camped in the little valley near the railroad shops. Large Sibley tents[4] had been erected, each with a capacity of from twelve to fifteen men. The ground under the tents was covered with straw, which furnished bedding. Nothing had yet been issued in the way of military equipment, no uniforms, blankets, guns or knapsacks. Blankets had been secured from some source to make beds but not much was needed in the way of covering as it was hot August weather. I was given space in a tent where Spencer and I were together.

When we reached camp we found that 80 men had reported but that we were still short 20 men for a full company. Some of these had already enlisted but not reported. Our Company was to be from the three townships of Fort Ann, Dresden, and Putman. Our officers were: Captain John Barron, 1st Lieutenant Alexander Anderson, 2nd Lieutenant Edward Quinn.[5] The non-commissioned officers had not been appointed.

---

[4] Large, conical, easily erected tents which took their name from their inventor, Major Henry H. Sibley.

[5] John Barron (1828-1863?) came from Ft. Ann and served as Captain of Company D until dismissed from service February 22, 1863 for being absent without leave. Alexander Anderson of Putnam, N.Y., the First Lieutenant of the company

After we had been in camp three days Captain Barron sent me back to Fort Ann to enlist more men. This I did and 14 men joined. I was at this work for about a week and had an opportunity to go home, make a visit, and again say goodby. When I returned to Salem, our Company was full and numbered 104 officers and men. The non-commissioned officers were then elected by the men and their action approved by the Colonel. I was elected a Corporal.

I will not go into much detail of our stay in Salem. There were some attempts made at drilling but there was no parade ground as the field on which we were camped was small and nearly covered with tents. Every day the friends of the new soldiers kept coming from all parts of the county. Since they were in great numbers and swarmed over the camp, military order or discipline was next to impossible. By September 1st recruiting was finished and all the companies had full numbers. Physical examination was then made and nearly all passed and were accepted. Then we received our uniforms and most of our equipment which included old-fashioned Enfield rifles. They were ungainly pieces having the look of old age. We carried these guns for some weeks but before going into active service they were exchanged for Springfield muskets, a much better weapon. With our other equipment we got our knapsacks in which we were supposed to place all our baggage and belongings. One of the puzzles that confronted us was how in that limited space we could carry all the good things our friends, with the kindest intentions, had given us. A list of the articles sent me would have made quite an inventory, and could I have packed them, it would have required a Samson to carry them. It was impossible to get half of them in my knapsack, so after sorting and discarding for a long time I finally sent home a larger bundle than I took with me. Even then my knapsack bulged on every side

succeeded Barron as Captain. Edward P. Quinn from Ft. Ann, the Second Lieutenant replaced Anderson as First Lieutenant upon the latter's promotion. Quinn was severely wounded at Culp's Farm, Ga., June 22, 1864.

and to an old soldier would have been an object of derision. Later experience taught us how little was necessary.

On September 4th we were mustered into the service of the United States. Orders came at once for us to leave by train September 5th. The news of our sudden departure was known in every part of the county that night and in the morning thousands of the people were in Salem. I am sure the village never before or since had so great a throng of visitors. The soldiers' relations, neighbors and friends were there to give the boys their farewell word, their goodby, their well wishes and to see them off on their long journey. With many it was to be the last farewell. It was not a happy day, it was a day of sadness. Finally, late in the afternoon, we shouldered our knapsacks and marched to the train, the great crowd following us. Then there was the last handshake and kiss. The train slowly started. The people lining the track were so wrought with emotions that they found no voice to cheer. They silently waved their hands while we could see their faces filled with tears.

When we moved away from the station and were out of sight of our people, a feeling of relief came for most of us were only boys and the love of home and friends was strong. We were leaving for the first time, not to go to some place to engage in a peaceful pursuit that we thought might better our lives, but going to a service of danger and privation and possibly death. Under any circumstances leaving home was a serious matter but on this day the presence of our families and friends, although they did try to hide their feelings, was very trying and we were glad when the parting was over. The boys were themselves again, and jokes and songs could be heard in every part of the train.

We were to go to New York City without change, so cooked rations were issued for one day, but as our haversacks were filled with good food our own friends had brought us from home few drew these rations. We were not in love with the meals the contractor had furnished us in Salem. It was a slow train and it was well on in the afternoon of the 6th when we

reached New York. It had taken us nearly twenty-four hours
to cover the 200 miles from Salem, but in those days that was
fast time. I am not sure just where we landed in the city, but
think it was at the site of the present 42nd Street Station.[6] We
then marched to Broadway and from there to the City Hall
Park near which there had been constructed barracks where
we were housed for the night. We were not a striking sight as
we marched down Broadway for we were undrilled and
hardly knew how to keep step, but there was a great crowd
on the sidewalks who occasionally gave us a cheer. We were
fed at the barracks but were not enthusiastic about the meals.
Some months later we would have considered them banquets.

On the morning of the 7th, after a good night's rest, we
had an early breakfast and resumed our journey, marching
down to the Battery where we took a steamer[7] for South
Amboy. It was a pleasant trip on the boat and then by rail to
Philadelphia where we arrived at one o'clock in the afternoon. We were marched to the Philadelphia Soldiers Restaurant (The Cooper Shop)[8] where so many of our regiments
passing through the city were fed. Then we marched to the
Baltimore Depot[9] where we waited some time. After a while
the train was made up and we were steaming away as we gave
"three cheers and a tiger" to the "City of Brotherly Love",
certainly not misnamed. It had been all that to us. In the
early afternoon we passed through Wilmington, a smoky but
thriving city, and later reached Havre de Grace. There we
crossed the Susquehanna River in a rather novel manner as
there was no bridge. Our train was run on to a very large
steamboat[10] fitted with tracks for cars and then we were
ferried over the river, which I would judge was a mile wide.
From that point we moved rather slowly and it was night

[6]   Grand Central Station.
[7]   The 741-ton side-wheeler *Transport*.
[8]   The Cooper Shop Volunteer Refreshment Saloon, Oswego Street below Washington.
[9]   Washington and Broad Streets.
[10]   The 238-foot iron-hulled, side-wheel train ferry *Maryland*.

when we reached Baltimore. Our train was stopped in the northern side of the city and to reach the Washington Depot[11] we had to march the whole length of the town. It was hot and close and I do not think I ever suffered so much from heat and thirst. There did not seem to be a great deal of enthusiasm displayed by the citizens at seeing us pass through the streets, still, many American flags were displayed and no insults were offered.

In several places women, generally Negroes, came out with pails of water. The water was very acceptable to me but some of the boys would not touch it fearing it might be poisoned. It was said that a regiment the day before had several men poisoned that way. How much truth there may have been in this I do not know, but do not doubt there are secessionists in the city who would do as barbarous a thing. As for myself I was so tired and thirsty I did not then consider the results and drank freely without any bad effects. However, while waiting at the Washington Depot one of our Company was taken sick and had to be left in Baltimore.

Late in the evening we left Baltimore but not now in passenger cars. We were packed closely in cattle cars and a hot, sweaty, hungry lot of men we were. The only food we had was what many had left over in their haversacks brought from Salem. It was stale enough but it was what we had to eat or nothing. We were stowed away, as mercilessly as though we were dumb brutes, but our patriotic ardor was running high and not many complaints were heard. All seemed willing to suffer in the good cause. I managed by a lot of strategy to get in a horizontal position on the floor of the car and was weary enough to sleep well until morning. I found on waking up we were in Annapolis Junction. We had gone only eighteen miles during the night. There were all sorts of absurd rumors about the conductor of our train. He was said to be a secessionist; how in the middle of the night he had stopped the train intending to deliver us into the hands of some

11 Camden Station, Camden and Eutaw Streets.

guerrilla band which failed to come through in time. The story was generally believed and some of the boys thought the conductor ought to be hanged; but nothing serious happened to him.

At the junction we first saw actual soldiering, a brigade of old soldiers was stationed there guarding the railroad. Their little white tents were arranged neatly in streets and made a fine appearance. As we were there early in the morning before any drilling could be done, the men were idle. Crowds of them gathered close around our cars to see the new recruits and to recount their hairbreadth escapes in battle. They encouraged us by saying there were some fine experiences coming to us later. A few maliciously wanted to know if we were $140 men.[12] This, however, was taken in good part by us and all personalities were laughed off. From Annapolis Junction until we reached Washington we saw camps scattered along the railroad, the men of whom came out to cheer us as we passed by. Near Washington, we found that a great camp of white tents seemed to surround the city.

About noon our train was stopped outside the suburbs about a mile from the depot. When we left the train we were at once marched to the Soldiers Home[13] for dinner. On reaching it dinner was not yet ready and the whole Regiment was driven into and locked in an attached yard to wait until the dinner was ready. The yard was hardly large enough to hold the men and was the most filthy place I was ever in. It was roughly floored and actually crawling with vermin and rats which scampered in all directions. We were in this hole nearly an hour before "dinner" was ready and then were marched to the dining hall and seated on rough board seats

---

[12]   Term of contempt for men who joined in order to secure Federal and state enlistment bounties.

[13]   Bull is in error about the name of the building. What he describes is either of two large structures called the Soldiers' Rest and the Soldiers' Retreat which served as feeding and lodging stations for transient troops. The Soldiers' Home was a pleasant, airy establishment on modern 7th Street, NW much enjoyed by President Lincoln as a summer retreat.

and at rough board tables, set with tin and iron plates and cups. We were hungry enough to eat almost anything but this dinner was the limit. We had bread, no butter, salt pork, very salty, and a mixture called coffee which would defy anyone to tell by its taste whether it was tea or coffee. It must have been a mixture of both. Well, we ate because we were faint and had to but I can tell you it was a tough meal. It was a notorious fact I found that the Soldiers Home in Washington was the worst conducted institution of its kind in the whole country. As Washington was the headquarters of the Army and everything could be had in plenty, it would seem as though the first reception of our country's defenders should have been at least liberal. Surely it should not be indecent. In fact it was not liberal or even decent at this feeding shed, which has become a hiss and byword with every soldier, and has been given the name of the "Soldiers Prison." After the dinner we were marched from our jail to the street near the Capitol and there stood in line for some time waiting orders. From that place we could see what was going on. Everyone seemed busy, the streets were filled with people. Soldiers, many with their crutches and canes, were around the Capitol which was being used as a hospital. Hundreds of wagons were going in every direction. The Capitol looked unfinished, the dome was about one-half constructed, the lower portions of the rotunda being surrounded by an immense staging. No work was now being done on the building as it was used for a hospital.

After resting for some time, we proceeded in an easterly direction going up a hill at the south of the Capitol, then east to a large open space that extended to the bay that set back from the Potomac River. I think they called it East Branch. On this area,[14] a large number of troops were camped; infantry, cavalry and artillery. They were mostly new organizations that would remain there only a short time and then be assigned to a brigade for active service or sent to some

[14]   Camp Chase.

other field for training. There was ample space here for
drilling large bodies of men, so the ground was hard and
smooth from the constant tramp of soldiers. We were directed to a place near the east end of the plain, not far from the
East Branch. As soon as our company streets were laid out by
our officers each man was issued a tent cloth, and with these
strips of cloth were directed to construct shelter tents; "dog
tents" was the name given them.

Usually three men would occupy a tent as the three cloths
could be so arranged as to enclose, when finished, the three
sides of a tent, in which they could lie. These tents were to be
used chiefly for sleeping, as one could barely sit erect at the
highest place in the center. They were far from comfortable
living quarters. Yet they were the only kind of shelter we
would have in the field during our term of service. For three
years this thin cloth tent would be our cover from wind,
storm and cold. The tents were kept erect by driving a stake
at each end, the stakes extending about three feet above the
ground, and about six feet apart. They were connected at the
top by a light pole over which was placed two of the tent
cloths, buttoned together and stretched as much as possible
at the sides. The third cloth covered the back of the tent. The
head of our bed was at the back where we used our knapsacks for pillows. For our beds we would first spread our
rubber blankets, on top of which we placed one woolen
blanket, for covering we used the two other blankets. In fair
weather we stacked our guns in the street but when it was
stormy took them into the tent to keep them dry. When the
weather was dry and warm our tents were comfortable sleeping quarters but in wet, cold times they were anything but
satisfactory. They would shed rain when it came gently but if
the storm was heavy the rain would come through, at first
like damp mist and when the cloth was well soaked would
run through in big drops like a leaking roof. In rainy weather
we had either to stand out and take it full force or lie wet in
our tents. As soldiers we had to get used to anything, discomfort, food, clothing and shelter, and we soon became used to

the little tents and were thankful to have them. Experience taught us to always trench around our tents if we were to use them for any length of time, so we would not be flooded out in case of a storm.

At this Capitol Hill Camp we had our first experience in camp engineering. The ground was level and our streets nicely arranged. Our tent cloths were new, so the tents looked white and attractive. In our ignorance we did not ditch around our tents so were washed out of house and home within forty-eight hours by a hard thunder shower. This taught us early never again to neglect to drain our camp.

We remained in this place just one week. Here we were first issued rations in bulk for the Company and arrangements were made for company cooking and distribution of food to the men. First we had to have dishes and company cooking utensils. Each of us had a tin cup and spoon, and knife and fork. The company cooks were issued the necessary, pots, kettles, etc. No meal was served us on the day we arrived in Washington except our "banquet" at the sheds, and we did not want a second. At ten in the morning of the 9th, the cooks, who had been appointed, announced that our meal was ready. All fell-in with plate and cup in hand. We received a spoonful of boiled rice, a square chunk of salt pork, one slice of hardtack,[15] and in our cups a dark fluid that was called coffee. The rice was badly burned and unedible; the hardtack, the first we had ever seen, was of good quality but we had not yet learned to appreciate its value. It seemed like biting into a wood shingle and had not much taste. The pork was very salty and the coffee had not been made by an expert. There was not much enthusiasm over the meal but we were nearly starved so nibbled at the hardtack,

---

[15] Hardtack is a hard biscuit made without salt. Since it did not spoil or shatter it could be easily carried by soldiers on the march and made edible by immersion in water, coffee, or any similar liquid. Soldiers with strong teeth were known to gnaw on a piece much in the manner of fishermen eating sun dried codfish and with about as much pleasure.

ate a little of the salt pork and drank the coffee. Our hunger was not satisfied and many of us would have been happy to drop into Mother's pantry to eat the left-overs from supper.

One of the greatest and most trying hardships of our early soldiering came from army food which to us was at first almost unbearable. Most of us who came from homes where food was plenty and of the best quality found it hard to get used to army rations. It seemed at first we would starve. The hardtack was absolutely tasteless and so hard and tough one could hardly chew it. To us then it was almost unbelievable that one could eat enough of it to sustain life. We soon learned that it was real food and, if not tasty, it was very nutritious. Later it came to be our main dependence when we were in active service in the field.

At the Capitol Hill Camp we had a good opportunity to see other regiments as they maneuvered and to get points from them. Ours was chiefly a company drill but during the afternoon Lieutenant Colonel Franklin Norton[16] would give us a lively regimental drill for an hour or so. While in this camp I visited the city two or three times, going through some of the public buildings. At that time Washington was a dirty city with its streets badly cut up by army wagons, which could be numbered by the thousands, going in every direction. The city was filled with sick and wounded soldiers from the Army of the Potomac. I saw an army wagon coming from the basement of the Capitol and was told that the basement was used as a bakery to supply bread for the hospitals.

To the right of our camp was located a battery of light artillery. Their drill was quite exciting. There was plenty of room for full battery practice. To see it maneuver and change front, with the horses on a keen run, then unlimber and begin firing was fascinating.

---

[16] Franklin Norton (1834-1863) served as a captain in the 77th New York prior to his election as Lieutenant Colonel of the 123rd. He was mortally wounded at Chancellorsville, May 1, 1863 and died in Washington eleven days later.

On the morning of September 16th we were ordered to
pack up, strike our tents, and be ready to move at once.
Before noon we fell in and headed for the city. We marched
by the Capitol, went down Pennsylvania Avenue several
blocks, then turning south passed the Washington Monu-
ment. It was unfinished and looked like a chimney the construction of which had been abandoned. Soon we reached
the Long Bridge over which thousands of our soldiers had
crossed. Many of them would never return. It was more than
a half-mile long but we were only a short time reaching the
other side, there treading for the first time the sacred soil of
Virginia. The ground was hard dry clay, on its good behav-
ior. It gave no indication of its ability in the way of mud-
making the first time we saw it. From the bridge we went in a
southeasterly direction for two miles and halted near Fort
Albany,[17] one of the forts erected west of the Potomac for
the defense of Washington. The place selected for our camp
was on rough uneven ground, well covered with bushes and
small trees. Before we could put up our tents the ground had
to be grubbed and leveled. This was a hard job and it was two
days before our camp was made in a satisfactory way. We
were surrounded with thousands of new troops, who as soon
as they reached Washington and location was provided, were
sent to Arlington Heights to be drilled, disciplined and prepared for their work as soldiers. General Silas Casey was in
command of this great training encampment.[18] He was an
old officer, a rigid disciplinarian, and was expected to give
these new regiments a thorough training so that after a few

[17]   Fort Albany stood on Arlington Heights near the present junction of Washington Boulevard and Shirley Highway.
[18]   Silas Casey (1807-1882) was a regular officer who had graduated from West
Point in 1826 and served in both the Seminole and Mexican Wars. He became a
Brigadier General of Volunteers in August 1861 and took part in the Peninsular
Campaign. After promotion to Major General in May 1862 he commanded portions of the defenses of Washington and oversaw the training of troops in the
area. His training manual Casey's Tactics was adopted in 1862. He later headed the
board which selected officers for the new Black regiments.

weeks they could be assigned to active service at the front. When this was done the new regiments would usually be sandwiched between older ones that had seen service.

Near us was a regiment from Massachusetts that had been well drilled by a competent Colonel. While we were at Arlington they received orders to go to the front. Before they started they were visited by President Lincoln, Secretary William H. Seward and the two Massachusetts Senators, Charles Sumner and Henry Wilson.[19] A great crowd of soldiers from the surrounding regiments gathered around the carriage of the visitors and after cheering called on the President for a speech. He arose from his seat and spoke for five or ten minutes. He was serious and tried to impress upon the soldiers the responsibility that rested on them, saying that it would be their efforts alone that would save the country. He looked thin and worn and one could see that he was troubled and anxious. He remained some time after he spoke so many of us had an opportunity to take his hand and have a word of greeting.[20]

While at the Arlington Camp our Captain Barron disappeared. Why, no one knew. One morning he was missing and he never returned to the Company. He did not return to Fort Ann and no one so far as I know ever heard from him. As I look back on the conditions prevailing in Washington at that time it would have been an easy thing for someone to have done away with him and his death would never have been traced. Lieutenant Anderson succeeded as Captain and

[19]   William Henry Seward (1801-1872) was a New York lawyer and political leader who was one of the leading contenders for the Republican presidential nomination in 1860. Senator Charles Sumner (1811-1874) was a noted opponent of both the Mexican War and slavery. Senator Henry Wilson (1812-1875) had served briefly as Colonel of the 22nd Massachusetts in 1861 and would be Vice President of the United States at the time of his death.

[20]   Only one Bay State unit was then stationed in the Fort Albany area. See James L. Bowen, *History of the Twenty-seventh Regiment, Mass. Volunteers, in the Civil War of 1861-1865* (Holyoke, Mass., 1884), 74-75. Apparently Lincoln's visit went unreported in the Washington newspapers and is not recorded in C. Percy Powell's *Lincoln Day By Day.*

was in command of the Company until the close of the war. He was a man of ability and character and was a brave and competent leader, loved and respected by his men.

At this camp we were kept busy drilling. There was a large parade ground not far south of us where regimental and brigade drills were held. General Casey conducted the brigade movements which were mostly in changing front. These were tiresome when we happened to be on the extreme flank and had to make the long swing to get into line. While there we had one review, in which twenty regiments took part. As they were all new regiments, with full ranks and bright new uniforms, we made a fine show. But, our marching was hardly up to standard. There was also picket duty on a line some two miles from the camp. This was not dangerous, as the enemy was no nearer than twenty miles, but it did give training. All were anxious to go on the picket line as it gave us a chance to visit some of the farmhouses located there where we could purchase a meal. This food seemed wonderfully good compared with our rations. While in Arlington I think we suffered from real hunger as much as we did at any time during our service; not that we did not have plenty of army food of excellent quality, but we had not yet reached the point where we could appreciate and eat the "stuff" as the boys called it. A certain length of time was required to bring us to the starvation point and we found it at this camp. When we had taken to the army ration we had no further trouble, for it was sufficient when we could get it. At Arlington the pie bakers were legion and it was amusing to see the boys line up to buy them as they were baked. They were so hungry they would stand in line for hours to get a pie which cost 25 cents. But it was at this camp that we passed through the childlike period of soldiering and became reconciled to our food and other conditions that we had to face in the service.

Our training period in the camp at Arlington lasted about two weeks. The weather was fine, we were becoming acclimated and the health of the men was excellent. Every day we learned something, not alone military evolutions. We were learning by experience how to care for ourselves and how better to overcome the conditions we had to contend with, which we first thought almost unbearable and unnecessary. We were now becoming reconciled to discipline and commenced to realize that we were only being fitted for the work before us.

The morning of September 29th we struck our tents, packed our knapsacks and by midday were ready to move. About three in the afternoon we started in the direction of Washington, crossing the Long Bridge at four. This was to be the last time we crossed the bridge until we crossed it to take part in the Grand Review of Sherman's Army three years later. Then there were less than half of those with us on September 29th. The others had died in action or from disease, or had left the service because of wounds or sickness.

After crossing the bridge we marched to the railroad station to take a train to some place unknown to us. That night we slept on the sidewalk as the train was not ready until seven the next morning. We left the city on flat cars, traveling slowly. There were many trains on the road and we spent much of our time on sidings. Just as night came we reached Frederick, Maryland. We stopped before entering the town and filed into the meadows where we were to spend the night. When we were dismissed we dropped to the ground where most convenient and spread our blankets for bed. It had been a hard day for us, crowded as we were on flat cars with no seats.

There had been no way to prepare meals so all we had to eat after leaving Arlington had been the hardtack that we had in our haversacks. Our company cooks made us some coffee which we drank with what was left of our hardtack. I felt as hungry as if I had not eaten for I had not yet reached the soldierly perfection when two or three pieces of hardtack and coffee could be made to satisfy my hunger. We remained two days at Frederick, where we learned that we were soon to join the Army of the Potomac in the vicinity of Harpers Ferry.

The Army was expected to advance soon. October 4th, we took train again and went to some station[21] near Harpers Ferry. From there we marched two or three miles up beautiful Pleasant Valley[22] and camped some three miles from the Ferry. We were to remain here until assigned to some Division of the Army. We would then enter active service after being in the Army only one month. Thus early and practically untrained we were at the front waiting orders for active field duty.

[21] Sandy Hook, Md., one mile east of Harpers Ferry.
[22] Across the Potomac from Harpers Ferry and east of Maryland Heights.

CHAPTER TWO

The Beginning of Real Soldiering

October 4th, 1862-April 25th, 1863

Following the battle of Antietam, September 17th, 1862, the Army of the Potomac remained inactive for quite a long time in the vicinity of Antietam Creek. It was encamped along the north bank of the Potomac River for many miles, its left as far east as Harpers Ferry. This was the location of the Army when we were waiting at our camp in Pleasant Valley for assignment to some division. In this valley many thousand troops were camped. Looking down the valley was an inspiring sight as one could see scores of camps in the near and far distance. In the morning, the bugles sounded the Reveille, followed by the countless regimental drum corps beating the morning call, we saw on those bright autumn mornings the glory and pomp of army life at its best.

In a day's time we had made a fine camp and spent an enjoyable three weeks before we moved. We were close to the east side of the mountains[1] upon which we did picket duty, for practice, as no enemy was near. These mountains were at least 1000 feet high with steep sides. A wagon road led to the top where our pickets were posted on twenty-four hour details. On the summit was the burial place of forty Confederates who had been killed in the engagement when Harpers Ferry had been captured by General Jackson[2] a few weeks before we arrived. Because the ground was hard and stony the graves had been made so shallow that many of the bodies were partly uncovered by the rain, so that hands and feet and even heads were visible. This was a gruesome sight for new soldiers. The view from the mountain top was extensive and beautiful, especially of the valleys to the south and west on both sides of the Potomac and Shenandoah Rivers that seemed walled in by mountains on every side. On bright days the view spread out for a distance of forty miles. It was wonderful. The weather was ideal and we began our first systematic drilling.

On October 10th as advance of the Army was begun, we were ordered to be ready to move, but were held in camp until the 9th Army Corps which was in our rear had passed and crossed the Potomac some miles below. This took about two days. We then marched to Harpers Ferry, where we found that the 12th Corps,[3] to which our Regiment was to be attached, was not included in the order to advance but was to remain and guard the line of the Potomac River, for a time at least, and to occupy a part of the Shenandoah Valley. This

---

[1] Maryland Heights.

[2] Thomas Jonathan Jackson (1824-1863) had graduated from West Point in 1846 and served in the Mexican War before joining the Virginia Military Institute faculty. Joining the Confederate Army he received a Brigadier General's commission in June 1861. After distinguishing himself and earning the nickname "Stonewall" at Bull Run he became Lee's most successful subordinate. He rose to Major General in October 1861 and Lieutenant General a year later after his masterful Valley Campaign. Jackson was mortally wounded at Chancellorsville, May 2, 1863.

[3] Temporarily commanded by Brigadier General Alpheus S. Williams following the death of Major General Joseph K. F. Mansfield at Antietam. Major General

was to protect the right flank of our Army as it made the advance and also to protect Maryland and Pennsylvania from raids by the Confederate cavalry who, if not prevented, might come from the Valley and in a few days cover a large territory and do great damage to the canals, railroads and other property.

As soon as the Army of the Potomac had crossed the river the larger part of the 12th Corps was transferred to the south side. When we reached Harpers Ferry we went to Bolivar Heights to a camp south of the town where we overlooked the Shenandoah Valley. The summits of the surrounding hills were rough and rocky but not as high as on the Maryland side, north and east of the Ferry. We were at this camp about two weeks and while we were there we were sent on an expedition to Ashby's, one of the gaps in the Blue Ridge. The purpose was to prevent any Rebel force from coming through the gap to strike the flank or rear of our Army when it was advancing on Fredericksburg. We remained there some days and there we had our first taste of real soldiering on the picket line in the face of the enemy. There seemed to be no large force in our front but the country was filled with guerrillas who were capturing and shooting any of our men that had wandered from their camps. Some of our own boys were chased and fired on but were not shot or captured. After ten days our Brigade[4] returned to their old camp near the Ferry.

Soon after our return we were moved to a new location where it was said we were to go into winter quarters. It was now November, the weather was cold in the mountains and our "dog tents" were uncomfortable so we welcomed any change that would give us an opportunity to build cabins.

Henry W. Slocum assumed command October 20. The division commanders were Williams, Brigadier Generals George S. Greene and John W. Geary.

[4] The regiment, along with the 124th, 125th Pennsylvania, and 20th Connecticut, formed the 2nd Brigade, 1st Division, XII Corps under Brigadier General Thomas L. Kane.

Two happenings while we were in Bolivar Heights have remained in my memory. First, my tentmate and friend Spencer was taken ill with typhoid fever. I had left him sick in the tent when we went up the Shenandoah River and he had not been on duty for several days before we started on that trip. When I returned I found that he was critically sick in the hospital located at the Ferry.

The second was the burial of the first man of our Regiment to die. He was the first of several hundred who died from disease while we were in the service. The funeral was sad and depressing. The whole Regiment, with arms reversed, followed the body to the grave where a salute was fired and the Chaplain[5] spoke feelingly about the soldier. As soon as I learned that Spencer was in the hospital I made an attempt to see him but could not. I was told, however, that he was getting on as well as could be expected and that he was free of fever.

November 15th we broke camp, crossed the river, and went into camp on the south side of Loudoun Heights, about two miles from Harpers Ferry. It was very cold and we were ordered to construct shanties for winter quarters. The Company was divided into squads of six men as the houses were built for that unit. As we had no lumber we constructed our buildings of logs, which we cut from the nearby woods. The logs were notched, fitted at the ends, and then laid up log fashion. The space between the logs was plastered with mud which in Virginia is almost as good as mortar. On the rear we built the chimney; the base was built of stone, the top of small limbs of trees laid in mud. The roof was made with our tent cloths in place of shingles. We built bunks for six, and used cracker boxes for a table. Our group purchased a small sheet iron stove which was a great luxury, but it furnished all the heat we needed in the coldest weather. Each company's quar-

---

[5]   Rev. Henry Gordon from Salem, N.Y. served as regimental chaplain from August 22, 1862 until April 18, 1863.

ters were laid out in streets, with the officers located at the head. When all was finished it made a fine appearance.

By this time I heard that my friend in the hospital was not gaining so I saw Colonel McDougall and he gave me a pass to visit the hospital at once. It was in an old abandoned cotton mill, located on the bank of the Shenandoah River. It was a large building some four or five stories high and each story contained a ward. It had only recently been organized and everything seemed in confusion. There were no wounded men there for it was for the treatment of diseases only. Many were ill with typhoid fever, dysentery and malaria fever contracted in the swamps of Chickahominy. Many had been taken sick on the march and had at first been left in barns and houses along the way. They had little care and when brought to the hospital were in an awful condition, filthy, dirty, lousy, and most of them so low as seeming past hope of recovery. When they reached the hospital they were placed in different wards, separating the most hopeless from those in less serious condition. Before placing them in wards, the men were stripped, cleaned as far as possible and given clean underwear. All were weak and many delirious. There were about two hundred cots in a ward. I found my friend had had a very severe run of typhoid fever but was much better from it. Gangrene, however, had developed in both feet. He was overjoyed to see me and insisted that I must stay and nurse him. I thought that was unnecessary as I could see that his fever was gone and reasoned he would soon be out. He was so insistent that I went to see the Surgeon and asked his opinion. I was shocked to learn that his condition was critical and that in all probability he would not recover. The Surgeon explained that his feet were mortified, that his only hope was to have good care, and that this was not available in the hospital at that time. I asked if I could be of any use in nursing him and if I would be permitted to remain in the hospital. He said he would be glad to have my help. Then I told Spencer that I would see the Colonel and if I could get a pass would come back to nurse him for a few days. When I left the

hospital I went at once to the telegraph office and wired his
brother in Cleveland, Ohio, of his condition and that he was
needed. It was late when I reached our camp, but I went
directly to the Colonel who willingly gave me the pass, and
directed me to stay at the hospital as long as I could help or
until his brother came. In the morning, I returned to Harpers Ferry, and the Surgeon gave me instructions about how
to clean the wounds in his feet, which he seemed to regard
most essential, and gave me medicines and directions as to
what he could eat. I brought all my belongings, knapsack,
gun, blanket, etc., as there was no certainty as to how long
our Regiment might remain where it was.

Spencer was glad to see me. He had been in low spirits but
said now that I was with him he would have some chance to
get well. The bunks in the ward were spaced three feet apart.
I placed my gun and equipment under the bed and my knapsack on the floor between him and his neighbor. At night I
spread my blanket on the floor with my knapsack for a pillow. Bunking this way I could reach my patient at any time to
care for his wants. At first he was nervous and uneasy and I
was up many times during the night. We were located in
what the attendants called the "death ward" in which were
placed those who were not expected to live. Nearly every
morning from five to ten who had died that night were carried out. We were almost surrounded by dying men. This
was depressing for me but worse for my patient.

I remember one night after I had gone to sleep on the
floor I was suddenly awakened by someone tramping over
me; then I heard a crash of glass. I sprang up and saw a man
with his head out of the window struggling to throw himself
out. I caught him by the shoulders and pulled him away. As I
did he collapsed and fell to the floor. By this time one of the
attendants came and we found he was one of the patients
who had typhoid fever. He was badly cut by the glass and
bled freely. He never regained consciousness and died before morning. There was little sleep for anyone that night.
The horrors soon made me decide that I had no further

desire for such service. The attendants were all green men picked up from anywhere. They knew no more than I did about a hospital.

There was one redeeming effort made in the presence and loving service of an old Quaker woman, the only woman nurse I saw in the place. She was almost constantly in our ward; night and day she was with the sick. She read to the men, wrote letters for them, advised them, and prayed for them. She was loved and respected by all as she went about doing her humane Christian work.

From the time I commenced to nurse my patient he began to mend. After I had been with him two days they amputated some of his toes and his feet began to heal and he to improve. Shortly after, his brother came and stayed until he could be moved. General Williams[6] granted him a furlough for his return home. Spencer's days of soldiering were over. We carried him on a stretcher to the railroad station, and placed him on a train going east. Then I shook his hand and watched the train as it crossed the bridge to take him home. To me it was a sad ending of our comradeship for we had been boyhood friends and had hoped to share the service together. When the train had disappeared on the Maryland side I returned to the hospital, shouldered my knapsack, took my gun and equipment, bid goodby to the Surgeon and some of the attendants and started for my Regiment. Before going the Surgeon asked me if I would like to remain and help them in their work since they were so shorthanded. Nothing could have induced me to continue in that work. This had been my first experience in the horrors of war as shown by our terrible Hospital Service. It made a deep and lasting impression not easily forgotten.

---

[6] Alpheus Starkey Williams (1810-1878) was a Michigan lawyer who had served in the Mexican War. Appointed a Brigadier General of Volunteers in May 1861 he commanded brigades and divisions in the II, XII, and XX Corps. He temporarily commanded the XII Corps following the death of General Mansfield at Antietam and the XX Corps during Sherman's March to the Sea.

On return to my Company, I reported to Captain Anderson and was assigned to duty. The Regiment had settled down to the routine of camp life. It was work and drill from morning to night. We began with guardmount, then squad and company drills until dinner hour; in the afternoon it was battalion or regimental drill, varied once or twice a week by brigade drill. At sundown we had dress parade and on Sunday inspection. Then we were required to have everything clean and in fine order, our guns in good condition, our clothes brushed, our shoes blackened and streets and quarters well kept. We were busy all the time, but congratulated ourselves on the prospect of a comfortable winter. Our anticipations were early dispelled.

On December 9th orders came for an early forward movement. The next day the wagons were loaded and made ready. Early on the 12th, we packed our belongings, stripped our shanties of the tent cloths, and by eight in the morning had fallen in and were ready to move. Soon we were off in an easterly direction. The road was dry and hard and smooth so we marched briskly. That afternoon we passed through Leesburg, a large old-fashioned town with many fine residences. The people were very "secesh" and did not seem to enjoy our coming. We gave them all the music we had; the fifes and drums, and sang "John Brown's Body" as well as we knew how. Only a few colored people showed themselves in the streets and the houses were fast closed. We camped that night beyond the town, footsore and lame. Being still new at soldiering we carried more baggage than we should and this added to our fatigue. After the evening meal we spread our blankets on the ground, and as the night was cold built fires from the fence rails along the road to keep warm, but it was damp and every bone ached. The Reveille sounded early the next morning. We were lame and sore, and our feet were blistered; we commenced the march after breakfast like a regiment of cripples. However, before we started our knapsacks were lightened by our discarding everything not absolutely needed. Our route was through a beautiful country and on the 14th we reached Fairfax Court House where we camped for several days. The village and surrounding country was filled with troops. They were mostly new regiments, waiting to be assigned to various brigades. The most notable building in the town was the old Court House which had a history. Sutlers tents were numberless and they were a great temptation to such boys as had any money to spend. In a short time we were sent to Fairfax Station, some three miles beyond the town, where we went into camp in the pine woods near the railroad.

When we left Harpers Ferry it was generally understood that we were to join the Army of the Potomac at Falmouth. General Burnside[7] was about to cross the Rappahannock and attack General Lee.[8] We were to get in close touch with our Army and in case of success the 11th[9] and 12th Corps were to lead a further advance against Lee. Burnside made the attack[10] and it was unsuccessful so it was not necessary for our Corps to go to the front, and so we remained massed in the vicinity of Fairfax. Here we expected to remain until spring and were directed to construct new winter quarters. This was easier to do than at Loudoun Heights as we were in the midst of a pine forest where the trees were straight and from six to ten inches in diameter, just right to build log houses. Instead of camping in this place for the winter, we only remained a month; but we were there to spend our first Christmas in the service. Many received boxes from home

   [7] Ambrose Everett Burnside (1824-1881) graduated from West Point in 1847 but resigned his commission in 1853. He became a Brigadier General of Volunteers in August 1861 and led his brigade in operations along the North Carolina coast. He joined the Army of the Potomac after promotion to Major General of Volunteers in March 1862 and commanded it from October 1862 until January 1863. Thereafter he led the Army of the Ohio and the IX Corps.
   [8] Robert Edward Lee (1807-1870) graduated from West Point in 1829 and served with distinction in the Mexican War. After resigning his federal commission he became a General and Military Advisor to the President of the Confederacy in June 1861. He assumed command of the Army of Northern Virginia a year later.
   [9] Commanded by Major General Franz Sigel. Its divisions were commanded by Brigadier Generals Julius Stahel, Adolph W. Von Steinwehr, and Carl Schurz.
   [10] Battle of Fredericksburg.

that were shared by all. While there, Mosby raided Fairfax
Court House and captured General Stoughton and his staff.[11]
This caused great excitement for a time as it was thought
there might be a large body of the enemy in our rear. We
expected to be ordered out but it was soon discovered that
the raid was a small affair.

While in this camp I paid a visit to the 125th New York
Regiment at Union Mills, five miles from us. I had a cousin,
Charles German, who was a Sergeant in Company D. I stayed
with him overnight and we had a happy time talking of
home. When I bid him goodby it was our last farewell; he
was killed in the Wilderness, May 6, 1864.

Several members of our Company E were fine singers and
every evening E street was filled with the boys listening to the
singing. It was a treat to hear their concerts. The glee club
sang at Sunday service that wonderfully pathetic "Tenting
Tonight on the Old Camp Ground." It was new and none of
us had heard it before. Those who listened were deeply affected; even now, after fifty years, in any gathering of old
veterans let that song be sung and you will see tears.

On January 18, 1863, orders came for an immediate
movement. The roads were then fairly smooth and dry and
we made good time, camping that night near Dumfries. Our
way that day had been through a bare country with few
houses, many of them abandoned. The farms did not seem
to have been cultivated for many years. The fields were
mostly covered with dwarf pines and cedars; among the trees
could be seen the old rows where in past years either corn or
tobacco had been planted. We passed a place where some
member of the Washington family had been born. The house

[11] John Singleton Mosby (1833-1916) was a lawyer who joined the 1st Virginia
Cavalry in 1861 and organized his own Partisan Rangers in March 1863. He became
the most famous of the eastern partisan leaders. His best known exploit was the
capture of Brigadier General Edwin Henry Stoughton in his bed at Fairfax Court
House, Va., March 9, 1863. Stoughton (1838-1868) had graduated from West Point
in 1859 and been named a Brigadier General of Volunteers in November 1861. He
commanded brigades in the VI and XXII Corps.

had burned years before; the two big chimneys which on these southern houses were usually built on the outside were still standing. The place where the person was born was marked by a slab lying flat on the ground. It stated that on a blank date O. S. Washington was born. I gained the impression that it was either the birthplace of Washington's father or mother. Many of us wondered if in Washington's time the region looked as desolate as it did to us.[12]

That night we made our beds on the ground without putting up our tents. About one o'clock it began to rain, but as we were tired we took a chance it would stop and did not then put them up. The wind began to blow and the rain came down hard, then we faced one of the worst storms I had ever known. Then the weather got cold so we made fires with pine knots and stood around the rest of the night. We had breakfast in the rain and it was not a cheerful meal.

We did not start until after ten o'clock as it was next to impossible to move the trains and artillery, the roads were in such a wretched condition. There was no bottom to the mud which was a sticky, red clay. With only one road over which to move we could make no headway; it became a quagmire blocked by stalled wagons and artillery that settled in the mud up to their wheel hubs, and the mules could not move them. The drivers shouted, swore and lashed, but no use, the Army was stuck in the mud. This lasted two days more, was called the "Mud March" and was never forgotten by those who took part in it.[13] A movement of the whole Army was attempted at the time we started but had to be abandoned. To proceed, the Pioneers[14] aided by our troops corduroyed

---

[12]   No plantation near Dumfries fits Bull's description. He may be recounting a garbled version of the destruction of Pohick Church near Fairfax Court House.

[13]   The "Mud March" of January 18-20, 1864 was an attempt by Burnside to move his army to Banks' Ford on the Rappahannock in an attempt to envelop Lee's position before Fredericksburg. The two-day rain described by Bull forced abandonment of the project which so demoralized the Army of the Potomac that Lincoln had to relieve Burnside of command.

[14]   Engineers who preceded a column in order to prepare the road for troops, artillery, and wagons.

the road. This was done by cutting the pines growing along
the road and laying them across close together. This made a
very rough uneven footing, but the wagons and artillery
could move slowly over it. This march tested to the utmost all
those there for the work was hard, we were wet to the skin
and had little to eat. It was not until the 22nd that we reached
Stafford Court House. It had taken two days to come from
Dumfries, only twelve miles distant. Stafford was a rickety
old town having an ancient Court House, tavern, and a few
residences and stores. The buildings were mostly used by our
Army.

The intention had been to march the 12th Corps to Fredericksburg, but as the movement against the enemy had to be
abandoned because of the storm, we were ordered to camp
at Stafford. As the 11th Corps, formerly stationed here, was
now at the front and would not return we were directed to
move into their camp.[15] Their cabins were well built and all
we had to do was place our tent cloths over the rafters. Then
we made great fires, dried out our blankets, and stood before
the fire until the mud had hardened on our clothes. It
looked like yellow plaster and when dry would peel off in
flakes, and you could see the "army blue" underneath. The
march had been trying to us new soldiers, unused as we still
were to such hardship.

It was unfortunate that we moved into this old camp, it
proved to be a most unhealthy place. The 11th Corps had
been there for some time and the stream from which they
got their drinking water had been contaminated by their
closets.[16] Typhoid fever soon developed in our Regiment
and many men were ill. There were some who died, three
were from our Company. We remained in this camp until
March 1st; while there I had my only sickness while in the
service. I remember how miserable I felt, feverish, faint,

[15]   The quarters occupied were originally built by the 26th Wisconsin.
[16]   Latrines.

weak and with no desire for food. However, I determined not to give in to it as I had not up to that time missed any detail.

On February 22nd I was detailed for picket duty. The orderly Sergeant knew I was not well and wanted to excuse me but could not do so without the Surgeon's certificate. He asked me to get excused but I did not want to do that. The picket line was near Aquia Creek more than two miles from camp. It was an effort to get there but we reached the reserve post about eleven that night and relieved the old pickets. At the post quite a large shed had been built, using fence rails. On top of the roof were pine boughs, which kept out some of the wind and rain in bad weather. The front of the shed was open so a large fire built outside made the shed warm and comfortable. The officer in charge, seeing my condition, told me to go to the shed, spread out my blanket and lie down where it was warm; he would excuse me from duty. I hardly moved for twenty-four hours. I was weak and sick but the fire made it so warm and comfortable I had a real rest. I was surprised to find that ten inches of snow had fallen. About nine in the morning we were surprised to hear heavy cannonading away to the south that continued for some time. It was a celebration of Washington's birthday. All our batteries had fired a shotted salute in his honor aimed at the batteries on the opposite side. The Johnnies answered and there was an animated celebration for some time. I kept my bed until the middle of the afternoon, when the officer told me I had better get back to camp. He said the detail would not be relieved until the next day and it was not necessary for me to stay as I was unfit for duty. The snow was deep, making it hard traveling, and it was nearly dark when I reached camp completely done up. The boys put me to bed and sent for Dr. Connelly.[17] He gave me some medicine and said he thought I would have a run of fever. The next

---

[17] Dr. Richard S. Connelly from Easton, N.Y. served as regimental Assistant Surgeon throughout the war.

morning I was much better and in a few days was ready for duty again.

Conditions had become so bad by this time that we moved our camp a mile north on a hill which had not been occupied by troops. The ground was high and dry and there was water from a stream that had not been contaminated. All went to work with a will and we built new quarters. While they were not as fine as the ones we left they were comfortable and they were healthy. That winter we had already constructed winter camps at Harpers Ferry, Fairfax Station, and Stafford so we felt we were getting expert in that business. In this new camp the health of all improved at once and the depression that had settled on the Regiment passed away.

Just before we moved to these last quarters, General Hooker[18] was appointed Commander of the Army of the Potomac, succeeding General Burnside. He made many changes and improvements in the equipment and discipline of the Army. One that was appreciated was the issuing of more and better rations. Bakeries were established and we had bread in place of hardtack. Potatoes, onions, and other vegetables were supplied, giving a much greater variety of food. There was improvement in the Quartermaster's Department. We were newly clothed and shod. We looked and felt much better in our new uniforms. A badge was designed for each Corps: that for the 12th was a star which we sewed on our caps. For the 1st Division of our Corps each man had a red star that was to be our badge of honor.

There was little sickness in our Regiment and we resumed drilling. Every day we were kept busy at it, under Lieutenant Colonel Norton. He was an experienced drillmaster as he had had active service before he joined our Regiment. He

[18] Joseph Hooker (1814-1879) graduated from West Point in 1837 and served in the Seminole and Mexican Wars. He resigned from the Army in 1853 but was appointed a Brigadier General of Volunteers in May 1861 and a Major General a year later. He commanded a Corps at Antietam, a Grand Division at Fredericksburg, and the Army of the Potomac between January and June 1863. Thereafter he led the XX Corps and the Northern Department.

drilled us in battalion and regimental formations. At this time there was little in the way of excitement, for we were far from the enemy, and our picket lines were not in their front. Yet our rear had to be guarded against their cavalry who on a raid might do much damage. Aquia Creek Landing, only a short distance to the north, was our depot of supply for materials that came by boat.

On April 8th we had a Corps review. In the reviewing party was President Lincoln, who was on a visit to the Army, and General Hooker. Great preparations had been made. A field was cleared long enough for the whole Corps to stand in line and wide enough for us to march in company front. The Corps numbered some eight thousand men and when standing in line the infantry and artillery covered two miles. The troops were all in new uniforms. It was a spectacle not soon forgotten by those who were there. The music, the marching, the artillery salute, the splendid horsemen, were all very grand.

President Lincoln, on horseback, rode by the side of General Hooker. There was contrast in the appearance of the two men. Hooker was in full uniform, splendidly mounted, and on this occasion at his best. The President was on a small horse and although a good rider presented a singular appearance. He was in citizens' clothes except a military cloak. He wore a tall stovepipe hat, which he had difficulty in keeping on his head. He was so tall and his legs were so long that, while his feet seemed only a foot from the ground, his hat loomed higher than Hooker's head. Following came the General's Staff and the President's little son on a pony.

At the right of our line the party halted. Then the Corps marched in review. Each regiment gave three cheers as they passed the President. The cheering was not military but the men could not be restrained from so honoring him. He really was the ideal of the Army. The review took all day. It was the finest and the last made by the 12th Corps, that was now through its period of training and was ready to take the field.

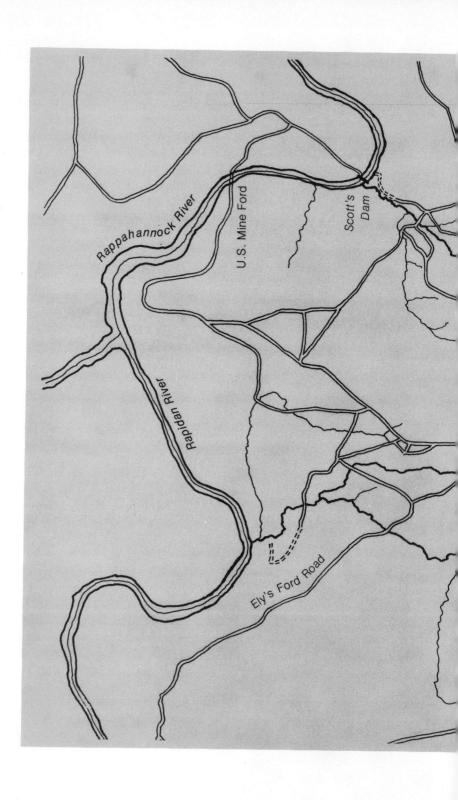

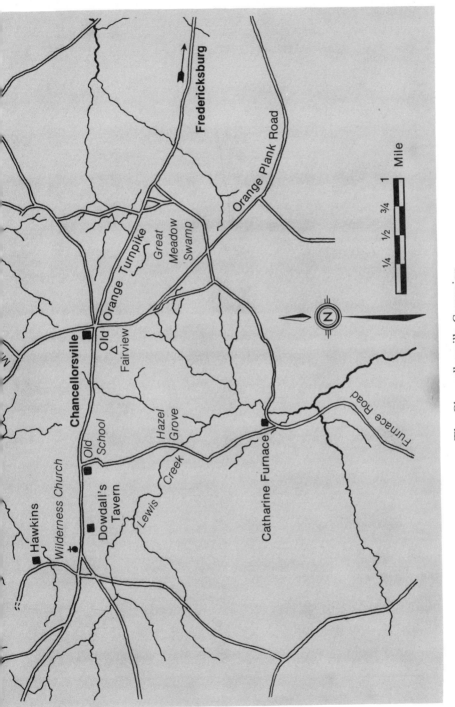

The Chancellorsville Campaign

CHAPTER THREE

The Chancellorsville Campaign

April 25th-May 15th, 1863

By April 25th conditions seemed favorable for an immediate opening of our spring campaign. The weather had become warm and pleasant. The rains, that during the winter months had been continuous, ceased. The mud that had so completely blocked our army movements had hardened and the roads that had been impassable were free to travel. There could be no reasonable excuse for further delay.

For at least a month our parade grounds had been in good condition, and we had been given intensive training, drilling every day in company, regiment and brigade movements. To this was added skirmish drill, an expert use of which was soon to become so essential. The drilling of troops ceased about April 20th, as the men were then required to prepare for the movement that was to be made by the Army.

To us in a regiment who as yet had only a slight experience in actual service the change from the monotony of our winter camping with all its ceaseless routine of drill and camp duty was welcome. To us new in the service, the knowledge that we were soon to face the enemy brought no fear or dread as we knew little about and but faintly realized what it meant. We were more than anxious to take part in a campaign where we would come face to face with the enemy. However, we did notice that the veterans in the regiments with whom we were brigaded, that had seen much active service and were well acquainted with its results, evidenced no great desire for the campaign to open. Their one or two years' active service had seemingly satisfied their fighting desires. While we were on guard and picket duty we often came in contact with these men and expressed our fears that we might have come into the service too late to see much actual warfare. They always advised us not to worry about not having plenty of chances to meet the enemy as we would soon get enough and plenty when spring came.

On April 24th orders were received to push the work that was required before our movement could begin. During that day and the following we were busy. Our Commissary and Ordnance trains were parked near us and wagons were loaded with such supplies as would be needed by an advancing army. The Ambulance train, with its accompanying wagons filled with medical stores, was lined up near our camp, fully equipped and ready to move with us. The old storage tents and depots for supplies used by our Corps at Stafford were taken down and moved to a central point.

During the day there were issued to each of us 80 rounds of rifle ammunition. As our cartridge boxes would only hold 40, the extra had to be put in our knapsacks. We were issued eight days' field rations consisting of hardtack, coffee, pork and sugar. Since our haversacks only had capacity for three days, the extra rations also had to be stowed in our knapsacks. We were notified that under no circumstances were we to part with either our rations or ammunition, except when their use became necessary. There would be no further issue of food or ammunition for eight days, unless ammunition became exhausted in action. By close packing we succeeded in getting the additional rations and ammunition in our knapsacks which after they were strapped in the usual way presented a very inflated look. When we slung them on our shoulders they were heavy.

Everything was done during the evening to make ready for an early start in the morning. All rejoiced to think we were now to see and know more of real soldiering than we had as yet experienced; that our days of drill and discipline which had become irksome and monotonous would for the time cease; and we would now begin the serious work of soldiering. In the evening after our work was done, we gathered in our company streets to visit and talk over passing events; we were all wondering and surmising where and when we would face the enemy in battle. When Taps sounded we were in our bunks for sleep, everything so far as we could tell was ready for the march. Up to this time the Confederates had been successful in holding the Union Armies in check. Now we felt the enemy would hardly be able to stand against the Army of the Potomac with its splendid equipment and the training that had been perfected during the winter by General Hooker. The General was regarded by many as the ideal soldier of our Army; he would surely lead the coming campaign to victory.

The morning of April 26th, Reveille sounded at four o'clock to give ample time to complete all preparations for an early march. Our breakfast was soon prepared and eaten. As it was supplied from our eight-day issue of rations, it somewhat lightened the load we had to carry. By eight we had removed our tent cloths from the shanties, after which our deserted winter quarters with their rafters uncovered looked like a burned city in miniature. By the time we had completed packing our knapsacks, which included many useless things, we were ready. Then we were called into line loaded to the limit with our heavy equipment. There were the delays usual in military movements and we stood a long time; other troops were to advance before us, and our many trains and artillery were on the road. It was nine o'clock before we had our place in the marching column. When we started our shoulders were aching from the heavy load under which we had been standing for nearly an hour.

When the order to march finally came, we, with cheers and all in the best of spirits, started keeping step to the music of our drum corps. The weather was all that could be desired. It was a beautiful spring morning with a clear warm sun shining down on us when we left the old camp at Stafford; none of us ever expected to see it again, much less ever again occupy it.

After we took our place in the line our drum corps stopped playing and we took "route step" and marched two hours before we halted. By this time the enthusiasm and hurrah with which we started was about exhausted for the severe exercise began to tell on our strength. Early in the day it became very hot. The load we were carrying was so heavy that many of the weaker men had fallen out and were straggling. We were all overheated and wet with perspiration.

As soon as we halted every knapsack came off our shoulders and a thorough house cleaning was made. Everything that was not absolutely necessary was sorted out and thrown away. Many foolishly discarded their overcoats and blankets; they thought it was so hot they would not have further use for them. Then we had a hasty meal and were on our way again but with a much lighter load than when we started. It was still heavy enough for we had to carry the large supply of ammunition and rations.

Our route was in a westerly direction through a poor country that was mostly uncultivated and covered with stunted pine and oak. We only passed a few good plantations or residences. The clearings were small and the houses for the most part were dilapidated log buildings. The people we saw were mostly "poor whites" but we did not see many either white or black, they seemed to keep under cover. There were some small peach orchards along the way. They were in full bloom and beautiful in marked contrast to the general appearance of the region. During the day our way had been mostly through forests. The trees were in full leaf and shaded the road; this did help keep us from the sun's rays.

Throughout April 27th and 28th we continued in the same westerly direction going from twelve to fifteen miles per day. The fine weather continued and since we were becoming hardened to the work could have marched much farther but for the delays caused by large numbers of troops and trains and artillery that were also using the road.

By this time we had learned that the right wing of our Army consisting of the 5th, 11th, and 12th Army Corps was in the movement, all three Corps keeping in close contact with each other. Late in the afternoon of the 28th we reached Kelly's Ford on the Rappahannock River where we were halted until a pontoon bridge could be laid. Then we crossed to the south side of the river where we camped on the hills that border the stream. The greater part of all the troops in the movement crossed the bridge and it was nearly morning before they were over.

So far we had not been opposed by the enemy. Before we had advanced our Cavalry had occupied the country over which we were to march. They had also at times covered most of the region that lay between the Rappahannock and Rapidan rivers. The distance between rivers was about ten miles and this area was held to be debatable ground for it was occupied at various times by both armies. These two rivers formed a junction some ten miles below Kelly's Ford. The land between the two streams was higher, more open and better farmed than the region around Stafford. The morning of the 29th, the hills on which we had camped the night before presented a martial appearance for nearly thirty thousand men were in that limited area. It seemed almost like magic for when we spread our blankets the night before only our Brigade had made the crossing. Early in the morning we resumed the march. Our Corps had the lead following the small body of Cavalry that always heads the march during active movements. Our Cavalry was about a mile ahead of us going in a southeasterly direction on a road toward

Germania Ford, which was one of the crossings of the Rapidan River. About three in the afternoon we heard scattered
musketry firing in our front. It was not heavy and stopped
after a short time. We pushed on rapidly and soon reached
the Ford where we found that everything had quieted down.
When we started in the morning opposition was expected
before noon, as it was thought the enemy had a Cavalry force
on the north side of the Rapidan. However, before we had
crossed the Rappahannock they had moved their force to the
south side of the Rapidan, except they had left a few men at
Germania Ford to collect timber for a bridge to be built later.
They were taken by surprise by our Cavalry and after a
skirmish their force of sixty men was captured.

Here we had our first sight of the results of active war.
Two of the enemy, who were wounded in the skirmish, and
the prisoners were sent past us to the rear. When we reached
the river the Cavalry was already on the south side, and a
regiment of Infantry was preparing to wade across. The
river was high and the current swift, so the passage was
dangerous. The Cavalry formed a line across the place where
the men would wade so as to catch any who might lose their
footing and be carried downstream. The river was some two
hundred feet wide. We watched them as they forded; the
water was up to their armpits and several were washed off
their feet and had to be rescued. We expected to follow and
made ready to go when an officer of our Regiment suggested
to General Williams, who was present, that we take the timbers that had been cut by the enemy and that lay on the bank,
and build a bridge. The General at once gave his approval
and the work was begun by our men assisted by the Pioneers
who had all the tools needed for the work. In two hours we
had the temporary bridge built; by night our Regiment had
crossed and then was followed by many other troops. In the
evening a pontoon bridge was laid and the trains and artillery crossed. The night of the 29th we camped on the hills to
the south and east of the Ford and by morning all our forces
were in the enemy's country. Up to this time we had had

splendid weather and the movement was successful in every way. We had crossed the Rapidan without opposition, were on General Lee's flank not twenty-five miles away, and this had all been done with scarcely the loss of a man.

The 30th was another fine day and we were on the march early. From Germania Ford we went in an easterly direction on the turnpike leading toward Fredericksburg. This road was parallel to the river, from three to five miles south of it. We soon entered the Wilderness, a rough, wild, abandoned country, covered with a thick growth of scraggly and stunted timber, growing in many places so rank as to be almost impassable to man or beast. There were some cleared farms and a few dilapidated houses but our whole day's travel was through a dreary and deserted country. In the afternoon while we were crossing a cleared field in the forest we were surprised by a strange noise that sounded like a great bird fluttering over the Regiment and then there was a crash in the woods beyond followed by a loud explosion. The enemy had discovered by this time that we were south of the Rapidan in force and their Cavalry had been sent to delay our advance as much as possible. They had placed a battery on a rise of ground far to the south of us and were shelling our line through the open space in the forest. The sound we heard was made by a shell, the force of which was almost spent, passing a few feet over our heads. It was the beginning of our experience under cannonading that was to last for three years. The boys took this baptism pretty well but this first shot was followed by others that hissed and shrieked over our heads and made everyone jump and duck, a nervous habit few ever fully overcame. The first shell came so suddenly, and the whole affair ended so quickly, no one had a chance to get scared but we breathed more freely when we had passed the clearing. Actually the battery was located so far from us it could not have done much harm as most of its shells fell short. Soon the battery was driven from the hill and it could no longer annoy the column marching on the road.

We moved very slowly and were now getting so near the
enemy's lines that we proceeded with caution for in this
wilderness we might get caught in some trap. By four in the
afternoon when we had not marched more than ten miles we
arrived at a clearing larger than we had seen since we crossed
the Rapidan. This was a plantation of several hundred acres.
It was better situated and showed a finer condition of cultivation than any we had seen along the line of march. The
cleared land was on both sides of the turnpike and near the
center was a large and rather pretentious mansion. The
property belonged to a family by the name of Chancellor, the
owner I believe had the title of Judge. The place was called
Chancellorsville although there was no settlement other than
the house and the rather unusual buildings connected with
the plantation.

On our arrival we marched into the fields south of the
house and soon the large open space at the right of the
turnpike was filled with troops who were massed in the field
as they entered the clearing.

Generals Hooker, Slocum,[1] Williams and other commanders, with their staffs, dismounted at the Chancellor House.
The Generals gathered on the large open piazza at the front
facing south; they seemed to be holding a consultation. We
stood at rest for some little time awaiting orders. In about a
half hour the Generals finished their conference and came to
the turnpike fronting the house where their mounted escorts
were waiting. After they joined their various commands, the
troops were soon moving in several directions evidently for
the purpose of fronting in line. Our Brigade marched in a
southerly way, passed through the open field by the Chancellor House and entered the woods. We advanced about a half-
mile where we fronted facing nearly south, the other Regi-

[1] Henry Warner Slocum (1827-1894) graduated from West Point in 1852 but
left the Army four years later. He led a New York regiment at Bull Run; became a
Brigadier General of Volunteers in August 1861; and a Major General the following
July. He commanded the XII Corps at Chancellorsville, Gettysburg, and in the
West.

ments of our Brigade forming on our right and left. To our right, but not connected with us, was the 11th Corps. On our left a battery was in position and then troops in line as far as we could see.

We were only about ten miles from Fredericksburg and might expect at any time to be faced by the Army of General Lee, who must have known by this time that a large force of our Army was on his flank. Where we were in the forest the trees were very close together with much undergrowth of bushes and vines and any movement from our front would be very difficult. A line was laid out by our Engineers and we were ordered to fortify our position. Axes and shovels were furnished and we were soon hard at work. To most of us this was an unfamiliar effort but before our service ended it was one in which we were to become proficient. But as farm boys we all knew how to handle both an ax and shovel and by ten that night had a good defense in our front. There was a lot of fallen timber that we gathered and placed lengthwise, then dug a trench behind, with the dirt thrown over the logs. The trench was over two feet deep, wide enough for the line to stand in and with the embankment the total depth was five feet. These works were quite strong and would protect the men against attack, for an ordinary projectile could not go through the embankment.

Early in the evening the Regiment had been called into line and a congratulatory order was read. It was from General Hooker and thanked the men for the success that had attended the campaign up to that time and further stated that we now had General Lee's army where it could not escape, etc. We were, of course, much delighted and cheered heartily. The only really disturbing feature to us green soldiers in this optimistic address was the thought that perhaps we would after all see no fighting as the enemy would undoubtedly retreat and the war might end without our having done much to bring about the result. Before the end of the next two days, however, our misgivings in regard to the premature ending of the war were to be relieved and we were to learn in our unexpected defeat what a short step there was between seeming success and utter failure.

By eleven that night we spread our blankets on the ground back of our newly-made trench. So we passed our first night in line of battle facing an enemy of whom we knew nothing and consequently feared less. Our sleep was sweet and only disturbed by the ominous cries of the whippoorwills in the forest around us. The night was clear and a beautiful full moon shone down.

We were up early after a good night's rest. It was Friday, May 1st. Our breakfast was not bountiful for our eight days' rations were running low. We found that the 3rd Corps had crossed the river during the night and had filled the gap between the 11th and 12th Corps. To strengthen our works we cut the timber in our front so as to make an abatis that would delay an attacking force should there be an assault on our line. We continued at this until ten in the morning; then we were ordered to fall in to take part in a movement against the enemy. We took all our baggage as we might not return if changes were made in the line.

The 1st Division of our Corps was to make a reconnaissance in the direction of Fredericksburg. Within a half hour we moved out of our works and then went in an easterly direction for about a mile; then halted and formed in line of battle. Skirmishers were thrown out and the line advanced. We at once entered the forest, but found the scrub pine so closely grown together with their branches extended out from the ground up and so interlocked we could not advance in company front. It was even difficult for a single man to move ahead in the thicket. We broke into columns marching by fours; even then we could not keep that formation. Then we went on as best we could in single file, breaking our way through the pine branches, many of them were dead and sharp as spears. After we had gone about a half mile our skirmishers began firing and soon the enemy's artillery opened on us, but we were so hidden in the forest they could not locate us and their firing was wild. Their shot and shell passed over our heads but made a terrifying noise as they tore through the tops of the trees.

I cannot say how far we advanced, or how long a time it took, but finally we were through the thicket, and entered a large cleared field. Our line by this time was broken and scattered. However, as the men came out of the woods they formed a line at once, rallying on the colors; but it was fully half an hour before we were ready to advance. While we were reforming our line skirmishing was lively in our front. We went forward up a slope in the open field to the crest of the hill where we were in sight of the enemy who then redoubled the fire of their batteries. We could see the line of yellow dirt that had been thrown up by them in building their fortifications and the location of their batteries from the smoke of their guns. I judged the enemy was nearly a mile away. The country between our lines was open with few trees to break the view but it was cut up by ravines. Since we could not take part in the action in our front we lay down to avoid becoming a target for their guns. This was our first experience in line of battle with an active foe in our own front, cannon booming, skirmishers firing, and Minié balls singing and whistling around us. It began to look serious but as the enemy was some distance away our fears were not greatly excited.

We had hardly dropped to the ground when one of our Division batteries came on the field, horses and men on the run, the horses plunging as they ran, guns jerking and jumping over the rough ground, with the dust rising like a trail of smoke behind them. They passed by our rear and going a short distance to our left wheeled into line, unlimbered, and before we realized that they had passed they opened up on the Rebel batteries that were shelling our line. The duel between the batteries continued for some time and was exciting to us who had never before seen such action. The enemy's shots were directed at our battery so mostly fell at our left where they could do us no damage. We could see where the solid shot struck from the dust they threw when they hit the ground. The shells were more spectacular because they burst in the air and the pieces flew in all directions singing and shrieking.

After a time the advance was called off and we were given orders to go back to our old place in the line where we had built fortifications. To return we took a direction to the west of the tangled forest and marched back to the Chancellor House, reaching there about six o'clock. If the objective had been to "feel" and definitely locate the enemy's line, it was successful.

When we reached the Chancellor House our Brigade was halted for a short time. Then all the Regiments except ours were ordered back to their old places in the line, but we were held back for other work. An advance was at once to be made by our picket line, south and east from our present front and our Regiment was to support the advance. We received our orders, then went in a southerly direction for nearly a mile. Much of the way was through cleared land and up quite a long hill which was then called Hazel Grove. This elevation was so located that it was of great importance to our line and was to become the scene of severe fighting the next day.

To the south and east of this hill was low level marshy ground through which ran a small stream. The enemy's main line was supposed to be on the south side of the stream with their picket line running through the low ground on the north side very close to our front. The object of our advance was to drive them back, and then establish our own picket line in the valley.

When we reached Hazel Grove elevation Company A was detailed to go on the picket line. They passed to the front of the Regiment, deployed, and went down the hill toward the valley. During this time we were standing at rest on the top of the hill, which was bare of trees and underbrush, and as it developed later we were in full view of the enemy's line. Suddenly, without the usual skirmishing that would have warned us to lie down, a volley was fired from the enemy's line and bullets began to whistle and sing. I was standing

next to Jerry Finch,[2] one of our younger boys. At the first
round Jerry's gun tumbled from his hands and he staggered
and fell at my feet. I stooped down and turned him over as
he had fallen on his face; when I spoke he gave no answer. He
had been instantly killed. We all dropped to the ground but
the musketry fire continued and it was brisk with the bullets
coming fast. Many were hit but we could not return the fire
as our skirmishers were in the line between us and the
enemy. Very soon they opened on our line with their artillery
and shells fell and exploded in the open field about us. We
were then ordered back to the woods on our side of the clearing where we formed a new front and remained until Company A was recalled from the skirmish line.

The effort to advance was abandoned for the enemy's line
was so close to ours that only a general engagement could
dislodge them. We lost thirty men killed and wounded.
Among the killed was Lieutenant Colonel Norton, who was
mounted when the action began. He was probably our most
valuable officer because of his previous experience in the
Army.

In the evening we were ordered back to our old place in
the line, reached there about eleven that night, and were
glad to get back. I found that the stock of my gun had been
hit by a bullet but not damaged so I could not use it; my
coffee pail which was strapped at my side on the haversack
was shot through by another bullet. Jerry's body was brought
back and buried behind our works in the woods with a
prayer by the Chaplain.[3] He was a fine young boy of character and a splendid soldier.

When we dropped on the ground to sleep at midnight we
felt that we had had our baptism of blood and commenced to
realize the gravity of our position. We had heard that day for

[2] Private Jeremiah Finch enlisted from Ft. Ann.

[3] Since Chaplain Gordon left the regiment before the start of the Chancellorsville campaign and his successor, Rev. Myron White, was not commissioned until
April 1864 the identity of the chaplain is uncertain.

the first time the "Rebel Yell" that was to become so familiar in the years to come. With our beds on the ground back of our works and our guns stacked where we could seize them at a moment's notice, we were so exhausted that we slept well.

On Saturday, May 2nd, we were up late refreshed by our night's rest. Nature was still kind, the weather was fine with a cloudless sky. This was the seventh day of the campaign and so far not a drop of rain. Our eight days' rations were nearly exhausted, many of the boys were without food. Those who had been prudent had some hardtack and pork left which was shared by all but this was only enough for a half meal.

Far away, at our left, during the morning we heard cannonading and some musketry firing but our front was quiet. There was nothing to indicate that upon our short frontage of less than five miles more than one hundred thousand men were facing each other only waiting for orders to join in bloody conflict. That morning we heard the usual noises of the camp; the bugle calls, the beating of drums, the shrill sound of the fifes, and the neighing of the horses and braying of mules, all the sounds we would hear in a friendly camp. In the morning General Hooker inspected our lines and as he passed, he was heartily cheered by the Regiment. It was reported that the enemy was on the retreat[4] with their main force, leaving only a small body to hold us in check while they escaped. The quiet on our front would seem to confirm this report. Near us were some tall pine trees. One of our boys who had been a sailor climbed to the top of one of them, from there he could see a wide stretch of country toward the south. He saw on a road some two miles away a large body of troops going in a southwesterly direction. This was reported to our Captain Anderson who sent the information to our Division Headquarters. These men seemed to be going in the direction of Orange Court House. It was

---

[4] The "retreat" noted by Bull was actually Jackson's march to the Wilderness preparatory to his devastating flank attack on Major General O. O. Howard's XI Corps.

thought they were on retreat to that place, this opinion seemed to be confirmed later.

At one o'clock we were ordered to move and started out of our works, again leaving them vacant. The 12th and 3rd Corps, under command of General Sickles,[5] were to advance in the direction of Furnace Road upon which the enemy troops had been seen, and were to engage them if they were contacted. The 3rd had the advance so the 12th was held back until they had formed their line and moved out of the way. We then formed on their right and rear, Knipe's[6] Brigade of our Division heading the advance, with our Brigade following them in columns of regiments, taking such distance apart that they could form a line of battle quickly. Progress was slow, it was nearly four o'clock before the advance reached the vicinity of the road. Then our skirmishers were soon briskly engaged. The enemy was steadily pushed back, there seemed to be no heavy force behind their skirmishers.

Our advance continued and their batteries on our left opened up on us and for a time it was noisy. No halt was made until we reached the road where we encountered quite a large body of the enemy and attacked them. They proved to be the rear guard of the large force that had passed on ahead of them, and put up a stiff fight. However, our troops on the extreme right came around their flank and cut them off from their main force, and as they were greatly outnumbered, they were forced to surrender. Five hundred prisoners were taken and sent back to the rear, near where we were standing in line. Our boys chaffed them a good deal,

[5]   Daniel Edgar Sickles (1825-1914) was a New York lawyer and politician who received a commission as Brigadier General of Volunteers in September 1861. He became a Major General in November 1862 and commanded the III Corps at Fredericksburg, Chancellorsville, and at Gettysburg where he lost a leg and gained a Medal of Honor.

[6]   Joseph Farmer Knipe (1823-1901) had been an enlisted man during the Mexican War and a Colonel of a Pennsylvania regiment in 1861. Promoted to Brigadier General of Volunteers in November 1862, he commanded brigades in the XII and XX Corps until wounded at the Battle of Resaca. Following recovery he led cavalry brigades in Mississippi. His brigade contained the 5th Connecticut, 28th, 46th New York, and 128th Pennsylvania.

giving them the laugh for being caught but they were not backward in giving us as good as we sent. Among other things, they said the laugh would be on us before night if old Jack got to us by then.

During the fight I saw a movement of the 2nd Massachusetts Regiment that I thought was wonderful. This regiment was in the front line crossing a cleared field, firing as they advanced. For some reason, probably to adjust the line, they were ordered to fall back. When they retired they never turned their faces from the front but backed off the field in perfect order, firing all the way. This regiment was considered one of the best drilled in the Army.

General Sickles had secured the road and had apparently cut the enemy's line in two as there was a force on our right as well as our left. By this time it was nearly six in the evening and we were halted and standing in line awaiting orders. The fighting in our front had ceased and we were wondering what the order would be. Suddenly there came to our ears heavy and unexpected cannonading on our right. It seemed far away. It began slowly but rapidly increased in volume and soon was a continuous roar. With it came the sound of musketry, beginning with volleys which settled into a continuous rattle and roar that comes when firing at will. At first the musketry seemed far away but soon came nearer and nearer; the battle was extending in our direction or our forces were being driven back. Every indication pointed to the development of a severe engagement. As soon as it became evident that a real battle was on, our Johnnie prisoners became excited and jubilant. They shouted, giving the "Rebel Yell" and tauntingly shouted to their captors, "Now old Jack is after you and you'ens will soon think Hell has broke loose. Now is the time for you to laugh for you won't feel much like laughing when old Stonewall gets through with you," etc.

Our Generals, who were near where we stood in line, seemed astounded and not to know what action was necessary. However, staff officers with orders soon began to arrive, their horses white with foam. Orders were given to return with all speed possible to the fortifications we left at noon.

It was at least two miles to our old works and we faced about and started at a double-quick. There was much confusion as all were striving to get back as quickly as possible. At times we would meet other troops moving in ahead of us and have to halt, but we made good progress and in about three quarters of an hour reached the valley south of Hazel Grove. Looking ahead we could see the high ground at the Grove, covered with our batteries in action, firing with almost incredible speed into the forest to the west, and could hear the rattle of musketry and the "Rebel Yell" that was not drowned out by the roar of our batteries. From the valley we came up on the high ground near the place where we were in action the day before, when we passed back of the batteries we formed in line of battle. The noise of the battle had become a pandemonium and it came nearer and nearer as we stood in line.

To the right extended an open field, leading to the near forest. After a short halt we marched across the field, toward the forest, there we witnessed a sight that beggars description, it was the panic and stampede of a part of the 11th Corps. They were coming from the woods in our front and fleeing across the field toward us. Their retreat was headlong; they had thrown away everything that was loose, guns, knapsacks, caps, and many had no coat and blouse and were in their shirt sleeves. Nothing could stop them. They were crazed and would fight to escape as though the enemy were close to them. We were ordered to stop them but we might as well have tried to stop a cyclone, they dived through our line regardless of our guns or bayonets. One can hardly conceive of the terror that possessed them. Further to our right the confusion was even greater. Soon the fugitives had all gone through our line, greatly to our relief, for their panic was nerve-wracking to troops new to the service.

By this time it was nearly dark and our line was moved up close behind the batteries for support. There were nearly fifty guns[7] trained on the enemy who were in the woods beyond the open fields. In the darkness that was coming on it was a grand and awful sight. The earth trembled, the noise was deafening and the darkness lighted up with the flash of each gun, while from the forest could be heard the "Rebel Yell." Fortunately they could not use their artillery; the forest was so dense it could not be brought to the front and if it was fired in their rear it would have endangered their own men. For two hours our cannonading continued, then gradually lessened and, almost as greatly disorganized but not so demoralized as our 11th Corps, the enemy fell back to rest and reorganize for the coming day.

The artillery action we witnessed[8] has since come to be considered one of the most notable and successful of the war. For more than an hour while General Sickles was getting his troops back from the Furnace Road they had, without any infantry support, held a large part of Jackson's Corps at bay. After the firing had ceased and all was quiet, we marched back to the open field in front of the Chancellor House. The breastworks we had so carefully built were in the hands of the enemy who had moved into them when we were with General Sickles that afternoon. The battle had resulted in a complete defeat for our Army, the right wing had not only been demoralized but destroyed. The surprise and retreat of the 11th Corps had placed in the enemy's hands all the line we had fortified; now a new one had to be constructed that night for it was certain that they would renew their attack in the morning. A new line was hurriedly located nearly at right angles to our old one; now we faced west and were on the west edge of the open field that faced the Chancellor House, and the forest was in our front. As soon as we were given a place in the new line we commenced to cut the timber in our

---

[7]   Bull, not unnaturally in the heat of battle, overestimated the number of guns. These pieces, hastily gathered by Brigadier General Alfred Pleasonton of the 1st Cavalry Division, actually numbered only 22.

[8]   The artillery successfully broke up an attempt by D. H. Hill's Division (Brigadier General Robert E. Rodes) of Jackson's Corps to overrun Hazel Grove.

front to make a barricade, trees as far away as fifty feet or more were cut to fall parallel to our front. This formed an abatis with the larger logs piled up so as to make a breastwork. By three in the morning we had strong protection that saved many lives when we were attacked the next day. It had been a trying time and after we reached our new line we had no rations for our eight days' supply was all consumed. We had been informed that rations would be issued at the end of the day, but none were to be had. It was remarkable how the men kept up without food; but in the excitement and nervous strain food was forgotten and we pitched in to protect our line without thought of how tired or hungry we were. After we had finished, our rations came issued for three days. Then we laid down to get such sleep as we could.

After midnight our troops on Hazel Grove withdrew; the enemy reorganized their shattered and broken lines and moved into the works there that we had so carefully built. Then they were not more than one half mile from us. The enemy's skirmish line was advanced close to ours which was posted not more than fifty yards away. Strange to say not a shot was fired by either side during the night.

At five in the morning, tired, I lay down as I ate my breakfast of hardtack and pork. My face was toward the Chancellor House. As I looked over the field between our position and the house I noted the batteries ranged upon the low hills in our rear that faced south and west. Some of the guns were protected by small earthworks thrown up by the artillerymen during the night. Some men were around the guns making them ready for the coming action, others in the rear of the guns were caring for the horses, the last time for nearly one hundred of the splendid animals. Between the batteries and the turnpike a brigade was marching toward us. They were marching without music, beating of drums or bugle call, as in pantomime.

Over and beyond this dumb show I saw in the east the sun just coming over the forest. Never was there a more beautiful sunrise, not a cloud in the sky. It was an ideal Sunday morn-

ing, warm and fair. It seemed to me like sacrilege that such a
sacred day should be used by men to kill and maim each
other.

As I looked and thought of these things, a single shot in
our front broke the stillness. It was the first, the "opening
shot" of the battle that was to break in fury on us. Most of the
men of our Company were preparing or eating their breakfast, others were lying down resting after their night's toil, a
few were sleeping. That shot brought every man to his feet.
There was no need for the order to "fall in." Before our
Captain could give any orders the men were taking their
muskets from their stacks on which hung our cartridge belts.
As we took our guns, the belt was thrown over our shoulders
and strapped in place; then gun in hand we faced the front.
Our haversacks and knapsacks were laid on the barricade
within our reach. Within a minute we were in line, facing the
front. Our guns that had been loaded the night before were
at half cock. We were ready for the action to begin; with our
hearts beating hard and fast we waited.

On the heels of the first shot there was a lull for a moment,
then followed another, and in quick succession many more.
At our right and left was scattered firing, increasing in volume every second. It was the action of the two skirmish lines;
the enemy's men advancing and ours holding back to give us
time to get ready for the assault that was coming. We had not
long to wait; our own skirmishers having held them for a
time were forced back nearer and nearer to our barricade,
and bullets began to sing and whistle over our heads. Then
for a short while the firing almost ceased; the enemy's skirmishers had done their work and halted for the attack to
begin. Our men, firing as they came back, climbed over our
works. I was near the right of our Company when one of the
skirmishers passed near me. He said: "Get ready, boys, for
they are coming and coming strong." He did not linger but
went to the rear.

In our front was a gradual ascent for some two or three
hundred feet to a low ridge beyond which the ground de-

scended; so in making their attack, the enemy would not come in range with us or we with them until they had reached the crest and were coming over the top. Soon their main line reached their skirmishers and the battle was on. The attack began, as it always did, with their yell, not a cheer, not a shout, or hurrah, but a shrill, long, continued, high-pitched yell that finally was drowned by the roar of musketry.

When the enemy began to yell, our batteries that had waited until that time to locate them opened up. As they were only about two hundred yards from our front, the fire from the many guns passed about fifteen feet over our heads and the shells exploded only a short distance beyond us. The noise was deafening as the shells went howling and singing over our heads, and we nervously ducked as they went by.

I noted back of our left center, some distance from our battle line, that our Surgeons with their attendants and stretcher-bearers had established a headquarters and every-thing was being made ready for their bloody work.

We continued standing unengaged in line, a trying time for even veteran soldiers, almost unendurable for us new recruits. I glanced down our line toward the left and could see, at the center of our Regiment near Company C (the Color Company), our flags just unfurled by the Color Guard. They were new and bright and beautiful. Our company officers were walking back and forth waiting for orders.

To the right of our line were the 27th Indiana and 2nd Massachusetts, old veteran Regiments. Their flags were un-furled but they were ragged and stained from their two years in the earlier campaigns of the Army of the Potomac. How different they looked than ours.

Colonel Colgrove[9] was the only mounted officer I saw that morning. When the firing began he was an easy mark and was carried back to the rear badly wounded. In our rear, the men I had seen earlier marching toward us were formed in a

---

[9] Silas Colgrove was Colonel of the 27th Indiana. He was breveted Brigadier General for service in August 1864.

second line to support us. It was the Jersey Brigade[10] of the
6th Corps. They presented a striking appearance, standing
in the open field with flags flying and guns glistening in the
morning sun. They were hardly given a glance from us on
the firing line for our eyes were to the front and our minds
on things more vital to us than watching other troops.

Looking down the line of our Company as the yelling of
the enemy came nearer and nearer to us, I judged that everyone felt about as I did; there was no levity now, the usual
joking had ceased and a great quiet prevailed. I could see
pallor on every face as we brought the hammers to a full
cock. I believe every arm trembled as we raised our guns to
our shoulders to fire but all eyes were to the front, not one
looked back. This was a testing time and there was not one of
our Company that did not pass the test.

Fortunately for us, the enemy began firing before they
reached the top of the hill so their first volley was over our
heads. We were warned not to fire before ordered to do so
but as soon as the Johnnies opened on us some of the men
commenced. Most of us, however, held our fire until we saw
the line of smoke that showed that they were on the ridge;
then every gun was fired. It was then load and fire at will as
fast as we could. Soon the nervousness and fear we had when
we began to fight passed away and a feeling of fearlessness
and rage took its place.

The enemy continued to advance, firing as they came nearly to the fallen trees. Finding our fire too heavy to face they
wavered and fell back over the ridge and we gave a "Yankee
shout and hurrah." We had a short breathing spell for perhaps five minutes, the musketry fire nearly ceased on our
front; but the artillery kept pounding away. After we all
loaded our guns we took a long breath and waited, but not
for long. We again heard their yell and they were coming on,
this time not making the mistake of firing before they reached

[10]   The 1st Brigade, 1st Division, VI Corps, commanded by Colonel Henry W.
Brown, consisted of the 1st, 2nd, 3rd, 15th, and 23rd New Jersey.

the top of the hill. There they gave us a volley and advanced on the run. When they reached the fallen trees they had trouble in making headway and their first line faltered and fell back but their troops were massed and their second line continued the attack. We loaded and fired as fast as possible but still they came on. The smoke was so dense we could seldom see them but we could see the flash of their guns as they advanced yelling. The crash of the musketry was deafening. Climbing over and pushing aside the fallen timber in their front they were soon not more than twenty feet from our barricade.

I had just fired my gun and was lowering it from my shoulder when I felt a sharp sting in my face as though I had been struck with something that caused no pain. Blood began to flow down my face and neck and I knew that I had been wounded. Ransom Fisher[11] standing next to me saw the blood streaming down my face, and said, "You are hit. Can't I help you off?" I said, "No, Ransom, I think I can get to the Surgeon without help." I took my knapsack that lay on the works in front of me and started to go to the left of our Regiment where our Surgeons were located. I passed in the rear of several Companies, all were firing rapidly, and when back of Company K felt another stinging pain, this time in my left side just above the hip. Everything went black. My knapsack and gun dropped from my hands and I went down in a heap on the ground.

I do not know how long it was before I became conscious but the battle was raging furiously; two dead men who were not there when I fell were lying close to me, one across my feet. Captain Wiley[12] of Company K was standing near by. I attempted to rise and when he saw my effort stooped over me and said, "I thought you were dead. Who are you?" The Captain was an old friend of our family but I was so covered

[11]   Private Ransom Fisher enlisted from Ft. Ann.

[12]   Captain Henry O. Wiley (1831-1864) came from North Granville, N.Y. He commanded Company K and was killed in action at Peach Tree Creek, Ga., July 20, 1864.

with blood he did not recognize me. I told him who I was and
asked if he could get someone to help me go to the Surgeon.
He had two stretcher-bearers come; they did not take me to
the Surgeon but carried me back about fifty yards to a small
stream that ran parallel to our battle line. Here was a depression some three or four feet below the general level of the
ground where the wounded would be protected from musketry fire. When I reached the stream its banks were already
well lined with many dead and wounded. Some had been carried there, others had dragged themselves to the place to die.
Many were needlessly bleeding to death. There was at that
time no Red Cross Association with our Army; no "first aid
appliances" were issued to the troops in the field that they
could use themselves if there was no Surgeon present. Many
died who would have lived if only the simplest treatment had
been in the hands of the men themselves. No Surgeon was
with us and the men bringing back the wounded were too
busy to give any aid. The wounded were very quiet as a rule
and it was exceptional that they made loud cries or seemed
excited.

I was left close to the stream so before Blanchard,[13] the
stretcher-bearer who helped me, went back to the line, I had
him fill my canteen. I was not suffering much pain but was
very weak as both my wounds had bled profusely. My face
was coated with blood and it had run down my back and
breast and saturated my clothes which were soaked from
head to foot, as my wound in the side had also bled freely.
After a time my bleeding nearly stopped. As far as I could
discover no bones were broken.

My mind was clear so I reasoned as I lay on the ground
that if it was possible it would be better for me to get farther
to the rear where there would be more chance to have my
wounds cared for. I raised myself to a sitting position but
found I was so dizzy and faint from loss of blood that I had to
lie down. My effort had opened my wounds and they started

[13]   The civilian clerk of the regimental adjutant, not otherwise identified.

to bleed again. I knew I could not get to the rear without help, so made no further attempt. Fortunately my canteen had been filled; my thirst had become great and I had some water to wash the blood from my face. During this time the battle on our front continued with unlessened fury; the Minié balls sung over our heads, cutting off leaves and branches from the laurel bushes that lined the stream. These bushes were ten feet high, and the tops were in range of the musket fire. The artillery on the ridge were pouring shot and shell over our heads into the Rebel line. Musketry made a continuous roar, the shouts of our men could be heard, and often the shrill yell of the enemy. It seemed to us wounded men that the battle went on for a long time. The ambulance men kept busy and not only brought men from our Regiment, but from the 27th Indiana and 2nd Massachusetts that were in line next to us.

As near as I can estimate it was about an hour after I was taken to the gully that the musketry firing gradually lessened, and shortly afterwards almost ceased. From the place where I lay, when no smoke filled the air, I could see back to our line. Shortly after the firing of musketry ended, the smoke cleared away and I saw that our men had disappeared; not an able-bodied man was to be seen.

It had been found that the line we had formed the night before was flanked by both the enemy's artillery and infantry and untenable; so an order was given to withdraw to a new line which had been laid out north of the turnpike in the rear of the Chancellor House, facing south with the flanks resting on the Rappahannock River. When our Regiment fell back it had not passed over the place where the wounded lay but had gone to the right in the direction of the highway. In our rear the artillery still continued in action in order to protect the troops as they fell back and to hold the enemy's advance, which was sure to follow as soon as they discovered the withdrawal. The batteries had depressed their guns and were firing grape and canister that made a fearful noise as they passed only a few feet over our heads.

After the artillery ceased firing, there was for a time comparative quiet; but soon there was a great commotion with men shouting and officers giving orders. Looking back in the direction of our abandoned line, which I could barely see as the smoke still hung low, was a scattered line of men coming toward us on the double-quick. They advanced to near where we wounded men were lying, as that in some measure put them out of range of our artillery which then seemed to be again working with redoubled energy. Coming to a halt they dressed their line, which was much broken, and lay down. They were not dressed in Union Blue but in Confederate Gray. They made a soldierly though not a handsome appearance, as no two uniforms were exactly alike in style or color or material. The officers were much better dressed than the men; they had light gray uniforms, well fitted. Many of them presented a handsome and soldierly authority over their command. The men looked to be well armed and equipped and so far as I could observe under rigid discipline. As a whole they seemed to be older than our men but a few were very young. Their first line was followed by a second that also dressed and lay down. The officers, who were all on foot, held a brief council near us, after which the men were ordered to cross the stream. They had to cross around or over the wounded and were cautioned by their officers to be careful not to disturb them more than was necessary. They passed over us carefully, without any unkind actions or words. A few asked questions as: "Well, Yanks, how do you like it?" or "Haven't you fellows got about enough of this?" Most of them seemed and acted as though they had troubles of their own and had no desire to annoy us.

After crossing the creek, they halted and again dressed their lines that were broken by the thick bushes; then continued their advance with the second line the usual distance behind the first. By this time our batteries had retired from the top of the ridge and had swung around and fronted on the south side of the turnpike near the Chancellor House, which was then burning from the action of the Confederate batteries. As our artillery was then lined up it had full sweep of the open fields in their front. As soon as the enemy that had passed over us went beyond the crest of the hill they met a murderous fire, losing many men. Some of their wounded were brought back near us.

It was not long after the enemy's infantry had gone beyond us that I heard bugle calls to the left of our old battle line and shortly a Confederate battery came and lined up in our rear. It was from the famous Washington Light Artillery[14] of New Orleans. They had six brass Napoleon 12-pound guns and made a fine appearance. The officers were mounted and handsomely equipped; their men were more uniformly clothed than the other Confederate troops we saw. During the action they had been located on the Hazel Grove elevation where they had been able to do great damage. From what I saw, the discipline of this battery was excellent. The officer in command dismounted and came close to where we lay looking for a place to cross the stream. Our wounded were alarmed, fearing that in crossing with the guns they would be injured. The officer, who was kind as well as capable, said not to worry as he would see that no one would be hurt. He found a place where the banks were low and had his men move any wounded who were in the way. This was done carefully and not one word was said that would wound our feelings. They then went over the brow of the hill where it faced the Chancellor House, unlimbered and went into action for about a half hour. Then all firing of artillery and infantry near us gradually ended. It was about noon, the battle for the day was over, our troops had been forced to withdraw, our Army was defeated. The line our command had laid out Saturday night had proved untenable as the enemy had early in the day been able to occupy the Hazel Grove heights which were so necessary to our success. When

[14]   A noted Louisiana militia unit, it consisted of a four battery battalion. Colonel J. B. Walton commanded it at Chancellorsville.

located there, they were on our flank, where their artillery caused great destruction and disaster.

In the afternoon there was little noise of battle. In the distance we could hear some cannonading and occasional skirmishing, but it was spasmodic and before two o'clock it was quiet. The Union Army was forming and fortifying a new line, while General Lee was hurrying the greater part of his Army back toward Fredericksburg to meet the advance of General Sedgwick[15] who, with the 6th Corps, was marching toward Chancellorsville.

With us for the time all was quiet. There was nothing to disturb us but the occasional cries and groans of the wounded; not a word of complaint was heard from most of the wounded. Nearly all knew we were not only wounded but prisoners and did not know what treatment we would receive.

Shortly after the battery went over the hill, we noticed the arrival of quite a number of the stragglers and bummers who follow in the rear of all armies. Seldom if ever do these men take any part in a battle; they can always be found in the rear when the action is fought. As soon as skirmishing begins they find some excuse to sneak away from their Company and do not return until all the trouble is over. They prey on the defenseless and are the authors of most of the atrocities and disreputable things that follow in the wake of an army.

The battle now being over in our part of the field, and all danger passed, these men thought they might begin on us. They came down into the open field and over to where we lay. They commenced their work by abusive and indecent language to the wounded, after which they began to rob the wounded and the dead. One poor fellow lying near me, who

---

[15] John Sedgwick (1813-1864) followed graduation from West Point in 1837 with service in both the Seminole and Mexican Wars. Appointed a Brigadier General of Volunteers in August 1861, he commanded a division in the Peninsular Campaign and at Antietam. He became a Major General in July 1863 and commanded II, IX, and VI Corps before being killed in the Battle of Spotsylvania, May 9, 1864.

was too weak to lift his hand, was robbed of his watch and money. However, before they got very far robbing the wounded the Confederate Provost Guard came on the field from the rear. They were mounted and evidently from some Cavalry Regiment, out to round up stragglers and skulkers and get them to their commands at the front. When the Captain reached us and saw what they were doing to the dead and wounded, he went for them with a will. Using the flat of his sword he struck some of them and cursed them with as vile names as they had used in abusing us. He gathered them in a squad and hustled them off to the front where we hoped they got their deserts.

From that time on, while we were in the Confederate lines, all the Johnnies treated us with kindness and with consideration for our feelings; they did all they could to make us comfortable. They had no means with which to help us much but were willing to do what they could. I came in contact with many of their soldiers while I was a prisoner and without exception found them kind and helpful.

The battle on this beautiful Sunday morning was one of the fiercest of the war and, although it lasted less than four hours, it was a major disaster to the Union Army. By twelve o'clock all was quiet. Where we lay many of the mortally wounded had died, no cry of suffering came from them. Most of the wounded were quiet, saying little; all were weak and helpless from loss of blood, and seeming to have little interest in what was going on around them. Some were sleeping regardless of their wounds.

The smoke had cleared away and with it the fumes of burning powder. The sun shown down on us and was warm and comforting as we lay uncovered on the ground. Fortunately, when our troops withdrew, two members of our Regiment remained to care for the wounded, they were John Larmon, a musician from CompanyI, and Blanchard, a clerk for the Adjutant, who was in citizens' clothes. Both were taken by the Provost Guard; later in the day Larmon was returned to nurse our wounded. He remained with us until we were returned to the Union lines. All through the battle he had worked heroically in moving the wounded back to the gully where they would have protection. As no Surgeon had remained on our part of the field, the responsibility of caring for our Regiment's wounded and many others who lay with us was his. Larmon had no medicines, surgical instruments, or knowledge of surgery, so all he could do was nurse, feed, and care for the men in an unprofessional way. He began by making as comfortable beds as he could from the material at hand. He laid our ponchos or rubber blankets on the ground, spread our woolen blankets over them; then after we were placed on our beds, he covered us with our overcoats if we still had them. So long as the weather remained fair and warm this made a comparatively good bed. He brought me water to wash my neck and face which were covered with caked blood. I could only get a little off as my face was so badly swollen and was getting sensitive.

The bullet that entered my right cheek had glanced along the jaw bone and came out of my neck near the jugular vein. My second wound was in my left side above the hip; the bullet came out near the back bone making a ragged wound. It was difficult to turn either way to seek a comfortable position as I had been hit on both sides. As yet there was little pain but by night my jaw was stiff and swollen, my side was commencing to give me trouble and I was hot and feverish. The clotted blood had hardened so my clothing was chafing and irritating my wounds every time I moved.

Larmon had a busy afternoon and I wondered how he could keep on as he did. Every man within call wanted something and he answered every call. He was also foresighted, for early in the afternoon he went back to our firing line and gathered all the haversacks he could find that had food in them, brought them to the creek, and hid them in the bushes. Toward evening, when it was evident that the Union Army would make no further movement that day, the Johnnies came back and began to wander over the battlefield, picking up such things as they could find that were useful and espe-

cially food. There was a mass of material scattered about,
guns, equipment, such as knapsacks, blankets, caps and canteens were everywhere.

In the afternoon a great number of Confederate wounded
were brought from the woods in our front to be carried to
their rear by way of the turnpike. When they arrived in the
open field they were loaded into wagons and ambulances,
chiefly in baggage wagons as they seemed to have few ambulances. I judged from the number that were brought in that
their losses in front of our line were fully equal to ours. Later
in the afternoon we were visited by a good many of our late
enemies; they were friendly and helped our wounded in
every way they could. Larmon had not been able to make
beds for all the wounded so the Johnnies aided him by carrying those who were so badly hurt they could not help themselves and placing them on the blankets he had spread for
them. Larmon could not have moved many of the men by
himself.

The afternoon slowly passed, a long and sorrowful one for
us; then the night came, the last night on earth for many who
died for the lack of the care they needed. For those not so
severely wounded nature was kind, the night was beautiful, it
was comfortably warm, and a full moon shone down on us,
making it almost as light as day. We were so far away from
the enemy's camps that we were not annoyed by them. We
could faintly hear in the distance the rumble of wagons
passing along the turnpike and the subdued faraway sound
of fife and drum reached us. But these sounds we did not
heed, for around us were suffering men and the air was
filled with their cries and moans. At last it was quiet for all
were so exhausted that even in their pain they slept. Before
morning many died; we heard their cries no more.

On Monday, the 4th of May, there was a beautiful sunrise
heralding another perfect day. Before daybreak we were all
awake. The little sleep had during the night helped us some
but our wounds were more feverish and painful than they
were before. I could not move my lower jaw or make any

opening between my teeth. It had been twenty-four hours since the battle began and it started before we had time to get our breakfast, so we had only eaten a hardtack or two, with no coffee or meat and had gone into the battle with nearly empty stomachs. Since that time no food had passed my lips. While I had been thirsty and had taken a great deal of water, I had not been hungry. I thought that I should eat something if I could to gain strength and tried to eat a hardtack. I found that I could not even get my teeth apart, to say nothing about chewing anything. I could only take food if it was in liquid form. Larmon did what he could to get some breakfast. He went to our old line where he found a kettle that had been left. He then took some coffee from our haversacks and we all had hot coffee to drink; those who could eat hardtack had food. The coffee did me good. After our breakfast those who were not desperately wounded brightened up and as far as they could were less despondent.

Early in the forenoon the Johnnies came around to visit us. They continued to help Larmon with work he could not do by himself, such as moving men who were helpless. Those who came were on the front between us and the Union Army; and were the troops that had fought us Sunday morning. They belonged to Ramseur's[16] Brigade, which was composed of the 2nd, 4th, 14th, and 30th North Carolina Regiments. This Brigade had a fine reputation as a fighting force, and our own experience with them Sunday morning had proven this true to our satisfaction. They were well appearing and their kind treatment of our wounded stamped them as a fine class of men. They might have felt ugly and revengeful for in the battle that brigade lost nearly nine hundred men, of whom more than one hundred and sixty

---

[16] Stephen Dodson Ramseur (1837-1864) graduated from West Point in 1860 but joined the Confederacy the following year. He rose to Brigadier General in November 1862 and commanded a brigade at Chancellorsville where he was wounded. He was wounded a second time at Spotsylvania and mortally injured at Cedar Creek, Oct. 19, 1864.

had been killed.[17] This was one of the highest percentages of loss in a single engagement suffered by any organization in the Civil War; yet these men held no grudge and were glad to do what they could for us.

The weather continued clear and warm; from ten in the morning until four in the afternoon it was hot where we lay on the ground without any shade. During the day a detail began to bury the dead; there were many among and around the wounded. They were given shallow graves by the side of where they lay with the dirt thrown on them after they were placed in the trench. One poor fellow from the 2nd Massachusetts who lay a short distance from me had a narrow escape from being buried alive. We all thought he was dead for he had been motionless for a long time. When they started throwing dirt on him one of the men saw that he was alive. He lived and later was carried into our lines with the rest who survived. His was a sad case; a bullet had struck him between the eyes and he was blind. His father who was a prominent citizen of Lynn, Massachusetts, came to get him, while we lay in the hospital at Aquia Creek.

About noon, a Confederate officer rode along the line of wounded and said that a detail had been organized to move all the wounded to a central point where we would be together. He told Larmon to do what he could to have the men ready to move when the detail arrived. The place we were to go would probably be near where our batteries had been located during the battle. This was not very far from where we were.

At three o'clock they began the work of moving the wounded. They had stretchers and a few ambulances to carry the helpless; those not wounded in the legs were helped to their feet and leaning on the Johnnies were slowly assisted up the hill to the new camp. The detail with us were from the

---

[17] Bull was misinformed. Ramseur's force lost only 151 killed, 529 wounded, and 108 missing during the entire Chancellorsville battle.

2nd, and 4th North Carolina Regiments. Isaac McNutt of our Company was so low and weak he was carried on a stretcher; I did not see him again, he only lived a short time. John Hall and I kept together. He was one of the older men of our Company; he must have been forty years old and was called "Father John" by the boys. Up to this time he had stood the service well, an exception to most of those of his age; he walked along quite well although badly wounded. When the Johnnie helped me to my feet I could hardly stand at first, I was so dizzy. I soon overcame that and told him that if he could cut me a cane I thought I could get on slowly. Taking his knife he cut one of the laurel bushes close to its root, trimmed it up, and gave it to me. It is fifty years since that day, but I still have the cane as a memento of my Johnnie friend. With our late enemies helping us along and carrying our baggage, we moved along slowly.

As the Johnnies were leading us along one of them said to me, "By going a little to our left, I can show you a sight that should make a man weep, and as it is not much out of the way I will lead you to it." We reached the place where the enemy's infantry had come in view of our artillery which was retiring but had swung around in the highway and opened up with grape and canister. The leading Regiment in the advance was raked by the artillery and nearly annihilated. The wounded had been removed, but the dead lay where they had fallen; they were so thick on the ground that one could have stepped from one body to another for the whole regimental front. The bodies were terribly mutilated by the grapeshot. It was the most horrible sight I looked on during the war. We did not linger long viewing that field of death and soon reached the brow of the hill where more than fifty of our own cannon had been in action Sunday morning. There another gruesome sight met our eyes; it was the bodies of nearly a hundred horses scattered around the field in the rear of where the artillery had been engaged; all were laying on their backs with their feet in the air, their bodies swollen enormously. Not alone had men suffered and died.

Near the center of the cleared ground, in front of where the Chancellor House stood, was a log cabin that had been unoccupied. There was no sash in the windows and all the outside doors were gone. It was a dilapidated place and during the battle it had been riddled by shot and shell. The ground around this cabin looked level but we learned later to our sorrow that it was in a depression with the surrounding ground draining toward it. The field surrounding the place had at some previous time been planted to corn or tobacco. The rows and hills left after cultivation were still visible with the hills at least six inches higher than the little valleys between the rows. To the north and east of the old cabin was a peach orchard; the trees were very old and most of them dying; yet there were some beautiful blossoms on the old limbs. To the east of the orchard was a burying ground surrounded by a frame fence that was either painted or whitewashed.

Farther to the east of the burying place was a small village of tents, the headquarters of General J. E. B. Stuart[18] who was in command of General Jackson's Corps in the Sunday battle. The Confederate Army was in line on the north side of the turnpike, well protected by works they had built Sunday night. The old log cabin was to be the center of our colony and around it more than five hundred wounded men lay. Here they were to suffer, and many scores die, during the next eight days. The building was some thirty feet long, twenty feet wide, and was partitioned into three or four rooms. In it were placed those thought to be most dangerously wounded and most needing surgical treatment. A Surgeon from the 3rd Corps though he had no medical supplies or instruments had remained with his wounded, many of whom were brought to the cabin. When we reached the

---

[18] James Ewell Brown Stuart (1833-1864) was an 1854 graduate of West Point who went south in 1861. He received his Brigadier General's stars in September 1861. Named a Major General the following July he commanded the cavalry of the Army of Northern Virginia until his mortal wound at Yellow Tavern, Va., May 11, 1864.

camp he was in charge of trying to establish some order. He spoke as encouragingly as he could, saying that soon Surgeons would be on the ground with supplies; that they would come from our Army under a flag of truce. Chaplain Ambrose[19] of the 12th New Hampshire remained with his wounded and was at the camp. He was one of God's Saints and I regard him as one of the heroes of Chancellorsville.

After many halts for rest we at last reached the cabin and found the space for some distance around already occupied and the building filled to overflowing. Our conductor looked for a good place and finally located us on a comparatively level spot about a hundred feet north of the cabin. There he spread our blankets. Close by we found William Dennison, Orderly Sergeant of Company H, badly wounded. Hall, Dennison and I decided to stay together; while none of us could do much for the others, we would be company. Our Confederate friend continued to be helpful. Each of us still had his tent cloth, so he proposed to put up our tent, saying we might be sure the good weather would soon be gone and we would need our shelter. He found and drove the stakes and stretched the cloths making a finished job. When we three lay inside we had comfortable quarters. Then he filled our canteens and as he started back to his regiment said he would be back in the morning if they remained where they were. We gave him our thanks, which was all we could give, and urged him to be sure to come and see us if he could.

Finally the night came but it did not bring any Surgeons or supplies to treat the wounded, many of whom were by this time in a desperate condition. The effort made in moving to the camp had opened the wounds of many; they were bleeding again, and were inflamed and painful beyond description. There was no food, no nursing, and no medicine to dull the pain of those who were in torture. The majority were

[19] Thomas L. Ambrose (1829-1864) had been a missionary in Persia before becoming the Chaplain of the 12th New Hampshire. He was mortally wounded at Petersburg, Va., July 24, 1864.

crowded together, had no covering tents, and many very little in the way of blankets to lie on or for cover. All were so weak they could scarcely move hand or foot.

The Chaplain and Larmon did all that two men could do. They put up tents for those who had cloths but most of the men had either lost or thrown their cloths away. Those who had no tents they made as comfortable as they could by covering them with such blankets as they could find. There was little they could do to provide food. They could make some coffee but there were very scant facilities to do that. The only food we had was hardtack; we had some left in our haversacks. As there was only a limited supply of coffee Larmon made a small amount that evening. My teeth were still set and my face swollen; both my face and side pained when I moved. Fortunately I was not hungry for I could not eat the hardtack. I was able to sip the coffee which warmed me and did me good.

Hall who seemed to be getting on in a fairly comfortable way until evening had a serious time that night. He had been shot through the breast, the bullet had passed through his lungs and out through his back; he commenced to have trouble breathing. His lungs were filling up and he could not lie down; he got up and stood outside the tent where he had an attack of coughing followed by a severe hemorrhage. This relieved him. He breathed easier and came back to bed, but was very weak. In the main, we rested fairly well but were once wakened by picket firing on our front. It could not have been more than one half mile away. In our nervous condition it was not a pleasant sound, yet it was evidence that our Army was not far from us, and it might drive the enemy back and we be again within Union lines.

The morning of May 5th was bright and warm but our wounds had become so sore and we were so stiff that those of us who were able did not feel much like moving about. Many had died during the night. They were gathered up and laid side by side in the rear of a lunette that had been built by our soldiers before the battle to protect our artillery. This collection of the dead continued every day while we were in the camp and when we left scores lay there unburied. As time went on we faced a terrible condition arising from the awful odor arising from the dead horses and men that were lying all about the camp. As time went on the stench became unbearable.

Early Tuesday morning our Johnnie friend came to see us and was just as helpful as before. We had a small quantity of coffee left in our haversacks and he made coffee. He was glad to get some himself; it was a great luxury for anyone in his Army. They never had any unless they got it from the Yankees. After doing what he could to help us, he sat down and we had a visit, he giving us his history. He was a young Irishman, only twenty years old. He had come to this country from Ireland about five years before, landing in New York. There he learned the trade of a carpenter. In the summer of 1860 the man he worked for took a contract to build a store house in Wilmington, North Carolina; and since there were not many carpenters in that city, brought his employees with him from New York. The work under contract continued during the fall and winter of 1860-1861, previous to the opening of hostilities. When it commenced to look serious after Lincoln was elected, most of the workmen from the North went home. Our Johnnie decided to stay in Wilmington; he had no relatives or close friends in New York and it made no great difference where he settled and work was plentiful in North Carolina.

When Fort Sumter was captured there was excitement and enthusiasm and a Regiment of Volunteers was at once recruited in Wilmington. He was urged to join; was told it would only be a fine vacation, and all the trouble would be over in ninety days. He then enlisted and had been in active service for two years. He said he had no prejudice against the North or sectional interest in the South; that his being in the Confederate Army was accidental; but now he was there he would fight it out to the end, doing his duty. He felt that the war would soon be over since they now had us so badly whipped. We could not deny that we had just been badly whipped but even then could not agree with him as to the final end of the war. All the Johnnies were very optimistic at that time and made their boasts with confidence. Many of them would visit us when off duty. They were pleasant and did not in the least object to our standing up for our side of the argument over the war.

One of our men[20] from Company B they especially liked to visit. He was a good singer, witty, jolly, and could tell a story well. He did not seem badly wounded; a piece of shell had taken off part of his heel and not being able to walk he had been taken prisoner. He had not lost much blood so was quite strong; sang for our boys and the Johnnies, told stories, was cheerful, and did much to entertain all those around him. The Johnnies would try to have him sing "Dixie" and "My Maryland" but he would not do that. They seemed to respect him for his convictions. I remember one night they asked him to sing "Home Sweet Home". He sang it beautifully, or it seemed so to us who were there. When he finished the eyes of both the Northern and Southern boys were filled with tears. They all had home in common.

One morning a few days later we heard no singing from where he lay and I asked Larmon, what was the matter with Stover. He said that he was very ill, having been taken that night with lockjaw. There was no hope for his recovery; the following night he died, his voice hushed, his work done. He was a loss to us prisoners and many of the Johnnies who knew him expressed their regrets at his unexpected death.

The morning of May 5th, Surgeons, under a flag of truce, reported at the camp. There were four of them and they had several helpers. They began their work at once. They took a large door from one of the rooms in the log house for an operating table, placing it on barrels standing on end. The table was placed about seventy-five feet south of the house

[20] Private George Stover who enlisted from Kingsbury, N.Y.

under an old peach tree; even there it was surrounded by
wounded men, some of whom had to be moved to make
room for the table. The Surgeons then went among the
wounded looking for those that required amputation; they
said they could do nothing at that time for the other wounded. Coming to our tent, I told them about Hall's wound and
the great difficulty he had in breathing and asked them to
look at him. When they did, they said his wound should be
probed. They ran a probe through him from his breast to his
back, opening the wound so it discharged freely. This left
him in a weakened condition but in the end proved benefi-
cial. They found many that required amputation; the only
treatment they had for others was to give them a cerate with
which to rub their wounds. The Surgeons began their bloody
work at once in the immediate view of the wounded, some of
whom were not more than ten feet from the table. As each
amputation was completed the wounded man was carried to
the old house and laid on the floor; the arm or leg was
thrown on the ground near the table, only a few feet from
the wounded who were laying near by.

As the day wore on it became hot and sultry. Ever since the
campaign's start we had had wonderful weather, warm with
almost cloudless sky. About noon thunder heads began to
form in the west and south and before one in the afternoon
we heard the sound of thunder. In the days past we had
heard the artillery of men, now we were to have nature's
artillery.

By a strange coincidence as the storm was coming up from
the west, the Union batteries at our front opened up on the
Rebel lines, a reconnaissance being made by our troops.
There was first sharp musketry firing, then the batteries; but
their roar was almost drowned by the greater thunder discharge from the clouds when the storm broke. Several of the
shot and shell passed over us, one striking the ground nearby
that threw dirt high in the air. The only damage was to excite
and terrify the wounded who were so weak and nervous.
The attack was only a feint that was soon over.

It was about two in the afternoon when the storm started; it lasted about two hours. The thunder and lightning were terrific and the rain came down in sheets. I had never before witnessed and certainly never experienced one like it. When the storm was over we found the area surrounding the log cabin was a pond. All the rows left between the hills that had been made when the land was cultivated were filled with water with the little hills dotting the top of the dirty water. Where most of the wounded lay it was from four to six inches deep. Our tent was nearly one hundred feet from the cabin on higher ground and for some time we were fairly dry, but as the storm continued it drove the rain and spray through our tent cloths and we were soon as wet as we could be. We were fortunate that the water did not, at once, run into our tent; however, the ground underneath was soon soaked and our blankets wet.

The condition of most of the wounded was deplorable. More than half had no tent covering, so had to take the full force of the storm. Many could not move without help; they lay in the gutters between the rows, and were half submerged. A few had the strength to sit up in the muddy pool but the greater part lay sprawled in the mud and filth with nothing between them and the ground but their soaked woolen blankets. Many did not even have a blanket. I saw many men lying in from three to five inches of water. We were told, though I did not see this, that on the east side of the cabin two men were drowned. They were lying close under the eaves and were unable to move when they were covered by the water that fell from the roof.

If it had cleared after the storm and warm weather followed the rain might not have done so much damage as the water would have seeped into the ground and the sun would have dried out our blankets and clothing. After the thunder shower the weather changed, became cold, the wind shifted to the north, and there followed a steady downpour that was so heavy there was no lessening of the water around the cabin. It is now more than fifty years since that day, but in my memory, I can yet see those wounded men as they lay on the ground half covered with the yellow mud and water. The night came and the rain increased. Those who were fortunate enough to have a tent sat up, back to back to brace each other, either shivering with chills or burning with fever from their wounds. There were no lights about the camp, the darkness was impenetrable, and the groans and shrieks of the wounded could be heard on every side. At last the dawn came but the clouds were low and the rain continued. Before morning Hall became so exhausted he could no longer sit up so laid down in the water that was then an inch deep in the tent. He gasped for breath and prayed that he might die. We feared he might be dying and did what we could to cheer him up. When the day broke and we could see each other he rallied and his breathing was better. He tried to sit up but did not have the strength. As he made the effort, he smiled and said: "I would be dead, only I am a Frenchman; nothing can kill a Frenchman." He was a wiry little fellow of French descent. In spite of his severe wound and exposure in the water he lived to return to the Union lines. His wounds healed but his lungs never regained their strength and within a year he died from the effect of his wound.

We had not closed our eyes that night and the morning found us chilled through and through and exhausted. Looking out of our tent we saw a desolate place; the water had mostly filtered into the ground and there was left a surface of yellow mud. Lying in this mud were hundreds of wounded men. They were quiet for they were too exhausted to do anything but lay where they were.

The Chaplain and Larmon were early at work. They looked discouraged and ill for they had labored all night to do what they could for those who were in the most desperate condition. When Larmon came to our tent to see if he could do anything for us he said he was heartsick for he had nothing to use to aid the suffering or feed the wounded. Many had died that night. Nearly all the hardtack and coffee that was left had been destroyed by the storm. Fortunately we had placed our small supply in one haversack and hung it on the ridge pole of our tent to keep it dry. This was in fair condition but it was so wet outside we could not make a fire for coffee.

The rain continued until noon and it seemed as though all nature had conspired against us. The storm had been so heavy that the Rappahannock River rose so rapidly and the current was so swift it threatened to carry away the pontoon bridge at United States Ford, the only crossing then available for our Army. The fear of the loss of this bridge was later given by General Hooker as one of the reasons for the withdrawal of the Army without renewing the conflict.

Early in the afternoon the rain stopped and we again saw the sun. Our good Johnnie friend came to give us the news and see how he could help us. His news was that the Yankees, as he called us, were gone. The Confederates had made an advance that morning and found the Union works empty and it was reported that our Army had recrossed the river. After giving us the "good news," as he called it, he started to aid us in every way he could. First he made coffee, building a fire near our tent that also warmed us, a comfort after the chilly night.

The coffee was wonderful. I again tried to eat some hardtack but could not chew it. Our friend then took our woolen blankets and hung them on the limbs of an old tree where the wind and sun would dry them. After that he opened the tent so the sun would shine on the wet ground. When night came the ground under the tent, while not entirely dry, was fairly so and our blankets had dried out a lot in the afternoon sun. That night we made our bed by spreading our rubber blankets on the ground and covering them with our woolen blankets. Our bed was still damp but we were in luxury compared with the night before and far more comfortable than most of those around us. The Chaplain and Larmon were still the only workers to care for the wounded who were not undergoing amputation; they put in a busy day getting the men out of the mud and to higher ground. When night

came the condition of all, as a whole, was better, except there
was no food and hunger was pressing. What those men did
that day was beyond description; only those who saw them
work could know what they did.

With few exceptions the night of the 6th passed quietly.
Hall seemed more comfortable and we got some sleep. While
our bed was still damp, the weather was warmer. We did not
mind the wet bed when we were not in a chill. There was one
exception to the quiet that came from the tent next to ours.
In it were two boys from the 12th New Hampshire, the
Chaplain's Regiment. He had been very helpful in looking
after them. This night one of them was in great agony. The
Chaplain came and remained a long time and while he was
there we could hear him pray for them. After that they were
quiet. One of them had died from lockjaw. He had been
wounded in the foot and the rain and exposure had brought
that dread disease. During the next two days there were
many cases of that disease and they were all fatal. Nearly all
who had lockjaw had wounds in their foot or knee.

On the morning of the 7th our Johnnie confirmed the
report he had brought the day before of the retreat of the
Union Army. He said that our troops were all on the north
side of the river and we could expect no rescue from them.
Now this hope was blasted we wondered what would become
of us; would we remain as we were until death claimed all, or
what? So far the Confederate command had given us no
attention whatever since they moved us to a central point.
Not a thing had been done officially either for or against us
who lay wounded. We were entirely ignored and were to all
appearance of no more consequence than the dead horses
that lay around us.

Starvation that had threatened for several days became
acute. The badly wounded were getting weaker every hour
and even the stronger were breaking down. Wounds were
feverish and festering and hunger was now adding to our
troubles; food was as necessary as nursing. Great numbers

were still laying in the mud, helpless. There were no privy vaults, but had there been the majority were too weak to go to them. There still remained nearly five hundred men in the camp. I must leave it to your imagination for I cannot describe these awful conditions, which were made worse by the stench from the dead men and horses. None of the men or horses had been buried. The horses lay where they died, the men lay in a row side by side south of the cabin in sight of all the wounded.

The Chaplain and Larmon realized how serious the lack of food had become and knew it must be had from some source or all would shortly die of starvation. The only place to get food was from the Confederate Army, so the Chaplain decided to appeal to the Headquarters of General Stuart, located a half mile from our camp. The General received him pleasantly but said he could do nothing as he was only temporarily in command and had no authority over the Commissary Department; but even if he had, he could do nothing as his own troops were on half rations. He referred the Chaplain to General Lee who might be able to help us. The Chaplain walked to Lee's Headquarters, that was two miles further on toward Fredericksburg, and found the General there. He made known his errand and asked for help; Surgeons, medicines, and especially food. General Lee told him he could furnish neither Surgeons nor medicines as they had not half enough for their own wounded, whom he said numbered from ten to twelve thousand, but he would see that a load of meal was sent to our camp that day. The Chaplain was thankful for even that but said that some of the wounded so needed food that he would like permission to carry back a sack when he returned to the camp. He was back in the camp at three that afternoon exhausted, for he brought with him a fifty pound sack.

I heard the Chaplain tell of his visit with General Lee who expressed his regrets that he could do no more than furnish the meal. They at once took the kettle that we used for coffee and boiled the corn meal in water making a thin pudding. By four they were giving it to their patients. I was thankful to get a little for it was almost liquid and did not require chewing; so I could take it in my mouth and swallow it. Up to this time I had not been hungry, but this meal tasted good, although it was cooked without salt. About dark that day the load of meal promised by General Lee came. It was the only food we had for the next six days.

After the rain ceased the Surgeons continued their work of amputation and during the whole of our stay did nothing as far as I could see to treat any of the wounded except those requiring amputation. I presume they did what they thought was the best but we wounded men thought that they should have given some attention to all the seriously wounded. Hall was an example. Shot through the lungs, he was in danger of suffocation if his wound was allowed to close without treatment to keep it open. There were many who had head wounds, who were delirious and needed attention. One fellow suffered unspeakable agony for several days before he died and begged the Confederates to shoot him and put him out of his misery. It seemed to us that our Surgeons should have had something to relieve such agony and have given some attention to those not requiring amputation.

One man for whom they did nothing was for several days the terror of the camp. He was shot through the head near the top of his skull. At the place where the bullet hit his brain protruded. He was wildly delirious at times, would spring to his feet and run blindly about regardless of the wounded in his path, tramping those in the way. When the paroxysm was over, he would sink down and lie like one dead. His end came at night, and was tragic. A gun was fired, probably accidentally, near the old cabin that was filled with amputation cases all lying on the floor. The man wounded in the head was on the ground near us. With the report of the gun, he jumped up and ran and entered the cabin through the front door. On the further side of the room was a large dish shelf about three feet above the floor on which was a lighted candle. The demented man must have seen the light, and started for it, tramping on the wounded men on the way. He laid down on the shelf and died before morning.

When he crossed the room he tramped on three men who had that day had their legs amputated. As no Surgeons were there they bled to death before help came. One of the men was Albert Doan of Company K of our Regiment, a boy only eighteen years old, the son of a widow . . . I could tell of incidents of this kind that occurred from day to day. One reading about our camp might think I was exaggerating for no one who was not there could imagine the conditions; wounds of every conceivable kind, the agony of mortally wounded men who lingered without aid until death came. Then there was the storm that flooded the camp and brought chills and death to many.

By May 8th our wounds had all festered and were hot with fever; our clothing which came in contact with them was so filthy and stiff from the dried blood that it gravely aggravated our condition. Many wounds developed gangrene and blood poisoning; lockjaw caused suffering and death. While the stench from nearby dead horses and men was sickening it was not worse than that from the living who lay in their own filth. Finally, not the least of our troubles were the millions of flies that filled the air and covered blood-saturated clothing when they could not reach and sting the unbandaged wounds. As days went by none of these conditions improved, except the cries of the mortally wounded gradually lessened as they, one by one, were carried away and laid by the side of those who had gone before them. In all these days whatever care we had was due to the Chaplain and Larmon.

I want to say again that the Confederate soldiers were always kind and helpful. They would do anything that the Chaplain might ask for they had great respect for him. They saw how faithful he was. I often think of him as one of the nameless heroes of the war, one whose service was never recognized.

After the storm was over, many citizens of the surrounding

country came to see the battlefield and get a view of the wounded "Yanks." They were mostly old men and women and children. These elderly people did not have the kindly feeling for us shown by the soldiers that had fought a few days before. The battle had, it would seem, created a feeling of respect on the part of the soldiers. Usually when these people came they were on horseback. They would ride up close to the wounded seemingly filled with hatred. They would give no words of sympathy or cheer and no word of kindly help. Some of them seemed to rather enjoy seeing us so badly off and would make sport of our wretched condition to the women and children who were with them. One fat old fellow on horseback rode up close to our tent and said in a loud voice: "What are you'ens doin down here fightin we'uns in our bush for?" Our Johnnie friend, who was with us at the time, turned on the old man and said, "You just keep quiet old man, don't you see these are wounded men. You have no right or business to insult them." The old fellow rode away without finding out why we were in his bush.

The days passed slowly. There was no food except the "mush," of which we had just enough to keep alive. The Surgeons continued their bloody work with no lack of subjects, many of whom had not been reached at the time we left for the Union lines. This operating place with its bloody cupboard door, its bloody Surgeons, with the stack of human arms and legs thrown behind them was an awful sight that cannot dim from ones memory.

Early Tuesday morning, May 12th, we were told that a Federal ambulance train was on its way to Chancellorsville to take us back to our Army and friends. We had been nine days wounded prisoners, a fearful experience. When the news came there was a faint cheer, for help was at hand. That forenoon Confederate officers came and took a list of all prisoners, having each one sign a parole not to enter active service again until properly exchanged. At noon we were given our last ration of meal and water. Our Johnnie friend came over from his camp to help us make ready. He folded our blankets and packed our knapsacks, took down our tent and did everything to make us ready to go. It was nearly three in the afternoon when the ambulances came in sight over the road from United States Ford. All were excited and hope revived in even the weakest and most despondent. The placing of the wounded in the ambulances was slow and tedious, half of them could not help themselves in any way. Four badly wounded were placed on the floor of each wagon side by side; those who could sit up were closely packed on the seats. It was nearly five o'clock when we were ready to move. Our Johnnie friend stayed with us until we started, helping in placing our baggage where it would be convenient. He handed me the cane that he had cut when we left the battlefield for our camp and said to keep this to remember him. We shook hands, each wishing the other good luck. I little thought we would ever see each other again but I met him eight months later.

As soon as the ambulances were loaded, they started on their journey to the Union lines. We of the 12th Corps were to go to Aquia Creek, twenty-five miles from our prison camp. As we rejoiced at our deliverance we little realized what was before us in making that awful journey. The storm that had caused us so much suffering had brought havoc to the roads. Our Army had found them next to impassable and had been forced to corduroy them to move the artillery and trains. The ambulances had to use these roads to get us to the hospitals.

There could be no rougher surface than that of a corduroy road as made by soldiers in the Civil War. All kinds of available material was used in their building but they were chiefly constructed of logs, rails, and poles. These were laid across the road without regard to size; a log a foot through might be placed next a pole only three inches thick. The roughness of the road made no great difference in moving the wagons and cannon; all they wanted was to be held up from the bottom-

less quagmires in the surface of the road. Looking at a train
of wagons moving along one of these roads one would think
that they would capsize, as they rocked from side to side.

The distance from Chancellorsville to the Ford was only
about six miles. Our Army did not have to use this section of
road after the storm so it was not corduroyed. It was planned
that we would only go to the river that afternoon and make
the rest of the journey the next day. After we started we
found it was no pleasure trip for as our wounds were commencing to heal the least jar seemed to be tearing them
apart. It would have been painful enough had we been traveling over good roads; this primitive Virginia road was far
from that and we soon found that the journey would test our
endurance. We crossed the turnpike, over which we marched
before the battle, and took a road leading to United States
Ford. We passed the ruins of the Chancellor House; just
beyond were the works constructed by the enemy after they
had driven our forces from the field. The Confederates were
then packing up and making ready to move to some other
place, probably their old position at Fredericksburg.

It took at least two hours to reach the Ford. The river was
high, so pontoons had been laid for the ambulances to cross.
We were met by quite a large force of cavalry, all on the
north side of the river except a few who were waiting for us
to cross.

When we reached the little valley bordering the river, we
found an eager crowd of civilians waiting our arrival. They
had come from the North in search of, or to get information
about, their friends or relations who had been in the battle
and who were missing and probably killed or wounded.
When each ambulance crossed the bridge they would visit it,
anxiously looking at the wounded. They would not, however,
remain long as they could not stand the stench of those they
saw. Many turned away quickly, their stomachs could not
stand the pressure. We remained at the river only long
enough to complete the search for the missing. When this
was over most of the enquirers looked depressed and down-

cast for they had looked in vain. I wondered as I saw these prosperous men, for none but those who had means and influence could come so far to the front, what manner of story they would have to tell when they returned to their peaceful homes in the North. They would probably think they knew something of the horrors of war; yet how little they did know.

There are quite high cliffs on the north side of the Rappahannock. We were driven to the top and stopped there for the night. It had been a hard journey from the camp; the jolting about in the wagons had been almost unbearable. From an ambulance near where we were unloaded two men were taken out who had died on the way. However, we looked forward to better things after another day's travel. That night we were given hardtack and coffee for supper. I only drank the coffee for I could not yet eat solid food.

Early the morning of May 13th we again had hardtack and coffee and started on our twenty-mile journey to the hospital. Soon we were on the road leading toward Stafford and shortly reached the part that had been corduroyed; then trouble began. The ambulance rolled and rocked and it was with difficulty we could keep our seats, the men who had to lie down were thrown against each other and the sides of the wagon. As the wheels advanced they would strike a large log, go over it, and then fall to the next log perhaps a foot or more below. It was hard to control the horses, they would go over the large ones with a jump and that meant torture. One can hardly imagine the suffering of those who had broken bones, or who had their arms and legs amputated with the stumps not yet healed.

That afternoon we were surprised to receive a visit on the road from Lieutenant Willis Swift[21] of our Company. He had learned that the wounded of the 12th Corps were on their way to the Aquia Creek Hospital and came to see if there

---

[21]   Willis Swift, Jr. from Ft. Ann. Initially the Orderly Sergeant of Company D, he succeeded Quinn as Second Lieutenant.

were any Company D men in the train. Being shown our
ambulance he came to it but when told who we were he could
hardly believe us. Our wounds, our starved condition, and
our unwashed dirt and filth so changed us, he would not
have recognized us if we had not made ourselves known.
Swift said it was a great surprise to find us alive; we were
supposed to have been killed and had been so reported to
our people at home. When Hall heard him, he said with a
gasp, "Will, you can't kill a Frenchman." Poor John was game
but his wound got him even though he was a Frenchman.

We reached the hospital about five in the afternoon. It was
pleasantly located in a grove of pine trees; its large tents were
laid out in perfect order. Here was to be our home for some
time. In the tents each had a cot with mattress and blankets;
such luxury seemed too much for us. We were stripped of
our dirty clothes, thoroughly washed, our wounds cleaned by
Surgeons, and bandaged; then we were given food that we
could eat. We felt we were now again in God's Country.

It had only been seventeen days since we started from
Stafford on this disastrous campaign. A short time but an
eventful one for us. On our return many felt that during that
time of trouble and suffering there had come a crisis in our
lives. We had started out as boys with all the enthusiasm and
ardor of youth; we had returned feeling that we were men,
that the dividing line between boyhood and manhood had
been passed by us on the field of Chancellorsville. Not all of
those who came back from our prison camp would see further service. For some it was ended by their wounds, others
did not leave their hospital tent until they were carried away
for burial. In the tent where I was placed two died within a
week. One of them was Horace Howard, First Sergeant of
Company K of our Regiment. He had received a shell wound
in his thigh that crushed the bone and his leg should have
been amputated while in the camp. When he reached the
hospital it was too late, nothing could be done for him. I saw
a Surgeon examine his wound and remove more than a pint
of worms or maggots. Imagine the suffering this man must

have endured in the ten days on the battlefield and on the journey to the hospital.

Our Regiment was encamped only three miles from the hospital and many of the boys visited us. It was good to see their faces again. I gained strength rapidly and was soon able to walk about the encampment.

About June 1st, there was unusual activity in every department at Aquia Creek; transports were being loaded with all kinds of material that was then shipped away. The reason was soon known. General Lee had started his Army on the Gettysburg Campaign and his advance was already in the Shenandoah Valley. The Army of the Potomac was waiting for Lee to develop the course of his campaign and would then be on the move. Then our line on the Rappahannock River would be abandoned and that would make it necessary to move the hospital.

Furloughs were issued to all wounded men who were able to travel. On June 3rd I received mine for thirty days and soon after with many others I boarded a steamboat for Washington. From there I took a train homeward bound.

CHAPTER FOUR

Return to the Regiment for Service in Tenn. & Ala. Prior to Atlanta Campaign

May 13th, 1863-May 5th, 1864

On return to Stafford, after the battle, the Regiment's list of killed and wounded and missing was compiled, and my family was notified that I had been badly wounded, it was thought mortally, and I was left on the battlefield. Great was their joy when two weeks later, after they had abandoned hope of my being alive, they received a letter from me sent from Aquia Creek, telling of my arrival at the hospital and my expected furlough home. I was welcomed with rejoicing by my family and neighbors, and everything was done for my comfort. It was good to be home again.

While I was mending my wounds our Regiment was at Gettysburg and then sent on its way to Tennessee. Naturally I looked forward to returning to active service as soon as I was able. While my wounds were not completely healed; my furlough was about to expire, so I decided to return though I could probably have had an extension. Sidney Weer of Company E, who also had been wounded at Chancellorsville and

was home on furlough, decided to go back at the same time.
On August 4th we took the train for New York and from
there went to Philadelphia, arriving there early in the morning of the 6th. It was our duty to report to the 12th Corps
Hospital from which we had been furloughed. On enquiry we
were told that it was probably still at Gettysburg. Weer had a
brother[1] who had been wounded in the battle and we supposed that he was there; so we took a train to that place. We
found that the hospital had been moved to Virginia. The
remaining wounded that had been left in Gettysburg were
housed in a church. We went to look for Weer's brother only
to find that he was dead and buried, having died from the
wound he received July 2nd. Weer was heartbroken; he had
not expected to even find his brother very seriously wounded. He found only his sword and belt. Although we both
required further treatment we could not have it at Gettysburg; that temporary hospital was full to overflowing. The
Surgeon advised us to go to Baltimore and kindly gave us a
letter to the Surgeon in charge of the hospital there. By this
time we were both nearly used up; as neither of us was strong
and his brother's death had unnerved Weer. We started at
once for Baltimore and reported at the hospital that evening.
At first the Surgeon said he could not take us in as they had
more patients than they could house and properly care for;
but after reading the letter, he decided to admit us.

I have no record of the name of this hospital,[2] but it was an
old established institution near the center of the city. We had
good beds in a large ward and were well treated. I rapidly
gained strength and on August 24th was transferred to the
U.S. Hospital located at Patterson Park[3] in the suburbs of
the city. As Weer's wounds were not fully healed he was not

---

[1]   Captain Norman Fox Weer (1836-1863) of Company E had been wounded at
Chancellorsville and was mortally injured at Gettysburg, July 3, 1863.
[2]   Probably the University of Maryland Hospital built in 1823.
[3]   Site of War of 1812 fortifications rebuilt in 1861 by the 10th Maine as Fort
Washburn. It was later used as a camp and hospital. The remains of some of the
fortifications can still be seen.

transferred with me. The buildings had originally been used to house regular army troops but had been refitted for a hospital. These barracks were located in a large park; the grounds were sandy and not well kept. A large number of patients were there at that time, mostly men who had been wounded at Gettysburg. I was held in this hospital for some weeks longer than I desired. I was a stranger to everyone, felt quite strong, and wanted to join my Company in Tennessee.

Early in September I made application to be forwarded to my Regiment. On October 1st I was released and with others sent to the Convalescent Camp[4] located near Alexandria where we were "herded" in tents to wait for transportation to our various commands. All who came to this camp were just recovering from sickness or wounds and should have had decent housing while waiting until a detachment was formed to take them to their organization in the field. At this place tents were used. They had been in service for years; were ragged, leaky and very filthy. Straw had at some time been placed to make beds but it had been there so long that it was as fine as chaff and was dirty and lousy beyond belief. As the weather was warm and dry, many of us doubled up and made our beds on the open ground outside the tents rather than fight the vermin.

The food was on a par with the housing. Had I not been able to purchase something to eat outside I might have starved. Our bill of fare, morning, noon and night, was coffee, hardtack, occasionally soft bread, and boiled pork. At the commissary tent they dealt out the food about as follows: our coffee was made in a large kettle, it was black and strong and sweetened with soft and very black sugar. The pork was pulled out of a barrel; it had evidently months before been boiled at some packing factory, laid down in the barrel and covered with the grease that came from the boiling. This

---

[4] Commonly referred to as Camp Misery it was south of the modern Shirley Highway near the Army and Navy Country Club.

pork was in long pieces and was pulled out with a meat hook; when brought to the surface the sound of the suction was like the noise made when one pulled his feet out of Virginia mud. The grease was then scraped off with a knife and the pork, which was fat and thick, was sliced and placed between pieces of bread or two hardtacks. If one had the stomach to want more he could have two. I could not even face one; just took the coffee and hardtack; and got one meal a day from a cheap restaurant. Luckily we were there only four days.

I have given this rather full detail of my experience in this Convalescent Camp in order to show the kind of housing and food that was given Volunteer Soldiers, who after having been sick or wounded were leaving the hospitals in the vicinity of Washington for further service. This was even as late as October 1863. In the light of modern sanitary requirements, this account might seem overdrawn, but it is true and is in no way exaggerated.

By October 6th there were enough men in camp to form a train for the West. Before leaving Washington we had another meal at the "Sheds" where our Government fed us when we first reached the city; it was the same shameful place. After we had eaten, the train that was to take us west was ready. It was made up of box cars. Although it was to be a long journey, they were not fitted with seats so we had to sit on the floor or at the best on our knapsacks; the cars were so full one could hardly lie down. Many climbed to the roofs of the cars and when night came made our beds there; to keep from falling off we tied ourselves with our tent cloths to the ridgeboards of the cars. In that way we spent several nights and slept well.

Our route was over the Baltimore and Ohio Railroad. On the fourth day we arrived at Columbus, Ohio, where we spent the night in the station yard. We had a chance to go to a restaurant and get a good meal. The only food we had on the way from Washington was the hardtack in our haversacks. No provision was made to feed us along our route. We were nearly starved when we reached Columbus.

In the morning those who had traveled on our train were broken up into various detachments as they went different ways to join their commands. Our squad was to go south through Cincinnati. During the afternoon about fifty took the train, arriving in that city on the evening of the fifth day of our journey. We were taken to the Old Soldiers Home to stay until we had transportation to continue. This was a comfortable place where we had an opportunity to wash and rest after five days of discomfort.

We were in Cincinnati two days, one of which was election day October 13th. The excitement was high; a Governor was to be elected, and the Copperhead candidate Vallandigham was running against Old John Brough.[5] I was out in the evening to see and hear what I could of the election returns. When it was known that Brough would have nearly 100,000 majority the people went wild. They paraded and kept shouting until morning. A Copperhead hardly dared show his face in Cincinnati that night.

On the 14th we took a boat for Louisville and had a pleasant trip down the Ohio River. The water was low and we scraped along over the bars, making slow time. I spread my blankets early on the lower deck; when I woke in the morning we were near Louisville where we landed at ten o'clock. Seven that evening we took a military train for Nashville. This was an accommodation train, mostly freight; but there were three old worn-out passenger cars. Poor as they were, they were palace cars compared with the box cars we started with in Washington. We traveled right through to Nashville, arriving there at two in the afternoon the next day. Here the train remained until dark, then continued on to Murfreesboro which was a supply base for the Army. When we reached there at ten that night we were taken to the Court House for quarters. This building had been used

    [5]   Clement Laird Vallandigham (1820-1871) was an Ohio Congressman who was the leading opponent of the war. He ran for governor against John Brough (1811-1865) and lost by over 100,000 votes.

by both the Confederate and Union Armies, and I do not think it had been cleaned since the war started. To say it was dirty would have been praise; it was overrun with rats and vermin and unbearably filthy. The rats seemed to live on the food the soldiers threw or dropped on the floor when they were eating. They were almost as tame as cats and ran in every direction under our feet. They had holes in the sides of the room and would dive in them like a flash if you made after them.

It was past eleven that night when we reached this model rooming house, and knew nothing about its permanent residents. Tired as we could be, we spread our blankets and tried to sleep but that was impossible. The rats were all over us and they squealed and fought. I was laying on the floor trying to get to sleep when the soldier next to me gave an awful yell. I asked him what was the matter and he said a rat had just run over his face. Then he jumped up and said he would not stay there. I said, "I am with you." We gathered our things, went outside and made our beds on the ground. It was not very cold so we had a good night's rest. The boys who stayed in the building said they got no sleep as the rats kept up the racket all night.

I heard that the Regiment was guarding the railroad some forty miles south of Murfreesboro. I was anxious to join my Company. We had been two weeks on the road from Washington and the journey had been anything but pleasant. In the morning I went to the officer in charge of our detachment and asked him to let me proceed to my Regiment. He said he would if he could locate it. He found it was stationed at a place called Decherd and secured my transportation. I arrived there before night and went to our camp that was near the station.

They were surprised and glad to see me, and I was sure glad to see them. Many of my old friends were missing; the Company now numbered less than sixty. Forty were gone, either killed, wounded, or sick and disabled. Those who were there looked well and contented; they now had become in-

ured to the conditions they had to meet in the service. Many
changes had been made in their camp life and they were living very differently than when I left them at Aquia Creek.
There were now no company cooks; rations were issued
directly to the men and they prepared their own food. The
three men who occupied a tent formed a mess, pooled their
rations and did their own cooking. This plan proved to be
most efficient as in this way a meal could be quickly had
when needed. The only mess utensils required were a spi-
der,[6] coffee pot, and hatchet; each man had one article to
carry. Under this system of feeding the men were more inde-
pendent, well satisfied, and much better fed.

I reported to the Captain who was happy to see me back. I
told him that I was fit for duty but would have to have a new
gun and equipment for some Johnnie was now using those I
had at Chancellorsville. The 12th Corps was then stretched
along the railroad from Nashville to Bridgeport, guarding it
from an attack by the Rebel cavalry, commanded by Forrest
and Wheeler.[7] Every bridge and culvert had to be protected
or they would be blown up or burned, making it impossible
to use the railroad. It was most important that nothing delay
the movement of supplies that were held at Stevenson and
Bridgeport until the line was opened to Chattanooga and
food sent to Thomas's[8] starving Army.

---

[6]   A cast iron frying pan with legs to allow it to stand among the coals of a fire.

[7]   Nathan Bedford Forrest (1821-1877) was a businessman turned cavalryman.
He became a Brigadier General in July 1862, a Major General in December 1863,
and a Lieutenant General in February 1865. An outstanding cavalry commander he
led the Confederate cavalry in the Chickamauga, Franklin, and Nashville campaigns. Joseph Wheeler (1836-1906) graduated from West Point in 1859 and joined
the Confederacy. He became a Brigadier General in October 1862 and a Major
General in January 1863. He commanded the cavalry in the Atlanta campaign and
during Sherman's March to the Sea.

[8]   George Henry Thomas (1816-1870) graduated from West Point in 1840 and
served in the Seminole and Mexican Wars. Named a Brigadier General of Volunteers in August 1861, he became a Major General the following April. He succes-
sively commanded a division, XIV Corps, and the Army of the Cumberland. He
earned the nickname "Rock of Chickamauga" for his stubborn defensive battle

I reported at Decherd just in time to be in a new movement, for the next day we broke camp and went further
south toward Stevenson, Ala., and for a week were advancing
nearer the front.

On October 21st while we were camped at a railroad station I saw General Grant[9] for the first time; he was on his
way to take command of the Armies that were gathering
there. His train stopped for some time to meet a train coming
from the south. When it was known he was on the train the
men grouped around his car and began to cheer. After a
little time he came out on the platform leaning on two
crutches, for he could not walk; he had been thrown from his
horse a few weeks before and was badly hurt.[10] He wore an
army slouch hat with bronze cord around it, quite a long
military coat, unbuttoned, no sword or belt, and there was
nothing to indicate his rank. His appearance would have
attracted no attention had he not been General Grant. When
the boys called for a speech he bowed and said nothing. He
could not lift his hat, as was usual for the officers to do, since
both his hands grasped his crutches. After bowing for a short
time he went back to his chair in the car. It was while in this
painful condition that he planned and fought the battles of
Missionary Ridge and Lookout Mountain, a campaign among
the most successful of his career.

which saved the Union army at Chickamauga but his reputation rests more solidly
on his defense of Chattanooga, the Battle of Lookout Mountain, and his devastating
defeat of Hood's army at Nashville.

[9]   Ulysses Simpson Grant (1822-1885) was an 1843 product of West Point who
served in the Mexican War. He left the Army in 1854 but was commissioned a
Brigadier General of Volunteers in May 1861. He captured Forts Henry and Donel-
son in February 1862 which earned him a promotion to Major General. After his
victories at Shiloh, Vicksburg, and Chattanooga he was promoted to Lieutenant
General and named General in Chief. Thereafter he directed Union war strategy
while accompanying the Army of the Potomac. He continued as head of the Army
until elected President in 1868.

[10]   While returning from a review near New Orleans in August 1864 Grant's horse
had slipped and fallen on him. Although no bones were broken the injury was
extremely painful and Grant was confined to his bed until early October.

On October 24th we reached Bridgeport, at that time the terminus of the railroad. From there to Chattanooga the road had been practically destroyed by the enemy. The bridge over the Tennessee River had been rebuilt and our Regiment was to remain there to guard it and the great quantity of supplies stored there for later delivery. The weather was getting cold so we built light winter quarters and were comfortable. There was little drilling, as up to November 15th our time was taken not only in guard duty but in helping in the Commissary and Quartermaster Departments in unloading and storing freight as it arrived. After the 15th when the "Cracker Line" was opened near to Chattanooga, we helped in loading and shipping supplies by the little steamboat that we had built while at Bridgeport. While we were there the 11th Corps and the 2nd Division of the 12th opened up the railroad to within eight miles of Thomas's Army. This helped in sending food to those who had been starving in Chattanooga as previous to that supplies had to be carried over mountain roads for a distance of sixty miles.

While we were at Bridgeport, I again met my Confederate friend, who had done so much for me when I lay wounded at Chancellorsville. One afternoon I proposed to my tent mate Nat Rowell[11] that we go over to the island to see the Johnnies captured in the battles of Lookout Mountain and Missionary Ridge. They were in a dilapidated condition; the weather was cold and they built large fires to keep warm. As we passed along the edge of the crowd just outside of the guards, a Johnnie about fifty feet inside shouted to me: "Yank, Yank, come over here." The guard let me pass and about half way I met my young Irish friend who did so much for me in our prisoners' camp at Chancellorsville. He had been with his regiment at Gettysburg, after that they came west with Longstreet's[12] command. He had been in both the battles of Chickamauga and Chattanooga and was captured in the latter.

---

[11] Private (later Corporal) Nathaniel S. Rowell came from Fort Ann.

[12] James Longstreet (1821-1904) graduated from West Point in 1842 and served in both the Seminole and Mexican Wars. He joined the Confederacy, being named

He said, "Why you and I have changed places. I am now a
prisoner but thank God! I am not wounded." He was no
longer optimistic of Confederate success, saying he could see
that the South did not have the means to continue much
longer. He said, "Look at these men. They are good exam-
ples of our Army. You see they are in rags and many are
without shoes; for weeks they have not had enough to eat." I
asked him if there was anything I could do for him for I was
anxious to show my appreciation for all he had done for me.
He said he was in want of nothing; the prisoners were well
treated, had plenty to eat, and were to go north in the morning. He told me he would remain there as he had no special
interest in the South. I wanted to take him to our camp for
the night but that was not allowed. The next day the prisoners were entrained; many with bare feet had old cloths wound
around them. It was a pitiful sight. Fortunately my friend
was fairly well shod and again said he needed nothing. As the
train moved slowly away we again shook hands; it was our
last handshake and our final wishes of good fortune in our
future lives. Was it not strange that we should have been
brought together after eight months at a place more than a
thousand miles from Chancellorsville. I never heard from
him again.

On November 20th the Army of General Sherman[13]
known as the Army of the Tennessee, consisting of the 15th

a Brigadier General in June 1861 and Major General the following October. He led
a corps in the Shenandoah Valley, at Antietam, and Fredericksburg. Promoted to
Lieutenant General in October 1862, he commanded a corps at Gettysburg and in
September 1863 led two divisions to reinforce Bragg's army in Tennessee. He
rejoined Lee for the Wilderness campaign, being severely wounded May 6, 1864.

[13] William Tecumseh Sherman (1820-1891) was a West Point graduate of 1840
who served in the Mexican War and left the Army in 1853. Reinstated in 1861, he
commanded a brigade at Bull Run and became a Brigadier General in May 1861.
Promoted to Major General in May 1862 he took part in the Vicksburg campaign
and relieved Grant as commander in the West during March 1864. He conducted
the Atlanta, Georgia, and Carolina campaigns. He succeeded Grant as Commander
in Chief of the Army.

and 17th[14] Corps, passed our camp. It was on its way to reinforce General Grant, who had been placed in supreme command and was then with General Thomas. This Army looked
quite unlike our own that had originally been a part of the
Army of the Potomac. They all wore large hats instead of
caps; were carelessly dressed, both officers and men; and
marched in a very irregular way, seemingly not caring to
keep well closed up and in regular order. These were faults
in marching which we had been taught to avoid. They could
be excused for their loose marching, however, as they had
just made a three hundred mile movement on the way to join
Grant. We found their boast was that they "put on no style."
They were a large fine type of men, all westerners; it was
easy to see that at any serious time they would close up and
be there. As they passed by we viewed their line and a good
deal of friendly chaffing was done. They expressed their
opinion that we were tin soldiers. "Oh look at their little caps.
Where are your paper collars? Oh how clean you look, do
you have soap?" and so on. We took it good-naturedly. They
came to know and respect us later on, after the first battle,
where we stood in line together. As the war went on we had
no better friends than the men in those two Corps that were
with Sherman's Army in the Atlanta Campaign, the March to
the Sea and on until we finally parted after the Grand Review
of that Army in Washington.

We remained in camp at Bridgeport until January 5th,
1864. That was the longest stay in any place during our
service. We then received orders to go to Elk River Bridge,
back on the railroad toward Nashville, to relieve the 2nd
Massachusetts. This Regiment, whose term of enlistment had
expired, was reenlisting and first going home on furlough.

---

[14]   The XV Corps commanded by Major General Frank P. Blair, Jr. consisted of
the divisions of Brigadier Generals Peter J. Osterhaus, Morgan L. Smith, and Hugh
Ewing. Only Brigadier General John E. Smith's division of the XVII Corps took
part in the Chattanooga campaign. The remainder of the corps remained in the
Mississippi valley.

We were to use their camp but arrived a day before they started home. It was very cold, we had to stand around large fires all night to keep from freezing. The next day we had their comfortable quarters.

Shortly after we settled at Elk River I received a very unexpected detail. It was to go home for recruiting service. Four commissioned officers and ten sergeants, one from each company, were in the detail. Our Captain Anderson was one of the officers. I was not anxious to go and asked to have our Sergeant Joseph Bartholomew detailed in my place. For some reason Colonel McDougall insisted on my going. We had a pleasant time at home for the winter of 1864. We succeeded in enlisting some recruits and forwarded them to the Regiment. On May 2nd we started back, going by way of Buffalo, Cleveland, Louisville, and Chattanooga and from there to Ringgold, arriving there May 13th.

Our Regiment had advanced some distance beyond Ringgold. The railroad had not been repaired beyond that place, so we had to make the rest of our journey on foot. While we had been on our recruiting duty the Regiment had continued to guard the railroad in the vicinity of Elk River, where it had remained until the last week in April. Then with the whole Division it was ordered forward to join the 2nd Division, that had been in winter quarters near Lookout Mountain. We were all to take part in the coming campaign.

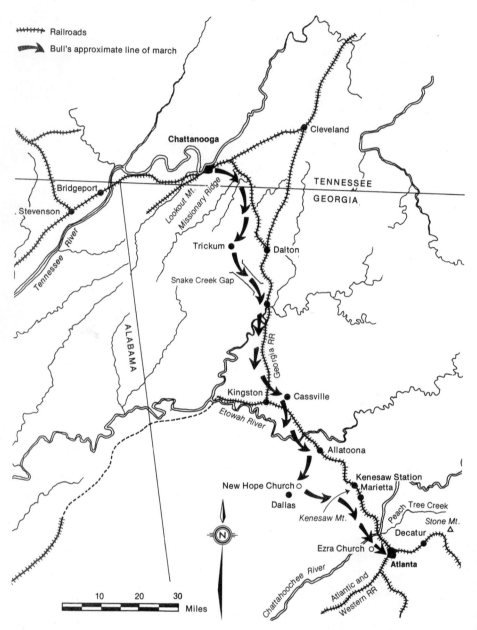

Cleveland

Chattanooga

TENNESSEE

GEORGIA

Bridgeport

Stevenson

Lookout Mt.

Missionary Ridge

Trickum

Dalton

Snake Creek Gap

Tennessee River

ALABAMA

Georgia RR

Kingston

Cassville

Etowah River

Allatoona

Kenesaw Station

New Hope Church ○

Marietta

Dallas

Kenesaw Mt.

Peach Tree Creek

Stone Mt.

Decatur

Ezra Church ○

Atlanta

N

Chattahoochee River

Atlantic and Western RR

10   20   30

Miles

The Atlanta Campaign

CHAPTER FIVE

The Atlanta Campaign

May 13th-November 15th, 1864

In the early spring of 1864, before the opening of the Atlanta Campaign, General Sherman reorganized his Army. Among other things he consolidated the 11th and 12th Corps into a large one named the 20th Army Corps. This new corps was placed under the command of General Hooker, then familiarly called "Fighting Joe Hooker." The Corps was attached to the Army of the Cumberland, about one-third of that part of Sherman's Army under the command of General George Thomas. The other two-thirds comprised the 4th and 14th Corps. Had we reached Ringgold a day earlier when we returned from our recruiting service we might have joined our Regiment there for they passed through that town May 11th.

At that time our Corps was part of a force that was starting on a flanking movement far to the left of the Confederate front; they were marching hurriedly in the direction of Snake Creek Gap. This action was well advanced when we got to Ringgold where we found that our Regiment was with the

troops assigned to this work. It was a major action that
included the 15th, 17th, and 20th Corps under the immediate command of General McPherson.[1] This force was known
to be close to the Army of General Johnston[2] which had
made a stand at Resaca, after falling back from its fortified
position at Dalton.

Lieutenant Colonel Rogers,[3] who commanded our detachment remaining at Ringgold, found that our Brigade
train was to start that day for the front, so we decided that we
would follow along when it started in the afternoon. We kept
up close to the wagons and made good progress; about sundown parked for the night at the little hamlet of Trickum. It
was warm so we camped in the open. The next day we were
up early as we had a long trip ahead of us for the supplies
were needed; the train had orders to make haste and reach
the Brigade that night. We learned that it was in front of
Resaca, nearly thirty miles from Trickum, that the enemy
were in line of battle facing them and an engagement might
commence any time. We had no rations so we had to beg
food from the Commissary in charge of the train; he issued
us hardtack and bacon and directed the teamsters to give us
coffee.

Our road was south through a beautiful valley on either
side of which were high mountains. This part of Georgia is

[1] James Birdseye McPherson (1828-1864) graduated from West Point in 1853
and became a Brigadier General of Volunteers in May 1862. Promoted to Major
General in October 1862, he commanded a division in Tennessee and the 17th
Corps before Vicksburg. He succeeded Sherman as commander of the Army of the
Tennessee and was killed in action before Atlanta, July 22, 1864.
[2] Joseph Eggleston Johnston (1807-1891) graduated from West Point in 1829
and served in the Black Hawk, Seminole, and Mexican Wars. He resigned his commission in April 1861 and accepted a Brigadier General's one in the Confederate
service the following month. He led Confederate forces in the east until wounded at
the Battle of Seven Pines in June 1862. After recuperating he took command of the
Department of the West and then the Army of Tennessee.
[3] James Clarence Rogers served as a captain in the 43rd New York before
becoming the Major of the 123rd on its organization. He succeeded Norton as
Lieutenant Colonel, May 13, 1863, and Stevens as Colonel, February 20, 1865. He
was breveted Brigadier General on May 13, 1865.

mountainous, the ranges usually running north and south between narrow fertile valleys, or valleys that would be if they were well cultivated. The country was mostly wooded and there were few farms; the houses were chiefly log cabins and the people we saw looked poor. The road was rough and narrow but the weather was dry, so there was no mud and we made good headway; as it was hot it took an effort to keep up with the train. We reached Snake Creek at two in the afternoon. Here a narrow gap runs through the mountains that lay on the east side of the valley we had traveled. There was a much larger valley on the west side of the mountains; the railroad from Chattanooga to Atlanta is located in this valley. The gap is the channel in which Snake Creek runs and in it is also the highway. The length of the gap is about eight miles; it is very narrow with scarcely room for the stream and highway that lie below high cliffs.

Our forces had taken the gap with but slight opposition and had, twenty-four hours before we arrived, entered the eastern valley almost in the rear of Johnston's Army. This was evidently a surprise to the Confederates and they were forced to retreat from their fortified position in the mountains to Resaca where their Army was in line facing the Federals. It was a great oversight on the part of Johnston not to have had a force at the gap; it could have been held by a brigade against all of Sherman's Army. It was nearly six in the evening when we entered the eastern valley. We had come twenty-five miles already and it was yet seven miles to the nearest place where the 20th Corps was in line, for it was on the extreme left flank of the Army. I was weary and the old wound in my side was troubling me. The orders were imperative to rush the train through, so after a short rest to feed the horses and allow the men to eat we made another start.

When we left the mountains and entered the valley a familiar sound greeted our ears; it was the distant boom of artillery. It could be heard on the east and south, covering a long line. As we hurried on the sound of the cannon grew louder; soon we heard the rattle of musketry coming in such volume as would indicate much more than a sharp skirmishers' engagement. When we came to the rear of our line we found the 15th Corps; the 17th at their right and extending beyond all our Army deployed in line of battle. General Sherman had been feeling the enemy's line all day; there had been heavy skirmishing but no general engagement.[4] As we passed along in the rear the sounds were war-like enough, the boom of cannon, sharp rattling of musketry, shouts of our men, and yells of the enemy. During the early evening we continued on in the rear of the 15th, 14th, 4th, and 23rd[5] Corps and at last reached the 20th. At ten o'clock that night the train came to a halt. Finding we could not reach our Regiment until morning, we spread our blankets on the ground and after a meal of hardtack and coffee were soon sleeping. That day we had marched over thirty-five miles. It proved to be the longest day's march I made during my service.

The morning of the 15th was bright, clear, and warm with every sign of a fine day. Our train was going directly to our Division, only about three miles from where we were camped, so we continued on with it. It was after eleven when we located the 1st Brigade[6] and reached the 123rd Regiment which was then standing in line of battle waiting for orders to advance. Captain Anderson and I at once reported to our Company, he to take command and I my place in the line. The boys were all glad to see us and gave us a cheer but joked us a bit on getting back at such an opportune time; just in time, they said, for the fun that was coming.

---

[4] The battle of Resaca, which contrary to Bull's statement, was a general engagement that took place on May 14, and cost Sherman some 6,800 casualties.

[5] Commanded by Major General John M. Schofield, the corps consisted of divisions led by Brigadier Generals Alvin P. Hovey, Henry M. Judah, and Jacob D. Cox.

[6] Commanded by Brigadier General Joseph F. Knipe, it consisted of the 5th Connecticut, 123rd, 141st New York, and 46th Pennsylvania.

The whole Division was in line of battle, the 3rd Brigade[7] on our right and the 2nd[8] on our left. There was brisk skirmishing in our front and an advance was expected in a short time. We had hardly shaken hands and commenced to answer questions about the homefolks when General Hooker rode along the rear of our line and orders were given to advance. Everything was ready and the "Forward" sounded. Our line was in the woods in both directions; the timber was heavy so our advance was slow as we could not lose or sever our contact with the troops on our right and left. After advancing about a half mile we came to an open field an eighth of a mile wide that extended a long distance in our front. At the far end the Rebel breastworks were plainly in view, only a half mile away. When we came into the opening the enemy artillery brought us under fire. Our line was in such an exposed position we were ordered to "Right Oblique" to a knoll just ahead of us where we could lie down out of sight. Although they could not see us the artillery kept pounding away but most of their shots were over our heads. They did not do much damage but even for veteran troops it is trying to lie unengaged under artillery fire. We could do nothing as our skirmishers were in our front, so just hugged the ground. After about ten minutes one of our batteries entered the field and in a short time silenced the enemy's guns. While this was going on our left was extended and was making a right wheel to get on the flank of the Johnnies. By four o'clock our force was well on their flank and they then had their choice; either come out and drive us back or retreat. They decided to come out and attack, so they jumped over their works and advanced. The skirmishing now became very heavy; we thought they surely would be on us and every-

[7] Commanded by Colonel James S. Robinson, it contained the 82nd, 101st Illinois, 45th, 143rd New York, 61st and 82nd Ohio.
[8] Commanded by Brigadier General Thomas H. Ruger, it consisted of the 27th Indiana, 2nd Massachusetts, 13th New Jersey, 107th, 150th New York, and 3rd Wisconsin.

thing was made ready to receive them. All along the line you could hear the click of the hammers on our guns as they were half cocked to attach the caps, which we did not place until we got ready to fire. Guns in hand we waited. The battery on our left now had a good target and fired rapidly at the charging line. When the Johnnies had advanced a third of the way toward our line, they filed off to the right and entered the woods, where they would not be exposed to the artillery fire; so they made their fight on troops to the left of us.

The fighting lasted two hours, the noise of the musketry and cannon was deafening and the shouts and yells of the forces engaged could be plainly heard. Our position in the open field we thought so unfavorable proved our salvation, as it kept us out of the severe fighting. After repeated efforts to break or drive our line back, the enemy fell back into their works that evening. It was too late to follow them so we halted where we were, expecting to continue the fight in the morning.

We were fortunate, our Regiment had only ten men killed and wounded.[9] One of the killed was a member of the detachment that had been home on recruiting service. He was killed within an hour of his return to the Regiment. All our casualties were either from sharpshooters or exploding shells. On our right and left the action had been heavy and the losses severe. The 2nd Brigade had captured a battery and carried the enemy's entrenchments. After dark we moved up close to our picket line and constructed earthworks until midnight. When we finished all were ready to drop down and get such rest as we could before the morrow, which had such a threatening look.

General Johnston during the night withdrew his Army and retreated in a southerly direction. At daybreak our pickets discovered there was no enemy in our front and entered the deserted works. Where the struggle had been fiercest we

[9] One killed, nine wounded. Three of the wounded later died.

found their dead unburied and many of their severely wounded left in farmhouses back of their works.

During the fight a rather funny incident occurred in our Company. One of the men whose name was Bill had a very large head, they used to hector him a lot about it. As we lay hugging the ground they could not keep from having their joke on Bill. Jim was constantly teasing him in a good-natured way. He said, "If you don't look out, that big head of yours will get knocked off; dig a hole for it and drop in the hole, that may be the means of saving your life." Bill lay quiet and made no answer. Suddenly he jumped to his feet and went for his tormentor. "Now see here," he said, "I will stand a lot of your talk but I won't stand for you throwing stones at me." "Why Bill," said Jim, "I have not thrown stones at you." "Well you or someone else has, and I won't stand for it. I will thrash the man who did." As Bill was a powerful man and dangerous when angry, the joking ended. That night the stone throwing was explained as Bill unrolled his blanket. He found about twenty holes in it. The blanket had been rolled and strapped to the top of his knapsack, and as he lay on the ground it stood a trifle higher than his head. A bullet had gone through it, not over two inches above his head. "Now Bill," said Jim, "You see I saved your life by telling you to get down." It was a long time before Bill heard the end of it.

In the morning I joined my old mess and we had an early breakfast of bacon, hardtack and coffee. I was lame and sore from my two days' walk from Ringgold, for my old wound in the side was still tender from too much exercise. We had hardly finished our breakfast before Companies C and D were ordered to make an advance along a road running south and east. The purpose was to follow the route taken by part of the enemy and find if they had yet made a halt. We went through the abandoned works which had been so well constructed and marched down the road for two miles but found no enemy. There were many signs of their retreat but the main part of their Army had evidently gone to our right. Our orders were to go two miles and if we did not encounter

the enemy to return to our camp; we were back from where
we started by nine o'clock. Then we followed after the rest of
the Companies that had gone on a similar errand. When we
caught up with them the entire Regiment returned to the
camp. Early in the afternoon our Brigade started on a general advance, crossing a small river by a pontoon bridge, and
then continued on a road that ran south to Kingston and
Rome. These towns were some twenty miles distant and it
was reported Johnston had prepared a fortified position
there. We marched about seven miles and camped near another small stream; as there were other troops in our front
we did not have to form in line. During the day, away to our
right, we heard heavy artillery firing, indicating that some
part of the Army was in close touch with the enemy and that
they were slowly falling back.

Tuesday morning, May 17th, found us well rested for we
had a good night's sleep. There was no skirmishing in our
front to disturb us and as we were not to start early we were
late risers; further we had camped near a stream large
enough for us to take a bath. One of the hardest conditions
we had to face in the service, when in the field, was the lack
of opportunity to keep clean. When near a small stream we
could not bathe or wash in it as the troops along its banks
were using the water for drinking and cooking. To wash our
face and hands a comrade poured it for us from a canteen.
When we could get it we carried a piece of soap but none was
issued to us when in active field service. Usually in the field
there was little chance to wash or clean our clothes. It was ten
in the morning when we started to move in the direction of
Kingston. The weather was fine; we had an easy march and
went into camp early that afternoon. It had been quiet all day
on our front but occasionally we heard cannonading far to
our right where the Army of the Tennessee was closing on
the enemy.

That evening we were informed that there would be an
early start next day but were surprised when Reveille sounded before four in the morning. We were ordered to have no

delay in getting ready to march. It was the work of only a few minutes to make our fire and boil our coffee and fry our pork. In less than an hour we were ready to move. Since we had hurried we were anxious to get started but it was fully eight o'clock before we were on the march which we kept up steadily until four in the afternoon when we halted to camp for the night. As it threatened rain we began to put up our tents but before we had finished our Brigade Bugler sounded the Assembly. At first the men thought there was some mistake and hesitated in taking down the tents; hurried orders were soon given and in not very good humor. we pulled them down and were on the move.

We turned in an easterly direction, almost at an opposite angle from the way we had been going since morning. We were put on quick-step; there were few rests and the march was a weary one. Our final halt came at nine that night, having covered an additional twelve miles after we had stopped to put up our tents. In all we marched twenty-five miles that day; when we halted, we just fell on the ground to rest; many were too tired for further effort, and went supperless to their blankets. No tents were pitched that night and fortunately there was no rain.

The next morning we were allowed to sleep late, a luxury appreciated after the long march of the day before. The whole 20th Corps was in the movement and we were not far from Cassville, where it was expected Johnston would make a stand. He had laid out a line there previous to his retreat from Dalton and strong breastworks had been built. It was after nine o'clock when we fell-in as we were waiting the arrival of other troops. The 23rd Corps passed us going to the left and the 20th was being placed in position where it could easily form a line of battle. After making our start we marched slowly as there was every indication we were nearing the enemy. A body of cavalry was in advance acting as skirmishers to push away any small force that might attempt to delay our advance. We had gone two or three miles when skirmishing became brisk in our front. It became a more open country, having some large well-cultivated plantations; on one of these we filed to the left and fronted in line of battle. On our right and left other troops were coming into line and our artillery and ammunition trains were massing in our rear.

In half an hour the line to our right and left, as far as one could see, was formed and ready to advance. This was the only time in active service I saw the whole Division deployed. Usually our deployment was in the woods where only a small part could be seen from any point. As the Division stood in the open fields awaiting the order to advance, with flags unfurled it presented a striking appearance. When the troops had all been deployed and fronted an advance was ordered.

Company F of our Regiment was thrown out as skirmishers. Then the advance was across the open fields and into the wood in our front. There the growth of bushes and trees was so heavy we could not advance in line, so broke into columns of companies and that way were able to get through the tangle. Shortly after they entered the woods our skirmishers ran into a line of the enemy in rifle pits; they held our men back for a short time, then fell back firing as they retreated. We followed closely after our skirmishers and after going a half mile came out of the woods to open fields where we reformed our line. This took some time as the troops were so broken up by the thick underbrush. When we came out into the open, we were not only greeted by musketry but by shot and shell.

Our line was on a hill at the foot of which was a valley that was about a mile wide. Near us up close to the hill was a pretty village and in the houses were sharpshooters who were busy. On the opposite side of the valley was a range of hills; they were quite high and we could see that they were crowned with a line of fortifications. When we advanced the sharpshooters made for their line. Their batteries started shelling us from several places; their redoubts were where we could see them from the smoke of their guns. When we had completed our formation we lay down until our artillery could be brought to the front. To the right of us near the village was a hill much higher than where we were. Battery M[10] of our Division was ordered to this elevation and our Regiment was taken from the line to act as their support. The Battery started on the gallop and we followed on double-quick. The enemy could see what we were doing and commenced sending shells around us in a lively way, most of them passed over our heads. When we had nearly reached the position assigned the Battery a shell exploded directly in front of our Company, but only two or three feet above the ground. When these shells explode the tendency is for the pieces to fly down to the ground; this saved us from a great loss. However, we had four wounded, one seriously, by pieces of the shell that glanced up from the ground. I was in direct line and not over ten feet from where it exploded, but was only covered with dust and dirt. It was nearly dark before it quieted down and firing ceased; then at ten o'clock we went back to our line for the night. The weather was hot and we were exhausted. While there was skirmishing in our front we were too tired to mind that; we did not lie awake thinking about what the morrow might bring for those frowning breastworks looked ominous.

In the morning we found that we had a pleasant day before us, as far as the weather was concerned. It was very quiet and we thought it strange that there was no musketry firing but soon we learned the reason. News travels fast in the Army and it was known that the Johnnies had abandoned their works and gone. To say that was pleasant news put it mildly; it seemed too good to be true. The line they held looked so strong with fortifications so well built, it was unbelievable that it would be abandoned without a fight. We had felt that we could only drive them out at great loss to ourselves. The enemy had lines that were located just north of the small Etowah River, but their line at Cassville was some

[10] Battery M, 1st New York Light Artillery commanded by Captain John D. Woodbury.

miles north of that. However, they had retreated beyond the river and after crossing destroyed all bridges. The 23rd Corps followed the enemy to the river near Cassville but we were held where we were.

Our Army had been on the campaign twenty days and as it had had no rest, General Sherman decided to halt for two or three days. During that time the railroad in our rear could be repaired and supplies brought forward for the Army. In their retreat the enemy had destroyed the railroad in as far as they could by burning bridges, blowing up culverts, and tearing up the rails. It was wonderful how rapidly our men could make repairs as we advanced; unless there was unusual work to be done the whistle of the engines could be heard close by us every morning. The bridge over the Etowah was quite long and it would require two or three days to rebuild it. After our morning meal a good many of our men went to the village.

It was a fine little town with four churches, a female seminary, court house, many stores and at least one hundred residences, some of which were quite pretentious. The people had all left except one family. The stores had been ransacked and wrecked and nearly everything carried away or destroyed. As near as I could see only a few private houses had been disturbed but during the day some buildings containing Confederate clothing and supplies were burned. As a rule private property was not injured, however, some of the boys searched for tobacco and found a few plugs. The village did present a deserted, deplorable sight.

On May 21st, the day after Johnston's Army retreated from Cassville, we were informed there would be no movement for several days. This would not only give us a good rest but time to clean up and do our washing. In service in the field while we eliminated everything not absolutely necessary there were some things we had to carry other than what we had on our backs. Our additional clothes consisted of one shirt, one pair of drawers, two pair of socks, and three handkerchiefs. Our underwear contained wool and was thick and very heavy. It took time to wash and dry so we had to know we would halt for at least a day before we could undertake the job. As we were near a stream we could use without contamination to our water supply, Nat Rowell and I did our washing. We borrowed a kettle from the Regimental Commissary for the "boiling" and by ten in the morning were at work. It was a fine warm day so we had no trouble in drying our clothes, after which we took a bath. When we returned to camp that afternoon, wearing our clean clothes, we felt like new men.

Our last day in Cassville was Sunday; had there been any church service in the village many of the boys would have gone. We had, however, service in the open near our camp; our Chaplain conducted the service and there was a large attendance. When in camp we were often called in a body to attend church but in the field it was voluntary. It was surprising so many were at the service that morning. We had no Sunday inspection, so during the afternoon Rowell and I went to see the Rebel works. They were the finest we had seen up to that time and it must have taken much labor to build them. Johnston's Army could not have reached there more than a few hours before we were in front of them so they must have been constructed prior to the start of the campaign. They were no ordinary breastworks that could be built overnight but strong elaborate fortifications with redoubts and abatis in front. It looked strange to us that they would abandon such a line without making a defense.

On Monday the campaign was renewed with great vigor. The Reveille was sounded at three, before dawn. We were soon up, our blankets rolled and strapped to our knapsacks, our tents down and breakfast eaten. At four-thirty the "fall-in" was sounded and we were on the march in the direction of Kingston. After going south ten miles we halted long enough to get our dinner and have a short rest. We then continued on until we reached the Etowah River, quite a stream flowing toward the west. The Engineers had already laid a pontoon bridge which we crossed and continued on for

two miles where we camped for the night. It was only three
in the afternoon but with our early start we had made something like eighteen miles. Quite heavy cannonading heard at
our left told us that some part of the Army was up against the
enemy. All our Corps crossed the river during the afternoon
and evening and was lined along the ridge where we camped.

The next morning, which was the 24th, we started early in
a southeasterly direction, almost at right angles to the railroad that ran from Kingston to Marietta and Atlanta. Every
mile we marched we were getting farther from the railroad
upon which we depended for our supplies; and which we
had followed all the way from Chattanooga. From Resaca to
the vicinity of the Etowah the railroad runs almost due south
but after crossing the river it turns sharply in a southeasterly
direction and continues all the way to Marietta, which is
beyond the mountain range that centers around Allatoona.
Near Marietta there is a pass through which the railroad
runs. When Johnston left his position near Etowah, he did
not permanently halt his Army until he reached the hill
country north of Allatoona. Here he formed his line, built
strong fortifications, covering the railroad and extending far
to the east and west; then waited for General Sherman to
advance. However, Sherman did not follow the Confederates
into the hills, but leaving a force at Kingston to protect his
base of supplies, left the railroad and with the larger part of
the Army started for the town of Dallas. This place was at
least twenty miles from Johnston's left flank and was beyond
the hills that surrounded Allatoona. This movement was to
force Johnston out of his strong position so as to engage him
where the conditions were more equal. This was the flanking
shift used time after time in the campaign to compel the
enemy to abandon his well-selected positions.

We continued our march the morning of the 25th, starting
about eight o'clock and taking the road leading to Dallas. We
swung to the west to avoid the hills around Allatoona, and
were gradually working our way back toward the railroad
which had for a short time past been abandoned. Our prog-

ress was slow as the road was narrow and our trains were kept so close up to us. They filled the highway making it difficult to make any time. About noon we came to a large creek where our advance had run into a Rebel cavalry force; they retreated without a fight but burned the bridge. This was Pumpkin Vine Creek and like most streams in that region was quite deep with a muddy bottom so could not be forded. Engineers were brought up to build a bridge. It would take some time to do this and our Brigade as it came up filed into the woods nearby in close order. While waiting we cooked our dinner; coffee, hardtack, and pork, an unchanged bill of fare that did not take us more than a half hour to prepare.

After we finished our meal we had to wait for the bridge, which took quite a time as the timbers had to be cut and brought to the site from the surrounding woods. I spread my blanket on the ground intending to get some sleep when Sergeant James Cummings[11] of our Company came and sat down by me. Cummings was, I think, the finest soldier in our organization. A physical giant six feet four inches tall, well educated, a man of character, and a splendid soldier. He and I had formed a close friendship. I noticed he seemed melancholy and sad, the very opposite of his usual manner; and I asked him what was the trouble. He answered that for the last few days he had the feeling that he would not survive the next battle; he believed it would be soon and would not be surprised if it came this day. He said he had tried to shake it off but could not and now believed it was a warning to him. He told me that I was the only one he had spoken to, as he felt almost ashamed to say anything since we might think him cowardly, but he could not throw the feeling off. He said he had consecrated his life to his country's service and if it was necessary for him to die he would rather be killed in action than linger of disease in some hospital. He had strong reli-

---

[11] Private (later Sergeant) James Leroy Cummings (1839-1864) enlisted from Putnam, N.Y. He was killed in action at Dallas, Ga., May 25, 1864.

gious convictions and had no fears in regard to death or the future life. I tried to convince him that it was foolish to give credence to such feelings, saying we all had such "warnings" at times but they never came true; and it was more than foolish to think of an early battle as it was then so quiet one could hardly imagine the enemy within fifty miles.

While we were talking the "fall-in" sounded and we took our place in line. The bridge was finished and we crossed, our 1st Division[12] taking the road to the right and the 2nd[13] the one to the left. We marched cautiously through the forest and had advanced some two miles, when away to our left we heard the familiar sound of conflict, the first scattering skirmish fire that gradually increased until it was evident that the main lines were engaged with both infantry and artillery. Our Division was halted; soon couriers began to come and orders were given for us to counter-march. We about-faced and started back to the bridge almost at double-quick, then took the way to the left, following after the 2nd Division at full speed. We learned they had met a heavy force of the enemy about three miles from the bridge and had difficulty holding their line so we were being rushed to their support. As we neared the front there were all the evidences of battle, wounded men being brought back, ammunition wagons and ambulances hurrying to the front, cowardly skulkers who would not stay on the firing line except a bayonet was at their back getting to the rear, men, horses and even mules wild with excitement. There is nothing that tests men's nerves more than marching up to a line of battle that is already engaged; they know they are soon to take their place on the firing line. While making the advance they can see, hear, and think, but can do nothing to take their minds off the dreadful work they know is before them. Until their own battle line

---

[12] Commanded by Brigadier General Alpheus S. Williams and composed of the brigades of Brigadier Generals Joseph F. Knipe, Thomas H. Ruger, and Colonel James S. Robinson.

[13] Commanded by Brigadier General John W. Geary, it consisted of the brigades of Colonels Charles Candy, Adolphus Buschbeck, and David Ireland.

is formed and they are facing the front and firing their
nerves are almost at the breaking point; then the strain
relaxes and the fear and nervousness passes away. As we
neared the firing line the noise was deafening, the air was
filled with the fumes of burning powder; the lazy whining of
bullets almost spent, the shot and shell from the enemy
batteries tearing through the trees caused every head to duck
as they passed over us. With all this tumult could be heard
the shouts of our men and the yells of the enemy. We had
come three miles from the bridge when we halted just in the
rear of our battle line; but only long enough to get orders.
Then our Division was deployed to the right and left; our
Brigade went to the right at least a half mile through the
forest and was then brought to a front.

When all the formation was completed we advanced to
relieve the 2nd Division that had been in action for nearly
three hours. They had found the enemy in rifle pits and had
only been able to hold the position they had first taken very
close to their line. As we moved up to the front, our Colonel
McDougall was just behind our Company; he was on foot as
it was impossible for him to ride through the underbrush.
When we relieved the line in action they dropped back to
form the second line in reserve; at that time the enemy's
artillery located in our immediate front were firing grape.
After a discharge from their battery I heard a cry just back of
me; turning, I saw the Colonel stagger and fall. He was carried to the rear mortally wounded by a grape shot. We took a
position a little forward from the line we relieved and fought
from a reclining line to keep below the grape shot as far as
possible. In an hour the darkness came; our only light was
from the flash of the muskets and the greater light of the
artillery in action directly in our front. While lying there a
thunder shower that had threatened all day broke on us. It
was a furious storm, the rain came down in torrents, the
lightning was blinding; then the darkness so black it could
almost be felt. For a time the thunder drowned out the
sound of the artillery which continued to pound away at our

line. During the storm one of the boys, who was quite a wag, lying in a pool of water turned to Captain Anderson, who was just behind him, and said, "Now Captain, if you will just give the order, we will swim over and tackle the Johnnies." This illustrated the degree of familiarity that had become between our men and their officers. It is easy to understand this; our Regiment was made up entirely of men from Washington County and each Company of men from the same or adjacent townships; their officers were older men, the friends of their fathers and mothers. About nine-thirty the enemy's artillery fire gradually ceased but there was still quite active skirmishing and bullets whistled around us all night.

Most of the men continued lying on the ground, hugging it closely although the rain was still falling. I was near the right of the Company and as a file closer in the rear of the men. My friend Cummings arose from a place near me. He had been quiet during all the excitement of the advance and attack and as far as I could see had not been worried; he had hardly spoken to me. Firing had nearly ended when he arose and placing the butt of his gun on the ground stood facing the front. I said, "Jim you know there are orders not to fire, why do you stand and expose yourself." He answered, "I don't think there is any more danger in standing here than lying in the mud, I have had enough of that." He remained standing, leaning on his gun. I do not think it was more than a minute after I spoke to him that I heard a metallic sound, as though one had taken a hammer and hit a tree with it. Cummings's gun dropped from his hands and he and his gun struck the ground at the same time. A bullet had found its mark in his forehead, passing through his brain. We carried him back to the field hospital where he died before morning. In his death our Company lost its best soldier.

About ten that night we began to build rifle pits. We had to work quietly as the enemy would send a shower of bullets after any unusual sound. By morning we had works that would protect us from infantry fire. It had become almost a habit with us as soon as we halted close to the enemy to build

breastworks; every man would dig in as though his life depended on his work. In many cases it did. It was surprising
how quickly we could construct a trench that would protect
us from musketry. Each Regiment was equipped with spades
and shovels which in this campaign were carried by pack
mules. In most places the location of our line was in such
heavily wooded country that wagons could not follow up
closely, while mules could be kept right with us.

In this action our Regiment lost forty[14] men killed or
wounded including Colonel McDougall; he was succeeded by
Lieutenant Colonel Rogers.[15] Our Company D had one killed
and four wounded. The day after the battle, away to our left,
there was heavy skirmishing and artillery action indicating
almost a general engagement. In our front it was quiet. It
was now known that General Johnston was there with his
whole Army behind well built works that were far too strong
to be captured by direct assault without great loss. In the
battle of the 25th both sides had been heavy losers of men;
ours was probably the larger as we were the attacking force;
and we could not claim a victory as we were unable to drive
them back. However, we did establish a line close to them and
we then kept up a great racket with our skirmishers and
sharpshooters. This engagement is now known as the Battle
of New Hope Church; those who fought gave it the name of
Hell Hole. The night after the battle I was on picket duty.
There was not much picket firing. It was raining and black as
ink and neither side seemed to be desirous to make it more
uncomfortable than nature's effort; but it was a dismal time
and the night was long.

In the morning the pickets from our Brigade were relieved
as it was understood that we had marching orders. When we

---

[14]   The correct figures were one killed and 22 wounded. Four of the wounded
subsequently died.

[15]   Colonel Ambrose A. Stevens, formerly Lieutenant Colonel of the 46th New
York, held nominal command of the regiment between July 1, 1864 and February
19, 1865. He apparently never assumed actual command since the regimental
reports for that period were signed by Rogers as Lieutenant Colonel.

got back to the Regiment the men were ready to move but soon the order was countermanded and we were told to further strengthen our breastworks; so we went to work and continued well into the night. There was heavy skirmishing and cannonading all day. In the evening the Johnnies advanced on our pickets, driving them in; they came close to our main line where we gave them a volley that sent them back in a hurry. All our men were called into the line and were ready for the work that might come but they were only giving us a feeler to find if we were there, so it was all over in a few minutes. We remained on this line until June 1st. The conditions in our immediate front remained the same. The enemy holding their line with great tenacity; our men working closer and closer; deadly fire was almost continuous; and there was no safety for anyone, unless they lay close under the breastworks.

On June 1st, we received orders for an immediate movement; and at ten that morning a Division of the 15th Corps arrived to relieve us. These troops came from the vicinity of Dallas which had been occupied May 25th by General McPherson. This force had intended to connect with the right wing of General Thomas's command as soon as Dallas was reached but McPherson found this was no easy job. The Army of General Johnston was on his front in full force and he could not safely make the junction except by slow progress. He was four miles from Thomas's right and had he attempted to move his whole Army at once, he would have been attacked while on the march when not in order for battle. His only safe way was to move one Division at a time, from the right of his own line to the left. By repeating this movement, each time with a right Division, the line gradually moved to the left without being weakened. It took four days to make the junction.

After this connection was made on June 1st the same tactics were to be used by the whole Army to extend to the left until we reached the railroad which had been abandoned. It was now necessary to again make contact with the railroad for our supplies remaining in our wagons were running low. The 15th and 17th Corps were to relieve the 4th and 20th Corps while we passed by in their rear and formed a line on their left flank, thus extending the line as far as two Divisions could toward the railroad. Our extended line was heavily fortified as soon as occupied. By continuing the shift from the right to the left it would not take long to reach the railroad. However, this movement was not made without trouble. General Johnston was very wide awake and not a movement was made to extend our lines that did not meet with real opposition. Although we usually brushed it aside, it was not done without fighting and much loss to both Armies. There was hardly an hour that the sound of musketry and roar of cannon could not be heard.

We started our shift about ten in the morning and marched in the rear of the line some three miles back from the front, most of the time in heavily timbered forest that was almost impassable even for foot soldiers. We could locate the position of our front line by the constant sharpshooters' fire as we moved along. When we had gone about four miles we halted in the rear of the 23rd Corps which was then the extreme left of our Army. We then camped for the night.

From the beginning of the campaign until the Battle of New Hope Church we had fine weather. There had been little rain and no extreme heat; while it was dry and dusty it had been easy traveling. On May 25th the weather changed and I find recorded in my diary that for twenty-one days it stormed every day. It did not rain continuously but during some part of every day it hit us, usually in thunder storms of the most violent sort. It was such a time of great activity that these storms either caught us on the march or in breastworks where we had no protection. After one of these rains the men would be as wet as if they had fallen in a stream. As it was warm weather a wetting did not make us cold but the ground was so saturated with water it was almost impossible to find a place in which one could rest. We would cut limbs from the bushes and lay them under our tents to keep as much as we could out of the mud, but this did not make comfortable beds. Although the excessive rains retarded our movements we were active. Our trains were well up in front but could only be moved with great difficulty; the wagons would sink in the mud up to their axles and they could not be moved by the mules alone. The men had to take a hand, pry up the wheels and corduroy the road to solid ground. In these days of deluge there was no letup in the infantry's progress; we were slowly going toward the left. In a few days we had possession of the railroad and again the whistle of the locomotives was heard near our lines.

The enemy in the meantime was slowly falling back to a new position which was being prepared for them. It was strong, just north of Marietta, where their right flank would be on Kenesaw Mountain, and their left on Lost Mountain. Every step of the way back to this fortified line was contested by Johnston and line after line of breastworks had to be taken by our advance. These works were so strongly built as to cause us wonder when and by whom they could have been constructed. During the first twenty days of June, while we were facing storms as well as fighting the enemy, there was a sameness in what happened every day.

On Thursday, June 2nd, about noon our Division was moved still further to our left. After we had gone a mile we took a position in the second line as support to the 23rd Corps who were on the front. When the afternoon shower was over we began to build the usual breastworks.

At noon on Friday, June 3rd, the 23rd Corps moved out of their works going to the left; we were then the troops holding the front line. During the afternoon it began to rain, water filling the ditch back of our embankment. We were not only wet but muddy, and passed an uncomfortable night.

On Saturday, June 4th, at noon we had orders to get ready to move at once but the orders were countermanded as no troops came to take our place. Before night there was more rain. Everything was soaked with water. The Army was simply floundering in the mud and there was scarcely a time when our clothing was dry. Our shoes were cut low and were not well made so we had wet feet most of the time. Fortunately it was warm and we did not suffer from cold but it was hard to wear wet clothes night and day.

At eleven o'clock in the morning (Sunday, June 5th), we were relieved by a Division of the 14th Corps and marched about two miles toward the left, where we halted again in the rear of the front line and camped for the night. It was another cloudy disagreeable day with occasional showers.

The next day, Monday June 6th, we were again called early and at five-thirty fell in line and marched another three miles toward the left. We were evidently well on the enemy's flank as no opposition was made to our advance. As soon as we halted and formed our line we began to build our breast-works. This had now become almost second nature and the men needed no urging to do this. It was one duty that no one shirked; no matter how tired they would not rest or eat until they had a trench dug that would stop bullets. I was detailed for picket duty and started at once for the picket line.

We found the enemy not far away for they had extended their line as fast and as far as we had advanced. The officer in charge of our picket line pushed up as near to them as he could, establishing the posts under severe fire. We had shovels and our first work was to dig pits. There were two men to a pit and while one dug the other watched with gun in hand. Every few minutes they changed places until the pit was large enough to protect them. During the time we were making the pits there was more or less firing from both sides, but as the Johnnies were probably also making pits the firing was not heavy. Still the bullets were singing around. Our detail was on post all night so there was not a moment's rest or sleep for any of us. The only sound heard that night was the barking of the dogs in the enemy camp, which could not have been more than one-half mile away. We were thankful when the day began to break about four o'clock. To the right of us, the lines were closer together than in front of our pits; so close that the men could not only see each other but were in speaking distance. Early in the morning conversation opened between the lines and a treaty was made not to open fire unless there were orders to advance. At that time we did not know of this agreement but as the Johnnies did not begin firing in the morning we did not, so up to ten o'clock when we had been relieved there had been no skirmishing. Such agreements were not unusual with men in the advance lines but they were not encouraged or allowed by the commanding officers on either side. When the new detail was posted there was a change; they were ordered to open up on the enemy's skirmishers and June 7th was one of our noisy days. I spent the day in needed sleep.

On June 8th I received a letter from home. The mail service in the field, while slow, was fairly good and about once a week. No men ever hungered more for letters than we did. What a joy it was to hear from father and mother, brothers and sisters, and friends; letters with good news from home telling of work on the farm, the gossip of the neighborhood, and best of all advice and counsel from father and mother These letters were living pictures of the old home and of God's Country that we had left behind and hoped with God's blessing to some day see again.

At noon on June 10th we had a terrific thunder storm; the only cover[16] we had was our ponchos that were buttoned around our necks. They were no protection as the wind was strong and the rain came in torrents. After an hour it settled down into a steady downpour that lasted until night. Late in the afternoon we were notified we were to remain where we were. We were then as wet as we could be and the ground was a sea of mud and water so it was useless to put up our tents. Ordinarily we were not allowed to build large fires as they drew the attention of the enemy. We took chances that the Johnnies were just as uncomfortable as we were and would not unduly exert themselves; so we built fires of pine

[16]   The regiment was under orders, as it had been the preceding day, to march and had struck its tents.

knots and stood around all night. The rain stopped early in the evening so we were nearly dry in the morning.

June 11th brought another shower, not so hard as the one the day before but it was enough. When we marched at one o'clock we went in the direction of Pine Mountain, one of the enemy's strongholds. Two miles from our start we formed a line of battle in the rear of the 23rd Corps. Then we had another shower. It had been expected that an advance would be made by the 23rd and 20th Corps but it was called off because of the weather. The Army seemed nearly paralyzed by the rain and mud. We camped in the rear of the 23rd Corps and were so exhausted that we slept, although our clothing and beds were soaked.

The next morning (Sunday June 12th), the 23rd Corps moved from the line in front and we relieved them. We were then in the front line; the Army was being so stretched out, it left only one line of battle. This made it necessary for us to make our breastworks as strong as we could, so notwithstanding the rain and the condition of the ground that was sticky with mud we worked steadily all day. Our line was close under Pine Mountain, a hill some four hundred feet high covered with forest except at the top where a clearing had been made and a signal station located by the enemy. We could see the signalmen at times as they waved their flags but our artillery interfered with their signaling. The main line of the Johnnies was at the foot of the hill and was very strong. Skirmishing was noisy all day but no great damage resulted. At night it cleared up and looked as though the weather would be more settled than at any time during the past month.

On Monday, June 13th, there was no rain. There was a clear sky with the sun shining and although it was very warm we felt like new men. The despondency of the last ten days was gone and song and joke could be heard once more in the camp. There was no movement of troops on our front but it was lively enough. Our pickets were driven back by a heavy force and we were ordered to man the works; then we stood

in them for nearly three hours waiting for an attack that did
not develop. The Johnnies were only feeling our line. Several
of our batteries were located near us and they were busy all
day shelling the enemy's line and keeping the signalmen on
the mountaintop from making observations of that part of
our line.

The following morning everything was quiet. Not far to
our right was located a battery belonging to Geary's Division.
They had their guns trained on Pine Mountain; whenever a
Johnnie showed himself to make observations or give signals
with their flags, the shells began to drop on the crest of the
hill. It was, I judged, nearly three-quarters of a mile, a
good firing range. The boys located in the vicinity gathered
around the battery to watch the sport. The Johnnies could
see when the guns were fired from the smoke; we could see
them dodge out of sight before the shells reached them.
Often when a shell exploded or passed them they would
come out and wave their hats; they seemed to be as well
pleased as we were. That afternoon when I was watching the
practice a party of officers came out in the open space from
which the signals were given. The officer in charge of the
battery ordered three shots fired in a volley, which made a
great racket. When the smoke cleared away the party had
disappeared.[17]

We were ordered on Wednesday, June 15th, to get ready to
move at two o'clock; after we started it was found the enemy
in our front had abandoned their works. When we had gone
about a mile in the direction of Lost Mountain our skirmishers ran into the enemy, and our Brigade was quickly advanced in line of battle. They then retired to a new line that
had evidently been fortified for them before they left the old
one. We took a position on a ridge near their front and at
once began work with pick and shovel and axe to build breast-

[17] This appears to have been the meeting between Generals Johnston, William
J. Hardee, and Leonidas Polk during which the latter was killed by a cannonball
from the Union batteries.

works to protect ourselves. Geary's Division on our left was heavily engaged all the afternoon. We were lucky as we had no loss in our Regiment although it looked like a fight all the time that day.

At about daybreak on Thursday, June 16th, we left the position and went to the right about a mile; then advanced in line of battle up close to the enemy's works, halted, and began to build new breastworks. We worked hard at it all the afternoon. The infantry and artillery fire indicated at times almost a general engagement; our Regiment had several wounded by stray bullets that sang around and over us.

Early on the morning of Friday, June 17th, we made a general advance. We found the enemy's works deserted; they had retreated during the night. We advanced in line for another mile until we reached another range of hills. There again we found them well fortified. At one o'clock we halted in an open field on quite a high point. While we were at rest we were opened on by a battery located a long distance away. Most of their shot and shell fell short, but one solid shot that carried farther than the rest did us some damage. The shot was nearly spent and traveled so slow we could hear it coming and knew from the sound it would strike near us. It struck at the right of the Regiment, bounding like a ball, passed over the heads of the men in five companies and struck the ground in the center of Company K, wounding five men. Fortunately it was not an exploding shell. Our Brigade was in the reserve and we camped in the rear of the front line; pitched our tents and had a good night's rest.

From June 17th to 21st we were very active in the movements made by the Army. General Sherman so maneuvered his men as to force the enemy to abandon their line in front of Pine and Lost Mountains and concentrate around Kenesaw Mountain, the largest and highest of the three. In forcing Johnston back to this line the 20th and 23rd Corps had been chiefly used. It was a rapid and laborious job. We would advance to a point beyond their extreme left and make a left wheel on their line; after pushing as far as we could we would rapidly fortify with a large artillery force placed in the line with us. Well on the enemy's flank our batteries would have a cross fire on them and within twenty-four hours, generally, they would find their line untenable and fall back to a new position, we in close pursuit. From the 17th to the 21st this was twice repeated, two strong lines of fortifications were abandoned, and the enemy was forced back about four miles. On the 21st, we were well on the right of our Army and during that day were not moved. The 23rd Corps was chiefly in our rear but with some of its troops in the line on our right flank. We worked all day on our breast-works; the weather was hot and we were exhausted.

On the evening of the 21st we were notified to be ready for an early start in the morning. Our ammunition boxes were to be full and we were to carry ten extra cartridges in reserve. Fortunately we had a good night's rest, and by six o'clock were packed, had our breakfast of pork, hardtack, and coffee, and were ready to move. It was a bright morning, with little air stirring and all the signs for a hot day. Our 1st and 2nd Divisions were at the front in line of battle with the 3rd Division[18] in reserve. From early morning everything indicated a movement by our right flank of the Army. Ordnance wagons and ambulance trains were well in front, guns in the batteries were ready for their horses that were feeding nearby, couriers and staff officers were busy carrying orders. It was fully nine o'clock before everything was ready and the order to advance given. Our Regiment was taken from the line to act as skirmishers for the entire Division. We marched by the right flank to the outer posts which were about a half mile in advance of our battle line and near where our pickets were posted. There we deployed right and left, relieving the pickets who returned to their commands.

---

[18] Commanded by Major General Daniel Butterfield and composed of the brigades led by Brigadier General William T. Ward, Colonels Samuel Ross and James Wood, Jr.

We spread ten feet apart, deploying the entire Regiment. As we were in heavily wooded forest, it took time to complete the work. At ten-thirty we were ready for the signal but it was nearly eleven before the bugle rang out "forward." We then moved through the underbrush, slowly and cautiously feeling the way as we knew we were near the enemy. In less than a half hour we ran into their picket line and firing began. For some distance we drove them through the woods, they retiring slowly and contesting every foot of the way. By noon we had forced them through the forest into a large clearing which was east of the woods.

This open space was a large plantation owned by a man named Culp. It had been cleared in the usual way used in north Georgia; by girdling the big trees and then leaving them to die, and in time decay. There were many of these trees still standing and their dead limbs pointed in every direction made a weird appearance. The fields in which the plantation was divided were hilly and cut with ravines; this made it an ideal place for skirmishing for the side that was on the defensive. Where we came out of the timber we were on quite an elevation, the cleared lands descending for at least a mile; then there was another forest gradually rising to another range of hills, beyond which ran the railroad to Atlanta. As we advanced through the open country the Johnnies held to every protected spot as long as they could. They clung to every hill and ravine until our men on the right and left advanced so far as to endanger their capture then they would crawl back to the next hill or ravine. While this was going on we were using every protection there was to give us cover. One looking lengthwise of our line would have seen men behind trees and stumps, others lying flat on the ground behind some hummock, and many in the little gullies and ravines. From twelve-thirty in the afternoon we continued the skirmish in the open field; the sun was shining brightly and it was terribly hot but in the excitement we did not notice this. By this time we had forced them back to the woods beyond the clearing; there we saw a line of rifle pits that were well protected from our fire. When they dropped into the pits they gave us a big yell; which was saying, "Now get us if you can." In front of their breastworks and about a hundred yards from them was a ravine running for a long distance parallel to their line. On our last rush we were ordered to take the ravine. To get there we were in the open and while we covered the ground in record time, we lost several men. It was now four in the afternoon and we were as close as we could get to the rifle pits with a skirmish line. For more than an hour we remained in the ravine and the firing was lively as we waited for the battle line to come up.

While lying in this natural dugout there were two occurrences I well remember. The first was of a courier on horseback who was carrying orders from General Williams. He came down the rear of our skirmish line with a message for Colonel Rogers. Having further orders for an officer on our extreme left, the direct route would be to cross the open field behind us where he would be exposed to the fire of the entire enemy line. He was warned not to cross the field in that place if he valued his life but he paid no attention nor hesitated a moment in starting. At the left of our Company he came in full view of their line and was in perfect range. There he put spurs to his horse and flew over the field. I think every Johnnie in that line fired at him; while he took off his hat and shouting, waved at them. For fully a half mile he was under fire but neither he nor his horse was hit. After he passed out of sight there was a great yell from the enemy's rifle pits in recognition of a gallant deed.

My second remembrance was personal. Next to me in the ravine was Dan O'Connor, a young Irish member of our Company. Dan had been very industrious all day and was nearly out of cartridges; so I told him he had better quit firing for a time as he might need his ammunition more later on; then we both ceased firing for a while. As we were idly waiting, Dan began to notice his surroundings and looking out in our front discovered something. Turning to me he said, "R.C. (my initials and nickname) look at those berries."

I looked, and about six feet from us but out of reach were a lot of low-growing blackberries, the bushes full of berries. The temptation was too great for Dan to resist. He said, "I am hungry and I will take my chances in getting some of these berries." I was hungry as Dan, so I crawled out beside him and we picked berries as fast as we could, eating as we picked. As we glanced ahead we could see more and more bushes, and as we cleaned up we crawled further and further. Being greatly interested in our work we must have become careless for suddenly a bullet whizzed between our heads that were not more than six inches apart. It tore a hole through Dan's blouse at his shoulder but did not wound him. We slid back into our hole. He said, "Are you hit?" I answered, "No Dan, I am not hit but I think that bullet is notice that our blackberry feast is over." After we got back Dan insisted on firing on the pit from which he thought the shot came; although he did say the Johnnie was good to have let us eat so many berries. I relate this to show how men will grow indifferent to danger when they are constantly facing it.

The courier had brought orders for a forward movement of our Regimental skirmish line; Colonel Rogers at once gave orders for an advance. On our left this was impossible unless supported by the main line; our thin skirmish lines were as close as they could get. The right of our line was better protected by trees and bushes and could make some advance. The left half of our Company was in the ravine with no cover between them and the rifle pits. Captain Anderson divided the Company, leaving the left half with Lieutenant Quinn; the rest of the men proceeded to the right. I was near the center of the Company and he directed me to go with him. In front of us was a farmhouse with the usual outbuildings of a plantation. These were nearly surrounded by a peach orchard and other trees; this was the protection that screened us as we advanced. A short distance beyond the buildings was a forest, running in nearly a straight line with the one in which the enemy's skirmishers were located on our left. We found as we advanced that the ravine which we had occupied ran diagonally to the left after entering the woods and the enemy skirmish line followed the ridge on the east side of the ravine thus running off in an angle from the line we had been forcing back all day. We moved cautiously into the woods. There was at that time no firing on our immediate front but we halted on the west side of the ravine and took cover behind the large trees. The ravine was filled with trees and underbrush; and from where we were descended about seventy-five feet to a dry stream in the bottom and then up the other side to the same level we were on. Our advance was so quiet that the enemy on the other side of the ravine, not more than two hundred feet from us, did not know we were there. At first it was very still but soon we heard voices beyond the opposite hill. As we silently waited the noise increased in volume. I could hear men marching, the giving of orders in a low voice, the neighing of horses, and further back, bugle calls. I told O'Connor, who was still with me, to remain quietly behind his tree and listen; and not to fire unless they advanced. I would go back and report to Captain Anderson. I found Colonel Rogers with the Captain. After I had told them what I had heard, the Colonel went back with me and heard what was going on himself. He at once saw what the Confederates were preparing to do. Before leaving me he said, "They are massing troops and will probably attack. In case they advance have the men fire and then fall back."

During the afternoon the battle line had moved up very slowly, waiting, it was said, for Schofield's[19] 23rd Corps to come to the right of our 20th to protect its flank when the

---

[19] John McAllister Schofield (1831-1906) graduated from West Point in 1853 and became a Brigadier General of Volunteers in November 1861. Elevated to Major General a year later he commanded the XXIII Corps in the Atlanta, Franklin, Nashville, and Carolinas campaigns. He received a brevet Major Generalcy in the regular army for his activities at the Battle of Franklin. He served as Commander in Chief of the Army during 1888-95.

advance was made. For some reason there was a delay on the part of the 23rd in arriving at their position and it was nearly three in the afternoon before the line advanced. Then our troops in line of battle moved in to the open field and halted near its center where there was quite an elevation. Our 1st Division was located along the ridge, and the 2nd upon our left farther back. By this time it was nearly four o'clock, and as it seemed as though there would be no further advance during that afternoon, the men began to build breastworks a half mile back of our skirmish line but on much higher ground.

When the Colonel left us, we remained quietly on our post listening. There was no question what was going on in our front. The enemy was massing troops very rapidly and we could hear every movement as this went on. When the Johnnies came in we noted the warning commands of their officers, the orders to halt, front, dress, etc., orders familiar to us. The massing of a division[20] cannot be made under any conditions in less than an hour and it was fully five o'clock before their work was completed and they were ready to advance. To us on the skirmish line who were waiting for them to move it seemed as though they would never start. Our guns were cocked and we were ready to fire at sight of them.

Shortly after five a bugle sounded "forward", then we heard low commands given by their officers, followed by the rustle of many feet, as they marched through the underbrush. They had not far to go before they reached the crest of the hill on the opposite side of the ravine where we could see them. They came without skirmishers which meant an attack in force. We fired and dropped back through the woods and plantation grounds and into the open field over which we would have to retreat for nearly a half mile to reach our battle line on the hill. The men there were working with

---

[20] Probably that of Major General Carter L. Stevenson.

pick and shovel, as men will work whose lives depend on constructing barricades to stop bullets. Back of them we saw our batteries being wheeled into place. Everything was being done that could be for the fight that was coming.

The Rebel line advanced rapidly for they were in light marching order. We skirmishers were loaded with our full equipment, knapsacks, etc. This made it harder for us to retreat than for them to follow. When we reached the Culp buildings we halted long enough to load our guns but the enemy were so close we continued to run, with them calling on us to surrender. As soon as they were in front of the buildings they commenced firing on us as we retreated. As their bullets would strike in the sand around us, little fountains of dust would rise two feet in the air. On our way back on the run we came to a knoll and halted on the crest long enough to fire our last volley; then we started for our line, every man for himself.

By this time the enemy were in view of our forces; and several of our batteries opened fire with shot and shell; we were in their line of fire and for a time in as much danger from them as the enemy, so we tried to file off to the right and left out of range. Winded, we made a last effort and struggled through our lines. Everyone fell to the ground exhausted, and many were in a dead faint. We had lost forty-eight men killed and wounded; four were wounded in our Company, including Lieutenant Quinn, whose wounds were so severe that he did not return to duty. One of our Company, Oliver Smith, was captured and spent the rest of his service in Andersonville Prison.

The attack was made by Hood's Corps and lasted until after eight that night. There were three or four charges, all unsuccessful and with great loss to the enemy. The farthest advance on our line as measured by the dead was within two hundred feet. Fighting in defense behind our works our Division only lost two hundred and fifty men, of whom forty-eight were from our own skirmish line. The enemy's loss in killed and wounded was some twelve hundred. Many of their wounded and a few unwounded prisoners were taken. From them, it was learned that the attack was made by Hindman's and Stevenson's Divisions of Hood's Corps, with Hood[21] in direct command.

On the 23rd, our Regiment remained as we were behind the line until the afternoon, so I had an opportunity to look around and see what had happened during the battle. Our artillery had been effective, as it could sweep the entire field over which the enemy charged. In the afternoon a new line was laid out for the infantry halfway between the hill where the battle had been fought and the Culp farmhouse. In the new line our Regiment was placed on the extreme left of the Division, in the open field over which we had skirmished the day before. When we reached this position we commenced to fortify our line. At this time the enemy was about a mile east of us behind heavy works; our location was some three miles southwest of Marietta and as we looked toward the northeast, the two peaks of Kenesaw stood plainly in view. At night the mountains were lighted by the artillery fire from the lines that ran along the side of the hills. We remained in this place until the 3rd of July. Nothing startling happened in our immediate front.

On Sunday, June 26th, we had divine service for the first time in several weeks. It was ten in the morning and we could hear the bells ringing for service in Marietta. We had no Sunday inspection; all we were expected to have in perfect condition were our guns and cartridge boxes. If we had a real inspection we would make a ragged show for our clothes and shoes were in the last stage of existence.

---

[21]   John Bell Hood (1831-1879) graduated from West Point in 1853 and joined the Confederate Army in 1861. He rose to Brigadier General by March 1862 and led the famed "Texas Brigade" in the east before being promoted to Major General in the following October. He commanded a division at Fredericksburg and Gettysburg, being wounded at the latter. He commanded a corps at Chickamauga where he lost a leg. After promotion to Lieutenant General in February 1864 he commanded corps and the Army of Tennessee during the Atlanta, Franklin, and Nashville campaigns.

On June 27, Schofield's 23rd Corps cut the road from Marietta to Atlanta while to the left three divisions from the 14th and 15th Corps assailed the Confederate positions on Kenesaw Mountain. They lost 2,051 men but failed to seize the peak. The Confederates had to abandon the position, however, on July 1 when Sherman shifted the 17th Corps to his right flank and enveloped it. The 20th Corps continued in its blocking position southwest of Marietta. All was not quiet, however, as Bull notes.

During the afternoon of Wednesday, June 29th, Henry Sartwell, one of my tentmates, was shot in the arm by a sharpshooter as he was standing behind our works, which were in range of their rifles. Every day someone in the Regiment was hit.

After sleeping, Nat Rowell and I had permission from the Captain for two hours' leave and took a stroll down the line to our right. Our Division was now holding the extreme right of the 20th Corps and we passed along the rear of our entrenchments; then went some distance behind the 23rd Corps who were on the extreme flank of the Army. They were all hard at work on their breastworks as they had not yet had time to build them since they had advanced to this position on June 27th. We came to the pike which was a wide straight road that ran toward Marietta. Soon after it left where we were located it entered and passed through the enemy's lines. An opening in the road furnished a good range for their sharpshooters; not knowing this we walked some distance along this road. We were soon greeted with wheezy, long-drawn-out sounds made by nearly spent bullets that were going slower than the sound was coming to us. It seemed the Johnnies with their English rifles had the range but it was a long one. Before we could get to the woods at the side of the road a spent bullet struck Nat on the instep. We got the shoe off and found it was only a bad bruise. His foot swelled so quick he could not get the shoe back and I had a slow time getting him back to camp. He was lame for several days.

So far in June we had made slow progress in pushing the enemy back. In direct line not more than fifteen miles; for we had made no attack that had been successful and they had only abandoned their lines when they were flanked by us. We had, however, worked under great difficulties, the chief of which had been rain. The first twenty days of the month it rained nearly every day; not light showers but fierce rains that covered the land with water and made roads next to impassable. Our trains and artillery were almost lost in the mud. The men were wet most of the time and many were ill. It was remarkable that so many kept well considering the weather in which they were constantly fighting, moving and working on fortifications.

During the time we were resting, movements made by others were soon to bring results. Following the failure to break Johnston's lines on Kenesaw Mountain, General Sherman began to stretch out our Army toward the right. We were by this time so strongly entrenched that a small force could defend our works, so our reserve in the second line was placed on our right, thus extending the line in the direction of the railroad. The afternoon of July 2nd, a large force passed our rear going toward the right; it consisted of the 15th Corps and part of the 17th, with General McPherson in command. That night our picket line was doubled with instructions to use great watchfulness. It was felt that General Johnston would either attack or retreat, as he could not allow us to strike him in the rear and get possession of the railroad. Our orders were to be ready to move at a moment's notice; so everything was packed but our blankets. At daybreak our skirmishers advanced and found that the enemy had retreated. Fearing that his communications by rail would be cut if he remained longer, Johnston abandoned the strong Kenesaw fortifications and made for his other prepared position on the north side of the Chattahoochee River only a few miles from Atlanta.

When the retreat was discovered we started in pursuit, taking a fast gait, through their abandoned earthworks. These were strong fortifications; including their picket rifle pits, they had three lines, two with abatis in their front. We followed the 14th Corps; it was extremely hot; I don't think we had ever marched on a more stifling day. Fortunately the road was through the forest most of the way so we were in the shade, but there was not a breath of air. There was much straggling and many had sunstroke. The sun beat down fiercely when we crossed a plantation where there was no shade. We saw scores of men from the 14th Corps lying by the roadside overcome by the heat. At three in the afternoon we came up with the enemy who, as usual, were behind breastworks. When we halted nearly a mile from them, many of our men expressed their satisfaction that we had struck something to halt our march in the awful heat.

Our troops closed up and formed a line of battle, our skirmishers advanced, and there was noisy musketry until dark. We did not fortify our line as our officers feared no attack, knowing that the enemy's stand was only to hold us back long enough for their trains to continue on in their rear. That night we spread our blankets and had a good night's rest, expecting in the morning to find the Johnnies gone. However, at daybreak July 4th, we found them still with us and as ready to fight as ever. Early skirmishing commenced and continued all day, both sides seemed trying to see how much noise they could make. There were more casualties than in a home-doings on July 4th.

In the afternoon we advanced about a half mile, well up under the hill occupied by the enemy. A little to our left Geary's Division was massed in the woods, and the report was circulated that it, supported by our 1st Division, would attack. Generals Sherman, Thomas, and Hooker were present and inspected the enemy's position. At noon the men of our two Divisions had been given a ration of whiskey; this led us to believe the charge was to be made. For some reason, the order, if given, was recalled but we remained camped close to the picket line. While there was no serious fighting along our front, the 14th Corps on our right was engaged. This was the first and only time I saw or knew of any stimulants being issued to the Army during my period of service.

The morning of the 5th found the enemy gone; their trains had passed to their rear and they were slowly following on the way back to their last line of defense, north of Atlanta; this was on the west side of the Chattahoochee River some five miles from the city. We packed and had our breakfast before six and were on our way before seven. Our route was through the enemy's abandoned works. As usual, they were strongly built with many obstructions in their front. It had become more and more a source of wonder how and when they had built such complete fortifications. They could not have been constructed in the few days that they used them. We followed the enemy slowly and were halted many times so the several divisions on our right and left could keep in touch with us and each other. At three in the afternoon our skirmishers sighted the Johnnies some five miles from where we started in the morning and about three miles from the river. Here we found they had another line of works with a frontage of five miles and both flanks on the river. We halted and deployed in line of battle; then as a matter of habit began to fortify.

At six that evening I was detailed with four others of our Company for picket duty. With the full regimental detail we reported at the picket reserve post at eight o'clock. At that time the whole line had not been established. The Officer of the Day who had charge of our part of the line was a major of some regiment in the 14th Corps. As there was no commissioned officer at the reserve post, he placed me in charge and I accompanied him as he laid out the line. I placed the men and made the connection with the other details on the right and left. Then the Major went to other parts of the line under his charge, saying as he left he would be back after twelve and make his headquarters with our reserve post.

All was quiet in our front; there was no evidence of the enemy. Our reserve post was in the open field and our pickets were placed in the edge of the woods beyond the field.

About twelve-thirty the Major returned. He was in a very nervous condition. He said he was not satisfied, for as yet he had no definite information regarding the location of the enemy; they might be near us and suddenly attack or they might be far away. It was so uncertain he would be anxious until he knew for a certainty where they were. At one-thirty we relieved the men on the picket posts with men from the reserve so as to give all the men in the detail a chance to get some rest. After we made the change the Major said to me: "I have decided to find where the rebel picket line is if possible." He then directed me to take six men and with them pass in front of our pickets and advance cautiously from our front and if we found we were in close touch with the rebels, draw their fire, and then return at once to our own line. If we did not contact the enemy we were to go at least a half mile before coming to a halt; then I was to send back a messenger with such information as I had. It was nearly two when I took the six men, three of whom were from my own Company, and accompanied by the Major went to the advance post where he, after directing me to proceed as fast as I could, said he would return to the reserve post to await my return.

I deployed four of the men about ten feet apart, keeping two with me in the center, and started the scout. It was heavily timbered forest; and so dark we could see absolutely nothing. We had to go forward entirely by our sense of feeling, guided by such sounds as we might hear from time to time. The ground was rough and uneven and the undergrowth of bushes, vines, and briars was such a tangle and so matted together that in places we could scarcely move forward; but we stumbled along as best we could. The only guide we had to indicate direction was the neighing of the Major's horse, that for some reason kept it up all night; with that sound behind, we at least moved toward the enemy. Our advance was slow and the muttered curses as we stumbled on over the fallen timber and through the pools of water were only smothered because of the danger of being heard. To me the scout seemed as foolhardy and senseless as was ever given seven men to do. Along toward four in the morning it had lightened up so objects could be seen quite well. I judged we were a half mile from our picket line and had reached higher ground where we could see some distance ahead. In our immediate vicinity we heard only the song of birds but some distance beyond heard the sound of chopping, the ring of the axe clearly reaching us. We also heard men talking and dogs barking, a sure sign the Johnnies were not far away. I had an old envelope in my pocket and wrote a note to the Major stating that we had come the half mile, the enemy was just ahead of us but we had not yet drawn their fire, and asked for instructions. This note I sent back by Eddie Blanchard who was the youngest boy in our Company, only seventeen. He was timid about returning, fearing our pickets would fire on him, but I told him they knew about us and there was no danger. Three-quarters of an hour later he returned with a note from the Major for us to go forward at once, draw their fire, and then without replying return to our lines. By this time it was daylight.

While waiting we had kept a sharp lookout and there was every indication that there was a camp just ahead of where we were. There was more chopping, much singing and laughing, bugle calls, beating of drums and the other sounds usual in a camp. As soon as I read the Major's note we went forward through the woods and in less than five minutes were at a clearing enclosed by a rail fence. The field was planted with corn, which was heavy and stood at least five or six feet high. Through the center of the field ran a stream bordered with bushes. A small log house was on the other side of the stream and beyond the field was more forest. Coming out to the edge of the cornfield, I told the boys to halt so as to plan what was best to do for I was determined to take no chances of capture that could be avoided. I warned the men not to talk, when we reached the fence and climbed to the top to get a better view. While we were waiting and listening, Tim Crowly of our Company asked to go down to the stream to fill our canteens. It looked all right so he and another man went down through the corn. It was not more than a hundred yards and took only two or three minutes to reach the stream. Just then the fog lifted and we saw men surrounding the house. It needed no command to get the men off the fence, all dropped down behind and waited for what would come next. The Johnnies were shouting "surrender" and a volley was fired, the bullets whistling around us. The boys all itched to fire back into the crowd around the house and some did.

The mission of finding the enemy, so needed by the Major, was accomplished and we fell back through the forest with the enemy following us as far as the fence from which they continued to fire until we were out of range; but no one was hit. We went back to the top of the hill where we had halted when I sent the report to the Major; there we met him with the advancing picket line. When I reported he seemed surprised to see me. I told him that I feared we had lost two men. He said he was glad that any of us came back, he had expected we might all be captured. He justified his action by saying that he had to know where the Rebels were and the scout was the only way he could find out for a certainty. He congratulated me on my escape. I found out later that this was not the first time this officer had such questionable and unnecessary work done. In front of Kenesaw he sent out six men on a similar scout and all were lost.

While talking to the Major, to my great surprise, the two missing men reported. They were well done up by the long run made to escape but were all right; they had the canteens they had taken to fill but they were empty. Tim told their story. He said they went down through the corn quietly and coming near the bushes that lined the creek were surprised to see a Johnnie, gun in hand, standing behind the undergrowth on the opposite side, not more than twenty feet away. With but a moment to make a plan of escape, Tim motioned his companion to stop, dropped his gun, stepped forward, and said, "Good morning Johnnie," acting as though he was surrendering. The Johnnie lowered his gun and then in an instant they jumped back in the corn and were lost to sight. Fortunately, at that moment fog came rolling up the valley and they got away although the entire picket line was firing and calling on them to surrender. We had been within one hundred yards of their reserve post when we were on the fence when the fog first cleared. Had we gone beyond the fence I can hardly see how we could have kept from either death or capture.

The Major told me the Army was on the move and that we could join our Regiment back in the reserves. We returned to our command through the line of the 14th Corps, as the 20th had gone to the left. We found that our Division was over four miles away and were so exhausted by our night's scout that we camped by ourselves in the woods that night. We joined the Regiment at ten the next morning and found the men as usual building breastworks; after a rest and feed we joined them. In our new position we did not seem near the enemy and it was quiet. Away toward the right nearer the Chattahoochee River, there was a lot of cannonading and it was rumored Sherman had a large force making a detour and it was to cross the river.

We were notified that we were to remain in our camp for a few days, waiting until pontoons were placed and the railroad bridge rebuilt. The water in the river was very high so the fords could not be used. That we were to get a good rest was news for we were in need of it. For two months, if we were not skirmishing or fighting, we were working with pick and shovel on fortifications, much of the time in rain with broken sleep. We were in this camp until July 17th. In that time we not only rested, but with needle and thread did what we could to mend our ragged clothing. On July 12th I had a bath and washed my clothes; our last washing had been on May 20th at Cassville.

By July 17th, about half the Army had crossed the river, over pontoons, and the railroad bridge was completed. Our rest was now at an end and the final struggle of the campaign was before us. The weather was very hot during the day but the nights were comfortable. The rainy season was over except for many thunder showers that we did not mind for the sun soon dried out both our clothes and the ground we slept on.

Early on the morning of the 17th, we received marching orders and three days' rations. By ten o'clock we were on the move and after going three miles we reached the pontoon bridge. The water was running almost bank full and the river was from three to four hundred feet wide. We crossed and turning to the left marched two miles up the river, where we camped. That day the entire 20th and 14th Corps crossed; the 14th connected on our right. The 4th Corps that had preceded us by several days was on our left and had already fortified their line. Atlanta, the goal we were striving for, was only six to eight miles away on the south. From nearby hills the steeples of the city churches could be seen.

The morning of the 18th we made ready to start early but did not get underway until two in the afternoon. Our advance was in the direction of Atlanta, but covered only two miles; there we halted, formed in line, and camped. The movement was slowly and deliberately made, as we were with the right wing of the Army and were marking time while the left wing, ten miles away, was making a great right wheel and so had to advance much farther each day than we on the hub of the wheeling movement.

On the 19th our march was almost a repetition of the day before. We were held in line, while the movement of troops around us continued. Then late in the afternoon, our 2nd Division that was on our left advanced about two miles, and we moved up to connect with them. Our line as we formed it there was on the north side of Peach Tree Creek, which though not large required bridging before we could cross. We were some four miles from Atlanta but as yet had not seen the enemy. Conditions seemed to indicate that they had retired to their fortifications, and that we would not meet them again before we invested the city.

Early in the morning of the 20th our Pioneers began

building bridges over the creek so our Corps could cross. A bridge was to be constructed for each Brigade. Where we were, the stream was not wide but it was deep with a sluggish flow, high banks, and muddy bottom. The trains and artillery could not have been moved without the bridges. They were finished and we crossed before noon. In our Brigade the 141st New York, having the lead that day, was first to go. We followed them and marched directly to the front for about a half mile, and there the Brigade was massed in the woods. The 141st, marching by its right flank, halted and closed ranks, came to a front and stacked arms. Our Regiment followed them, passed to their right and at a distance of fifty feet, fronted. We were followed by the 5th Connecticut and 46th Pennsylvania who, also going to our right, closed and fronted. The whole Brigade was completely massed, covering a frontage of only some two hundred and fifty feet. We were followed by our artillery. With our Brigade were Generals Hooker and Williams with their staffs and escorts; they halted and dismounted in the woods at our right. By this time it was noon and we were notified that we would halt long enough for our dinner. The Generals had their lunch prepared under the trees nearby. We made our little fires, fried our pork, boiled our coffee, and ate our hardtack. It was a bright day, though hot; after we had our meal we made ourselves as comfortable as we could. Some were soon sleeping, others reading books or papers, a good many were having a friendly game of cards using the greasy pack that always was handy when we halted. Thus things went on until three in the afternoon.

There had been so far no sign of the enemy, not a warlike sound broke the stillness; and were it not for the distant sound of cannonading far to our left, we might have felt we were on a pleasure trip in the most peaceful of lands. While we were resting the rumor spread that the enemy was on the retreat, and we were marking time and in all probability would enter Atlanta the next day. The attitude of our Generals, who were near us, would seem to confirm this opinion.

No orders were given to put our Brigade in position to defend itself in case of attack. During the campaign we had never been so massed while in the presence of the enemy unless a line of troops was deployed in our front and we were where we had time to form in line in case of emergency. But on this day, everyone from our Corps Commander to private soldier seemed certain that the enemy would make no stand until behind the entrenchments at Atlanta; so there was no need for placing our Brigade in line of battle. Our officers must have thought it unnecessary to use even the most ordinary precautions for the skirmish line was not advanced as far in front as usual. We were finally informed we would camp for the night as we were.

We were congratulating ourselves on this unexpected good luck when suddenly, about three-fifteen that afternoon, there was a rifle shot on our front. It was as unexpected as would be thunder from out of a clear sky. A look of surprise and almost consternation came to every face; we knew the critical position our mass formation put us in; but the feeling was only for the moment. The first shot was followed by others in quick succession, then came the rattle of musketry, and with it the familiar "Rebel Yell." We knew then for a certainty that serious work was ahead of us.

The action, known as the Battle of Peach Tree Creek, involved an attempt by Hood to destroy Thomas's Army of the Cumberland while it was astride Peach Tree Creek. The troops opposing the 1st Brigade were from Major General Edward C. Walthall's Division of Lieutenant General Alexander P. Stewart's Corps.

On the sound of the first shot every man jumped to his feet and into line. There was no waiting for orders, the men knew what was required to get where they could make a defense. It was but the work of a moment to sling knapsacks and take guns from the stacks; in far less time than it takes to tell it we were ready to march. Meanwhile the musketry firing was coming closer and closer, the yells of the enemy louder and louder, and the bullets began to sing and whistle around us and through the trees over our heads. We realized the critical position we were in and the necessity of immediate deployment into line of battle; should we be struck while still in mass formation it would mean both defeat and slaughter. It was not more than three minutes from the time we heard the first shot and while the Bugler was sounding the "fall in" that the 141st New York was on the double-quick to the right. We of the 123rd New York, whose place was to follow them, loaded our guns as we waited for them to clear the way then went after them ready for business. The 5th Connecticut and 46th Pennsylvania, the other two Regiments of the Brigade, went to the left and fronted to complete the deployment. The 141st followed a narrow wagon road, we behind them. We had not gone two hundred yards before we commenced to meet our skirmishers coming on the run, closely followed by the yelling Johnnies.

The forest was filled with smoke from the guns of the enemy; the 141st as they hurried on the road ahead of us ran head-on into them. All their field officers were mounted and riding at the right of the Regiment; every one went down, either killed or wounded, at this first contact. It was then their Colonel Logie[22] was killed; a Captain as ranking officer commanded during the battle.[23] When they met the enemy, the 141st swung around by their right, changed their front, and held that position during the action. As soon as the 141st halted, we closed on them and fronted just in time to repel the first attack. While we were racing at double-quick and before we fronted or fired a shot, several of our men were killed or wounded. Our line was on a hillside that descended quite sharply in our front for some distance to a ravine, beyond which the ground rose to about the same elevation as

[22]   Colonel William K. Logie led the 141st New York from June 1, 1863 until his death.

[23]   The young officer in temporary command of the 141st New York at Peach Tree Creek was Capt. Elisha G. Baldwin.

that we were on. In our view was a forest of scattered trees, but not much underbrush. Looking down the hill the enemy's line was not in sight. It was behind the clouds of smoke from their musketry fire. They were advancing slowly up the hill, not more than two hundred feet away. Their loud yells could be heard above the roar of their guns. As soon as we fronted every gun in our Regiment fired on the Johnnies' line. They wavered for a time and fell back, we loading and firing as fast as we could, as they retired over the hill so they could be out of our range and reform.

On the road over which we moved when we deployed stood an old log house; it was loosely put together and around it were some outbuildings of squared logs. They were located about fifty feet back of our Company. After we had repulsed the first attack and the firing had temporarily lessened it was suggested we tear down the buildings and use the logs as a barricade. This was no sooner thought of than half the Regiment was put on the job; and in a short time, before the second charge of the enemy, the logs were piled in front of our line. When our Regiment went to the right to deploy it was followed by Winegar's Battery[24] of six guns. They wheeled into line between our Companies C and D, opened up at once, and continued firing until after seven that night. They were an important aid in checking the massed forces that were hurled against the line we had to form so quickly.

When the gun next to us was being unlimbered and wheeled to position, one of the skirmishers who had been delayed in getting back came running up the hill toward our line. As he ran he was loading his gun, and when he reached us he turned to give the enemy a parting shot. He was a straight young fellow at least six feet tall and looked every inch a soldier; on his cap was "27," noting the 27th Indiana, one of

[24] Battery I, 1st New York Light Artillery, commanded by Captain Charles E. Winegar, fired the 3-inch Rodman rifle.

the few Western Regiments in our Division.[25] As he was bringing his gun down after firing I heard a dull thud and saw him fall. A bullet had hit him squarely in the forehead. He was dead, and as his body was in the way of the gunners it was carried back of the line. I have often wondered if his fate was known to his people back in Indiana. He was separated from his Regiment and none who saw him killed knew him. He died when men's lives were cheap; I doubt if any effort was made to notify his Regiment. He was buried with our own dead.

During the afternoon the enemy made five charges on our line, coming at times within one hundred feet; yet I did not see a single Johnnie. The clouds of smoke from the muskets of both sides and from Winegar's Battery poured down on us to hide everything but the flash of the enemy's guns that gave us their position. At no time up to seven o'clock, when the enemy retired, was there complete stoppage of firing, except for short times we would cease to cool our guns when the enemy's attacks were driven off. The gunbarrels would get so hot we could scarcely hold them and I saw many guns discharge as the powder from the cartridge was being placed in the barrel. One of the boys near me, after biting off the top of the cartridge, had placed it in the barrel and was ramming it down, when the powder exploded and the bullet and ramrod went together. He looked a good deal surprised, and shaking his fist in the direction of the Johnnies yelled, "Take that you ——— and see how you like it." This expressed the mental state of men on the firing line, no fear for themselves, just rage.

Shortly after six o'clock, following the last attack on our line, the 31st Wisconsin Regiment was ordered to reinforce our Brigade, which had been engaged for nearly three hours without relief. This was a new regiment and had up to that

[25]   The 27th Indiana was *not* "one of the few Western Regiments in our Division." Of 18 regiments in Bull's division, 7 were from the Midwest.

time seen no active service. They had joined us after we had crossed the Chattahoochee River but had not yet been assigned to any brigade. Their ranks were full, having nearly nine hundred men. On the march they looked like a full brigade. They had been the butt of endless chaffing by the men of veteran regiments, who seemed to delight in nagging the new recruits. The enemy attacks had been so heavy and long continued that soon after six o'clock General Williams ordered them forward to relieve exhausted troops on the battle front. They came down through the woods behind us in a long straggling line.

The men, like all new volunteers under such conditions, looked wild and excited, not knowing what they might do with their guns loaded. We felt that they were almost as dangerous as the enemy in our front. When they had advanced within two hundred feet of our line we realized that they had come to relieve us. Our men put up a great protest. We knew we had the Johnnies beaten to a standstill and were determined not to leave the line that it had taken so much effort to hold now the battle was won. So the men shouted, "Go back we don't want you! We can hold this line without help. Go where you are needed, you can't relieve us." The officer in command of the regiment, seeing how we felt, about-faced and went to some other part of the battle line. The 31st was the next day assigned to the 3rd Brigade of our Division. It developed into a fine regiment and remained with our Corps until the end of the war. It made a distinguished record at the battle of Bentonville, the last major engagement in which the 20th Corps took part.

At Peach Tree Creek, I fired seventy rounds of ammunition, some of the men said they had fired one hundred. At the end of the action we presented a strange appearance, smoke and powder stains had covered our faces and made them look as blue as indigo. The day had been hot and we were as wet as though we had been in the water. When we started to deploy, no brigade was ever in a more dangerous position to receive an attack. If every regiment had not been composed of experienced veteran soldiers, men who knew what to do under the most adverse and changing conditions, we would never have fronted in battle line in time to have made a successful defense against the heavy force that attacked so suddenly.

By eight that night all was quiet. The battle of Peach Tree Creek had been fought, the enemy was defeated, and retiring to their fortifications near Atlanta. The Corps of Hardee and Stewart had been engaged in the surprise attack and their entire force[26] had fallen on the 20th Corps. Our entire loss in killed and wounded was over two thousand;[27] that of the enemy must have been twice as much as they were the attacking force, and further, our artillery was used effectively, while they had none. Our Division's loss was six hundred, and our Brigade, which could not muster more than twelve hundred men, lost three hundred and forty-nine, of whom seventy-five were killed.[28] Our Company had two killed and four wounded. The barricade of logs saved us from great loss; nearly all of our casualties came before we made the log breastworks. Many of our Company were affected by the continuous roar of the artillery only twenty feet from where we were. For two days our hearing was almost gone; it was several days before it was again normal.

[26]   William Joseph Hardee (1815-1873) graduated from West Point in 1838 and served in the Seminole and Mexican Wars. He became a Brigadier General in the Confederate Army in June 1861 and a Major General the following October. He commanded corps at Shiloh, Perryville, Stone's River, Missionary Ridge, and the Atlanta campaign. He was promoted to Lieutenant General in October 1862. Alexander Peter Stewart (1821-1908) was also a West Pointer, class of 1842. Joining the Confederate Army in 1862 he rose to Brigadier General by November of that year and Major General in June 1863. He commanded a division at Chattanooga and during the Atlanta campaign. He was promoted to Lieutenant General in June 1864 and wounded at Mount Ezra Church, Ga., the following month. Bull is in error in stating that the 20th Corps took the full force of the attack since the assailants initially struck lines held by Howard's IV Corps.

[27]   The actual losses were approximately 1,600 Union and 2,500 Confederate dead and wounded.

[28]   The regiment's losses were 11 killed and 42 wounded. Five of the latter later died.

From prisoners taken during the action, it was learned that General Johnston was no longer in command of the Confederate Army; he had been relieved by General Hood. There was to be a new fighting policy, no more retreating; Sherman was to be driven out of Georgia. The day after the battle we strengthened our works as we did not know but the attack would be renewed. However, all remained quiet. It was soon learned that the enemy had retired to their works in the outskirts of the city, some three miles from where we were. We buried the dead in the rear of the line where they had fought. Where it was known, a headboard was placed with name of the dead and his Company and Regiment. We buried many Confederate soldiers who were killed in our immediate front. I visited our Division Field Hospital to see our wounded. As yet only a few tents had been erected, but more than five hundred of our Division wounded lay on the ground. When I looked down on them I thought of Chancellorsville and its horrors suffered by the wounded. Here the men were receiving all the attention that could be given in the field. I found those from our Company doing well and cheered by seeing someone they knew. One who was wounded in the arm asked me to write his people about his being wounded and to be sure and say, "We licked them well." That afternoon I wrote home and also to the boy's father.

After July 20th, the Confederates at once abandoned their defenses in our immediate front. Friday morning, the 22nd, we were ordered to make an advance; at eight o'clock we moved out and set our faces toward Atlanta. We found the works from which they made the surprise attack on the 20th deserted. From there we moved ahead slowly with our skirmishers well thrown out and with our brigades at such distance that they could quickly form in line of battle. The surprise of the 20th Corps at Peach Tree Creek had been a lesson to our command, who would not be caught that way again. It was very hot and we moved slowly with many halts into a more open country. By noon we had gone two miles and there was every indication we were approaching a town.

There were many houses, lumber mills, a tannery and other factories and some places of business where power was used.

Up to this time our advance had been without incident. There had been no evidence of any enemy in our front; again the report was started that the city would be evacuated and we were to occupy it that day. The slow progress did not warrant that conclusion. At one o'clock we were brought to a halt in an open field; our skirmishers had at last found the enemy, who could be seen in heavy works about a mile ahead of us. The Brigade was brought into a position where it could easily and quickly form in line of battle. Our Division commander, General Williams, was with us where he could view the situation. Evidently wishing to know for a certainty what was ahead of us, he ordered one of our batteries to occupy a hill in our front and open on the Rebel line. This battery came up on a run. It was commanded by a Captain we called "Old Leather Breeches," and he acted as though he was itching for a fight when he unlimbered and started firing. He did not have to wait long for an answer from the Johnnies. From a dozen points they opened on our little battery, sending shot and shell and showing that their works were manned with siege guns. As soon as the heavy projectiles began to drop around our battery it was ordered back. No further evidence was necessary to show that the enemy were in well-fortified works and ready for us. There would be no retreat on their part; before us was a long, tedious and dangerous siege.

We at once formed a line of battle and cautiously advanced. Some of their batteries opened on us when we reached points where we could be seen, however, the ground was broken with ravines and we could usually keep out of sight. By evening we had reached the ridge about one half mile from their works and had established a temporary line. Other troops were already there and they were fortifying their position; we were not required to entrench as the second line had not yet been located. During the day we heard active cannonading far to our left indicating a general engagement.

We learned later that the Army of the Tennessee had been in action.[29] General Hood had again taken the offensive as he had done before at Peach Tree Creek. This time he attacked our left wing but after a bloody struggle was driven back into his entrenchments in the outskirts of the city. In this engagement our General McPherson was killed.

On Saturday the 23rd, the second line was located and we were ordered to entrench three hundred feet in the rear of our front line. All our batteries, with the exception of a small artillery reserve, were on the front line where heavy works were being built to protect them. Our breastworks were strongly made. In appearance they resembled the enemy works we passed through earlier in the campaign.

During the night of July 26th we went forward about one half mile, relieving troops in the front line. The 141st New York was in the line to our right. It began to rain as we made the change and we had a wet and muddy experience. The line was in the open fields, our first experience of being behind fortifications not in timbered country. Looking to the rear, not a tree could be seen for some distance. The houses and factories were either occupied or demolished to provide material for the Army. Toward our left the line could be seen for a mile. Our right was in a ravine, the line running to the bottom and then up a sharp hill. The summit of this hill was much higher than where we were and on its crest, a large redoubt was being built to be equipped with siege guns. Our immediate line was on a low ridge, the ground descended gently for two hundred yards to a forest, then it rose to a ridge higher than where we were located. At the top of this ridge was the enemy picket line, where there were located several houses occupied by sharpshooters who could fire on us from the trees. Our Company was so located that its line crossed a road running north from Atlanta, and we could see the outskirts of the city. We had a good view of the enemy's

---

[29]   This was the Battle of Atlanta.

fortifications; where the road passed through their line they had a large redoubt with heavy guns. They could see our works through the opening in the woods and we furnished a good target. Their sharpshooters had long-range English rifles that would carry about a mile and made it hot for us.

The troops we relieved lost several men and the conditions were no better for our men. As soon as a man showed himself during daylight a bullet would come. Not more than one shot in fifty hit its mark, but it was nerve-wracking to know you could not stand erect without hearing a bullet hiss close to your head. In order not to become a target while out of the trenches, the troops that we relieved had dug ditches back from our line deep enough to protect them when they went to the rear. As we were on the ridge they only had to extend for a hundred feet and we could cook our meals and rest with comfort except it was very hot and we had no shade. On our left was located Battery I, 1st New York Light Artillery; they were protected by heavy works.

We were ordered into the works at two o'clock for inspection. General Hooker, his staff and escort were to ride back of our works to view our fortifications and the troops of the 20th Corps. About three o'clock the reviewing party appeared, coming from the left. At some place before they reached us, the General and his party had gone through an opening in the fortifications, so when he would pass by us he would be in our front and in range of the enemy's sharpshooters. Before he reached our position the General was notified of the danger and was requested to pass us in our rear; but having started to review us from the front he would not turn back.

When they came to the place they were in sight of the sharpshooters, they started firing and continued to blaze away as long as the party was in sight. The General was in the lead but did not hasten the pace of his horse, which was a slow trot. To all appearance he might have been in total ignorance that they were under fire. After passing our Regiment they were soon out of range of the Johnnies and then went through an opening in the line and continued on in the rear. The General's orderly, riding almost at his side, was severely wounded, several of his escort were wounded, and some horses were disabled. The General was angry and as soon as he went to the rear gave orders to drive out the sharpshooters. The 13th New Jersey[30] was standing in the line near the General and they were given orders to clear the ridge. Under command of their Colonel they climbed over the trench, dressed their line, and charged at double-quick on the Rebel picket line, cheering as they went. The pickets were soon driven back and the sharpshooters with them, two of the houses were burned, and the ridge was cleared with the capture of thirty-three Johnnies. As soon as this was done every enemy battery within reach opened furiously, forcing the 13th back to its works with quite a loss. Although our batteries all along our front were firing, they could do little against the large guns in the enemy redoubts. General Hooker remained until the Regiment had returned. The Johnnies were soon back in their rifle pits saucy as ever. This was the most spectacular exhibition we had witnessed during this campaign; while it was a small affair it was exciting while it lasted.[31] It was viewed by a large number of our troops who were ready and expected to be called into the fight. The charge of the New Jersey men, the shouts and yells, the musketry fire, the burning of the houses on the ridge, the final cannonading by the enemy that forced the 13th back to their works, all came in quick succession; there was not a dull moment for either the actors or audience.

Early in the afternoon of July 28th we were ordered into line as another effort was to be made to advance our pickets. The batteries opened up and we were ordered forward but

---

[30] Commanded by Colonel Ezra A. Carman, it formed part of 2nd Brigade, 1st Division, XX Corps.

[31] Commanding officers at the time of the battle did not consider the assault of the 13th New Jersey to be as dramatic as Bull inferred. *Official Records* XXXVIII, Pt. 2, 18, 72.

we were too weak to accomplish much. Shortly our skirmishers fell back to our old rifle pits and our daily effort to
dislodge the sharpshooters was over. The two picket lines
were now so close that ordinary conversation might be had
between them, if they wanted to talk.

The weather continued hot but there was no change in our
position or need to constantly watch the enemy; so we sweltered in our dog tents. Had we been permitted to go a short
distance back in our rear, we would have some shade, but
this was not possible as we were liable to be called into the
breastworks at a moment's notice to either repel an attack or
make an advance.

An attack at daybreak on Saturday, the 30th, was ordered
on the enemy picket line and, if possible, the ridge was to be
taken and held. We[32] were placed on the posts with the men
already there, doubling the usual force. The advance was to
be made at daybreak but we were not to fire during the night
unless we were attacked. There were to be no cheers or fire
until we reached their posts so as to surprise them if we
could. In the pits we could get no sleep and it seemed one of
the longest nights of my life. There was nothing to do but
wait for the dawn. Our line was in heavy woods, it was dark
and absolute quiet prevailed. It was nerve-wracking but the
longest night will have an end and just about four-thirty we
saw the darkness going, and wanted the action to begin and
end as soon as possible. We had been carefully instructed
what to do. We were to start quietly but after covering the
greater part of the distance between the lines rush forward;
and if the enemy was taken by surprise, run over the pits and
turn on them so none would escape.

Just as it was light enough we stepped out of our pits and
headed for the front; there was not much underbrush so we
could move without noise. The lines were not more than five
hundred feet apart and it did not take long to cover the
greater part of the distance; strange to say not a shot greeted

[32] Bull had been assigned picket duty the previous night.

us. When nearly on them we took to double-quick and just before we reached their line a few shots were fired but they were so wild no one was hit. We had given them a complete surprise and were over their trench. Many of the Johnnies were in their pits asleep and did not know there was any trouble until they were prisoners. A few tried to put up a fight but were soon disposed of, three or four were wounded but most surrendered at once without making any resistance. We captured their entire picket line of nearly two hundred men with scarcely any loss to ourselves; our troubles and losses came later.

After the pits were captured and the prisoners sent back to the rear we moved on to the summit of the ridge, where we established a new line and the digging of pits was begun. We had no tools at first but we had become adept at trenching and could use anything in reach to quickly dig and throw dirt ahead of us. We worked in pairs at each pit, first loosening up the ground with our bayonets and then using anything we could find to push the dirt to the front. Our hands and the dish we had in our haversacks would do this work when we had no picks and shovels. It was really wonderful how fast one could pile up material sufficient to stop bullets when they were singing about him. The ridge was quite heavily timbered and there were many trees that we used as much as we could for protection when the firing was brisk. Our Brigade Pioneers were sent up to aid us and together we worked with a will. Soon we had pits that were deep enough to cover us when we dropped into them.

As soon as the enemy in their main line found out what had happened, they opened on us with their artillery and advanced a strong line of skirmishers. Had it not been for the trees we had for protection before we finished our pits we would hardly have been able to hold the ridge. The location of the post where I had been stationed was just to the left of the road that passed through the woods, and was almost directly in front of one of the redoubts in the enemy's line. It was on a lower level than our pit and when standing in the road one could look down on it. This fort was equipped with heavy guns and during the morning sent many shots tearing through the trees, making a fearful noise and breaking down large branches, that when they fell were more dangerous than the shot and shell. At ten o'clock that morning a party of our sharpshooters was sent to our aid, and two were located near where we were. They climbed up in a tree and during the rest of the day kept it hot for the men who were working the guns in the redoubt; they nearly silenced them. Now with our new line we had the Johnnies under our guns and they would have to start ducking and crawling as we did when their sharpshooters were working on us. By noon the enemy had evidently given up hope of driving us out, but their artillery and skirmishing was lively all the afternoon. Now in pits that would protect us we could sit down, get some rest, and eat hardtack, feeling that we had done a day's work. We were glad when six o'clock came and we were relieved.

Our day's work had not been without loss. While we were fortunate in the capture of the pickets, when we were on the ridge digging the pits we met with artillery fire and skirmishing that was more deadly. Three of our picket detail were killed, two from the 5th Connecticut and one from the 123rd New York; there also were nine wounded, but none seriously. The prisoners were all from the Georgia State Militia. This may explain the ease with which they were taken; had they been old Confederate veterans they would not have been caught napping. This skirmish was a fair example of many that were fought during the investment of the city. They were nameless and unheralded battles and were fought by only a few men on either side; but they were just as deadly and full of peril as many a pitched battle.

On Sunday the 31st, the work and loss of sleep while on the skirmish line had left me tired even after a good night's rest; so after breakfast I went back to my tent and tried to "sleep it out" but found it impossible. There was no quiet and we had to man the works, fearing an attack. In the morning the Rebels undertook to drive our men from the ridge, using both their artillery and infantry. It was a very noisy action but they were unable to gain ground against our well built pits.

During August 1 a heavy rain accompanied by high winds blew over the tents and filled the ditch behind the works with water. Extremely hot weather, well over 100° on the 4th, dried the land but inhibited skirmishing. On the 9th Bull drew picket duty and had just relieved the old detail when it began to rain once again.

At ten o'clock the advance vedettes were posted. They were located about one hundred feet in advance of the picket line and when possible were placed behind trees when the line was in forest. These men watched and listened for any movement of the enemy and were the first to detect an advance. They remained on their posts until daybreak and then returned to the picket line. As the enemy also stationed vedettes, these men were close to each other. In this campaign a vedette from our Brigade on going to a tree where he was to be stationed met a Johnnie coming to the same tree. This duty was not sought; it was nerve-wracking, dangerous, and the safety of the Army depended on his vigilance. I had seen more than one man when he returned to the picket line in the morning in such condition physically that he was sent back to the camp. If one wants to know how long a night can be and how black the darkness may become, let him stand some night on the picket line in the face of the enemy. In the rifle pits no one sleeps, talking is in whispers, gun in hand, the men sit or stand peering toward the picket line of the enemy, listening as only men listen when their lives depend on their vigilance. It was little better at the reserve post.

It was quiet and the men in the reserve could spread their ponchos on the ground and slept. I could not close my eyes during the night, for our services would be required at a moment's notice should there be trouble on the advance posts. No fire was allowed at the reserve post except a small candle that was set back of a tree. The forest was dense and the night dark and dreary. While on the relief post there was nothing to do but watch and listen; if one remained sitting it was not only depressing but soon one would become sleepy. To keep awake I would walk back and forth behind the sleeping men, and I had ample time to think. My mind went back to the old times and my past life came vividly before me. I could see the old home farm with its meadows, woods, and orchard, the cultivated fields on which the crops were now being harvested. I could see the old farmhouse, our home built by my grandfather far back in the last century, where my father and all his children were born. I could see the mountains far to the west of our home; mountains that stand out so bold and strong, whose crest as a boy I had followed with my eyes toward the north where they joined the Adirondack Range. I had spent my boyhood days there; days not then appreciated as now when they seemed so far away. As I walked back and forth there came to my mind the verse of an old poem that was in our Fourth Reader that we boys often "spoke" in school. The first verse was:

I remember, I remember.
The house where I was born,
The little window where the sun,
Came peeping in at morn.

There came to my mind the old wood colored school house at the corner of the roads where I had acquired the greater part of my schooling, with its play ground. Then I thought of my old schoolmates, my boyhood companions, many of them scattered and far away in the service, some who had already given up their lives.

August 14-21 were quiet insofar as the 123rd New York was concerned. On the 17th, moreover, the pickets on our front made treaty of peace and parties from each side met halfway between the lines and bartered coffee for tobacco and exchanged newspapers. For a time it was quiet but I did not think it would last long. Such meetings were usually followed by sharp skirmishing.

On Monday, the 22nd, away on our right the sound of heavy cannonading reached us. We were informed by couriers and cavalry that passed our rear that general engagements had been going on for several days, that our lines were being constantly extended and that a crisis was sure to come soon. There were signs that some movement would shortly be made by our Corps. At the Commissary, the Quartermaster, and Ordnance supply centers, there was activity; they were cleaning up and loading their wagons with supplies. Captain Anderson told me that the Colonel had informed him that orders had been received to have everything ready for a sudden movement that might start any time. He thought we might be sent to the far right, following the other Corps that had passed us. We were now the extreme left of the entire Army.

No special orders were given us to make preparations to move; that was unnecessary. We had so little to pack that when haste required we could be ready to move in fifteen minutes. We kept all our supplies not in use in our knapsacks and haversacks. If called on to move suddenly we only had to roll up our blanket, take down our tent, strap our blanket and tent cloth to our knapsack, buckle on our ammunition belt, sling on our canteen, haversack, and take our musket and we were ready to fall in. We then had on our backs our house, our furniture, our bed, our clothing, our cooking utensils, our food for three days or more, forty rounds of ammunition, our gun and the many little things from home one has in his knapsack that he feels he cannot throw away until dire necessity forces him to do so. With that load of more than fifty pounds we had to march whatever the weather might be. If it rained we plowed through the mud, if it was dry we plodded over the dusty roads, when it was hot we sweltered under the load which after an hour found us without a dry thread of clothing. I often wonder how we stood up under the fearful load.

On Tuesday, the 24th, I received permission and a pass from Colonel Rogers to take a stroll from camp. I wished to see the heavy guns in action so I visited the fort where there were mounted four thirty-six pounders and one large seventy-two pounder.[33] They looked large to me. Every five minutes, and some times oftener, they dropped a shell in Atlanta. It required quite a large force to man the redoubt, which was strongly built, with heavy iron doors in front that closed when the guns were not in action. These siege guns were only used to shell the city.

A fine view could be had of the enemy's line from the hill where the redoubt was located. The enemy had no less than three lines, including their picket line. Their two main lines were protected by abatis built with poles about ten feet long, sharpened at the point, and firmly planted in the ground and spaced about six inches apart. From a distance they looked like great hair combs pointing toward us. Unless they could be taken by surprise these fortifications appeared impregnable against assault. A handful of veteran troops could hold them against an Army. The 20th Corps occupied the front both east and west of the redoubt, as far as one could see. Our works were much inferior to the enemy's, but we had no fear of attack as our force was much stronger.

During my wanderings I saw General Sherman making for some place in our rear. He was on the road going toward the Chattahoochee Crossing accompanied by only three staff officers and a courier. He was very plainly dressed and one not knowing him would never take him to have a rank higher than a Captain or Major, surely not the Commanding General of an Army. He was without sash and sword and wore a common loose blouse; the only thing that would indicate his rank were his ordinary shoulder straps. The General could not be called a handsome soldier; he was tall and thin with very plain features, his face covered with a full beard that

---

[33] Probably these were the four 32-pounder and a 10-inch smooth-bore siege guns manned by Captain Arnold Sutermeister's 11th Indiana Battery.

was rather light and sandy and cut close. I think he somewhat resembled President Lincoln, though not as large and not quite so plain looking. He seemed to care little for show and seldom had more than two or three of his staff with him when he made an inspection. Soldiering with him seemed to be a business, not a spectacular entertainment. General Thomas was also quite unassuming and had the respect and confidence of every man in his command. He was called "Uncle Pop" by his men and he had a fatherly interest in them.

Those of our Corps who served two years in the Army of the Potomac before they came west noticed the great difference between the two Armies, especially in the dress and conduct of the general officers, all the way from the Brigadiers to the General in Command. In the east our Generals, as a rule, made a real military show with brilliantly dressed staffs. They followed after the General who usually was in full dress with sash and sword and all the buttons allowed his rank. The staff officers were followed by an escort of Cavalry varying in number according to the officer they followed in the parade. In the Western Army I never saw such a gaudy show; there they seemed to avoid show of any kind.

On Thursday the 25th, I started to sleep soundly, but it was only a short time, when Orderly Sergeant John McLaughlin came to our tent and shouted to us to wake up. "What is the matter John," I asked. "Orders to move at once; strike tents and pack as quickly as possible; be ready to move in a half hour." I lighted my candle and looking at my watch saw it was fifteen minutes before two o'clock. At two-thirty our Regiment was standing in line ready for orders to move. The battery on our left was also ready. I was surprised that there were no troops to take our place and was told that the Cavalry had relieved our men on the picket line, so I judged they were to replace us.

As soon as we were in line we started; there was no beating of drums or bugle call and we were cautioned not to talk and no loud orders were given. After we had gone back a half mile we filed to the left and went in a westerly direction; this made us think we were on another flank movement and that sunrise would find us well toward the right of the Army. When we had gone a mile we reached the main road running north from Atlanta to Marietta; took that road instead of crossing it and continued toward the north to a point where a large force was being concentrated. Soon all were moving north, marching in haste, we knew not where, so wondered what it meant.

We were delayed by other troops and by wagon trains and artillery, all trying to use the road at the same time. However, we made fair headway and by six in the morning reached the vicinity of the Chattahoochee River railroad crossing. Here we were halted and soon the fields were filled with troops, baggage wagons, and cannon. Our Engineers were already at work surveying a line of fortifications and until they were finished we were at rest. This gave us time to get breakfast. By this time all the troops were there; they all wore the star badge; either red, white or blue; indicating that all came from the 20th Corps. As soon as the line was located we were assigned a place and at once began to build our fortifications with instructions to make them heavy and strong. We faced south in open fields about one-half mile from the river. Between our line and the river were the old Rebel works that faced north; had they been a little farther from the river we might have used them by facing them the other way.

As the weather was fine we got on well with our work; everyone dug in with a will as all felt that if we were to have trouble we wanted good protection.

From the 26th to the 30th, the Brigade worked steadily all day on our breastworks and built them so strongly that we did not fear any force that might be sent against us. The Corps now had a line about two miles long, flanked by the river on both ends. It was crescent shaped, with the center a half mile from the railroad bridge. Most of our artillery was in the front line protected by works. Our Brigade was on the front deployed from the right: the 141st New York, 46th

Pennsylvania, 123rd New York, and 5th Connecticut. Our Corps was expected to hold this position even though General Hood's whole Army should be thrown against us. This was the reason we built such strong works.

That day General Slocum came to the crossing; he was now to take command of the 20th Corps in place of General Hooker. General Slocum had been our Corps commander when we were a part of the 12th Corps of the Army of the Potomac. We were glad to be with him again.

On Wednesday the 31st, as we had no Cavalry, we sent out an infantry party every day to see if any enemy force had come in our vicinity. That day a detail was made from every regiment in our Division. In all there were more than five hundred men under the command of Colonel Cogswell[34] of the 2nd Massachusetts. I was in our Regimental detail. After passing our picket line at six in the morning we went in the direction of our old fortifications, going nearly to them. We captured one lone Johnnie who probably had deserted some days before and been hiding since our change in line. He knew nothing regarding the whereabouts of the enemy. We could have gone to our old works but Colonel Cogswell, a competent and careful commander, thought better not to do so; the enemy might have a Cavalry force in the vicinity and we were not strong enough to take chances.

Hurried orders were received on Friday, September 2nd, directing our Regiment to make preparations to make reconnaissance in the direction of the city. Only fifteen minutes were had for breakfast and we were only to take our guns, ammunition, and canteens. A guard was left behind to take charge of our knapsacks and any other belongings. Our breakfast consisted of hardtack and raw bacon; we had no time to make coffee. Within thirty minutes from the time we got the order, we were on the move with Colonel Rogers in

---

[34] William Cogswell (1838-1895) was a lawyer who rose from Captain to Colonel of the 2nd Massachusetts. He commanded 3rd Brigade, 3rd Division, XX Corps and was breveted a Brigadier General in December 1864.

command. Going in the direction of Atlanta, we traveled fast for four miles; then we waited for further instructions. We heard and saw nothing unusual; and as we had no orders to proceed, at noon we started to return to camp. The Regiment had only gone a mile toward camp when a courier met Colonel Rogers with orders from General Williams informing the Colonel that Atlanta had been evacuated by the Confederates, that a small force under Colonel Coburn[35] had taken possession of the city, and we were to proceed there at once.

With our faces toward the town, we covered the distance in record time. On the way all was quiet and peaceful. When we passed through the enemy's works we saw how formidable they were. They had no less than three lines, two of them protected by the strongest kind of abatis. I do not think it would have been possible to have taken them by assault. When we reached Atlanta, we were of course in the best of spirits and marched through with great cheering. Very few white people were in sight, but lots of Negroes watched us as we marched along. To the best of our ability we sang, "We will hang Jeff Davis on a sour apple tree." Colonel Coburn was there with part of his Regiment and some Cavalry. As he was first on the ground Colonel Rogers reported to him. Shortly after this General Slocum came and took command.

We remained near the center of the town until about four o'clock in the afternoon and supposed we would be ordered back to camp as we had no supplies. But soon after four we were marched out to make a camp at the old enemy line southeast of the city. We were told to remain there for the night; that our tents and everything we had left behind had been ordered sent us by wagon and we should get our things by midnight. We stacked our guns and hung our cartridge belts and canteens on the stacks. We were quite elated to think we were among the first to enter Atlanta. Then began

---

[35] John Coburn (1825-1908) was a lawyer and judge before becoming Colonel of the 33rd Indiana in 1861. He was breveted a Brigadier General in March 1865.

to wonder what we would do for rations and camp equipment before our wagons arrived. Our experience gave us little faith in the statement that we would have our wagons by midnight; if they came before noon the next day they would make fast time. We had started early in the morning with only a scant breakfast, had marched twelve miles, and did not even have hardtack to eat during the day. By six o'clock we were famished and there was no prospect of our getting any army rations. The officers decided to have ten men from each Company go out around town to see if they could purchase some food. However, before this was done some food arrived from camp. A few of the boys, myself included, had permission to go and we purchased a rather poor meal. Fortunately, it was a warm night and we had little need of our tents and blankets. At that, to lie down on the ground in September, even in the South, with nothing between one and the ground is uncomfortable; the dampness always seems to give one rheumatic pains. There was plenty of wood so we made fires and stood around a good part of the time. This was the way we spent our first night in Atlanta.

On Saturday the 3rd, we were feeling tired and hungry and hoping that our wagons would come early. I succeeded in getting a meal from a lusty colored woman who lived in a small cabin; gave her fifty cents and had a fine meal of fresh pork, sweet potatoes and "Pones."[36] Then I took a stroll around the main part of the town. It showed the effects of our bombardment; many business buildings and residences had been damaged. Quite a number had bombproofs in their yards for use when the shelling was brisk. During the last two weeks of our investment our long-range guns destroyed much property. This was a good-sized city, but ancient in appearance, and the business houses and residences were as a rule low and small. The signs one sees of thrift in towns of its size in the North were lacking although there were some very fine residences. The railroad depot and

[36] Cornpone.

shops and all buildings housing Confederate supplies as well as places where they manufactured ordnance stores were burned by the enemy when they evacuated the city. The ruins still smoked.

I went back to our camp before noon and found that our wagons had not yet come; but all the troops of the 20th Corps were being located on the right and left of our camp. We had a shower in the afternoon and as we had no cover had to stand and take it. When our wagons reached camp at six in the evening we found that everything was pitched into the wagons without order. We had a fine job to sort out our belongings but when that was done, we had supper of pork, hardtack and coffee; then pitched our tents, spread our blankets, and went to sleep.

Sunday the 4th was spent in locating and building our camp. It was near the place where we first halted but was moved back about three hundred feet from the Confederate fortifications that were dirty and full of vermin. These conditions we found in all the enemy camps we passed through during the campaign. When we could avoid it we never camped on ground that had been used by them. They could make the same criticism about the ground we camped on, for we lived in conditions equally dirty. Our Division was strung along back of these works, the regiments in close order. We were on the east side of the town outside of the suburbs and a mile from the business center. During the day a small part of the Army that had driven the enemy out of Atlanta passed in our rear and were given a noisy reception. With them were several hundred prisoners taken at the battle of Ezra Church; their condition was pitiable, they were ragged and looked starved. From Atlanta they would be sent north; perhaps many would be thankful that the war was over for them.

Within a week after the occupation of Atlanta by our Corps, nearly all the rest of the Army had abandoned the pursuit of the enemy and were camped in the vicinity of Atlanta, expecting to take a well-earned rest. General Hood's Army was some thirty miles southwest of the city. The only troops left to watch him were our Cavalry. General Hood was not one to remain inactive for long, so by September 25th he was on the move. He knew that the railroad in our rear was not guarded against such a large force as he could throw against it; so he moved around to the west side of Atlanta, crossed the Chattahoochee, and moved rapidly north, passed through Dallas and reached the railroad near Allatoona.[37] A part of his force was left there to attempt to capture the fort in which was stored a large supply of material that he needed. With the rest of his Army he continued on as far as Resaca, capturing several small posts and destroying the railroad as he advanced; thus he stopped the delivery of supplies to our Army in Atlanta.

The Confederates had hardly crossed the river before General Sherman with all the Army but the 20th Corps was in pursuit. We were to remain in Atlanta to hold the city and protect the railroad bridge. In addition to this garrison duty, we were to build fortifications so they would be available if needed, and construct winter quarters for use if we remained long in Atlanta.

We had one very difficult and unpleasant job in evacuating those civilians who had remained in the city. They were mostly old men and women who were almost helpless to care for themselves. With the railroad destroyed we had no food for them; there was a question as to how we were to continue to get food for ourselves. If they went north we could give them transportation; if they went south all that we could do was give them some food to take with them. Most of them went south. It was heartrending to witness their distress as these old people left their homes with so little to go with, as they said, among strangers. We did feel that they were going to their own people who would treat them with kindness as

[37] This was the start of the Franklin-Nashville Campaign which would culminate in the devastating defeat of Hood's Army at Nashville, Tenn., December 15-16, 1864, by Thomas's Army of the Cumberland.

martyrs to the cause. Our Company was detailed to go as guard to one large company as far as the Confederate lines, some six miles from the city. We did all we could to make them comfortable and show them how sorry we were that they had to leave their homes because there was no food, since we now had no railroad to supply food even for ourselves. The Negro servants were very loyal to them and we were happy that they went with these old white people.

By November 1st our Army again had repaired the railroad that had been destroyed by General Hood. Trains were reaching the city, bringing in food, supplies and ammunition; on their return north they were filled with all kinds of material that would not be needed in an active campaign. The hospitals were closed and everything connected with them, including the sick and wounded were sent back to Chattanooga and Nashville. By November 10th, nearly all material that was loose except what might be needed for immediate use was shipped north. By November 12th, all rolling stock had left Atlanta and with it all that remained of materials we did not require for the coming campaign.

Medical inspectors had been through the Regiment and all men unfit for duty and those who could not make a long march were sent back to Nashville. The men of our Company were in fine condition, only two failed to pass muster.

Troops began to arrive from the north on November 12th which indicated that now our movements were probably from Atlanta to the south and east. The troops coming from the north informed us that the railroad from Kingston to Atlanta was completely destroyed by them as they moved to the city. On the 13th we were at work wrecking the railroad from Atlanta to the Chattahoochee River.

On the morning of November 15th, all was ready for the next campaign, in which the 14th, 15th, 17th, and 20th Corps made their March to the Sea. Our Regiment was to lead the Brigade that day; and as we were the 1st Brigade of the 1st Division of the 20th Corps, we led the long procession out of the City of Atlanta.

CHAPTER SIX

The March to the Sea

November 15th, 1864-January 15th, 1865

November the 14th, we lay quietly in camp; it was to be our last day in Atlanta. During the day we were notified to make ready for an early start in the morning as we were to begin a new campaign. We were to carry three days' rations, full boxes of ammunition and as little extra baggage as possible since the march might be long. Our officers were placed under almost as great restrictions as the men in the ranks; no mess utensils or tents were allowed them, they could have only the minimum of baggage, and were to have such rations as were issued to the enlisted men. These restrictions were necessary because every foot of space in our wagons had to be reserved for our food and ammunition. We would be more than a hundred miles from our present base, so there could be no renewal of these supplies until we could reach another base. That could not be nearer than one on either the ocean or Gulf, some three hundred and fifty miles from Atlanta.

The morning of November 15th was bright and clear and pleasant. At four that morning Reveille sounded. The city

and surrounding country was filled with troops, not only the
20th, but also those of the 14th, 15th, and 17th Army Corps,
that had just returned from the pursuit of General Hood
and now waiting the order to begin the March to the Sea.
When the bugles sounded the Reveille that morning it was
followed by the hundreds of drum corps of the regiments
beating the morning call. They summoned an army of 60,000
men to make ready for the march that was to begin the final
campaigns of Sherman's Armies, that were to last six months,
cover four states and finally end in the surrender of the army
of the fine and capable Confederate General Johnston.

By six our breakfast had been eaten, our knapsacks packed,
and our neat little cottages dismantled; at seven the order to
fall in was given. We led the long procession, first through
the works that we had constructed, and then those of the
Confederates that we would not see again or face in battle;
singing as we marched the familiar "John Brown's Body"
putting especial emphasis on the chorus "Glory Glory Halle-
lujah." Thus we began the March to the Sea, headed to the
east as a part of the left wing of the Army.[1]

Looking back, but not like Lot's wife with any desire to
return, we could see the smoke and flames of the burning
city rise to the sky. It was yet early morning, there was little
wind and the smoke hung like a great pall over the doomed
town we had just left. All the public property and store
houses, factories and machine shops where materials had
been manufactured or stored for the Confederate Army that
still remained had been set on fire. Their destruction meant
the whole city; for when the blaze started there was no one to
prevent its spread to all the business and residential districts.
Soon we were out of sight of burning Atlanta but the smoke
rose in black columns and was visible all day.

---

[1]   For the March to the Sea, Sherman organized his forces into two wings. The
Right Wing, Howard's Army of the Tennessee, consisted of the XV and XVII
Corps (the latter less its 3rd Division); and the Left Wing under Slocum, sometimes
called the Army of Georgia, contained the XIV and XX Corps.

We were after a short time on the battlefield of July 22nd
where our own forces were surprised by General Hood;
there General McPherson was killed and but for the fighting
qualities of our troops, who were mostly western men, in this
action we might have been defeated. Here we saw low breastworks that were made while the battle was raging, broken
trees, empty ammunition boxes, parts of soldiers' equipment,
canteens, and haversacks scattered in all directions. The battlefield was soon passed and we proceeded leisurely toward
the east. The day was fine, the road hard and dry, there was
no enemy in our front, the march was made with ease and
really enjoyed by all after our stay in camp.

Our Corps was taking the extreme left in the advance. On
our right, but many miles away, the 14th Corps, which with
the 20th Corps constituted the left wing of the Army, was
deployed and marching on another road. Further to the
right, the 15th and 17th Corps, which were the right wing of
the Army, were marching on roads yet farther south of us.
All these roads ran nearly parallel with each other, and when
the Corps had come to their proper positions, the Army after
a day's march covered a front of some thirty to forty miles.
The length of each column, when made by a Corps deployed
in usual order with trains and artillery, would cover from
five to eight miles along the road. Our baggage train was
reduced to the lowest possible minimum; and we carried but
twelve days' rations of bread. No forage was taken for the
animals except a small quantity of oats; the country over
which we moved must supply all the hay and coarse feed.
There could be no cut in the amount of ammunition we carried. Ammunition could not be gathered as we went along,
nor could its loss be replaced, so enough was taken with us to
care for any situation we might have to face before we
reached another base.

Probably, never were wagons of an Army train more completely loaded with only the essentials required for a campaign or were the trains so complete in their equipment. The
wagons were the best, no horses were taken that had not

been examined and found in perfect condition. When we started the march, we had only picked men; everything that could be was provided to make the campaign a success. Nothing seemed left or forgotten that could assist and expedite the work to be done. In an ordinary campaign, where the base of supply is up close to the Army, it is easy each day to get what is needed; but in this movement everything had to be carried from the beginning to the end and must be guarded and conserved.

In order to move this Army with speed and safety a system of placing the various units in the marching column was planned and rules were made of the daily shifting of these units so that all would share equally in the duties required. As a rule, although exception would be made at times when the roads were bad, each Corps marched on a separate road. The column was formed in this order; two divisions with the artillery, headed by a small body of cavalry, had the advance, then came the baggage train, the long line of ambulances, and the wagons that carried the pontoons, that would be needed for bridging the rivers where we expected all bridges would be destroyed. At least a brigade of the remaining third division was sandwiched between the various sections of the trains, artillery, etc., to give protection from any side attack the enemy might make with their cavalry. Following the train came the remainder of the infantry of the last division; they covered the rear of the Corps, ready to repel any attack from the enemy. Then followed a few horsemen. We really had a cordon of cavalry surrounding the whole Army, on the front and rear and on both flanks. This cavalry was the eye of the Army; during nearly all our march, they did the skirmishing and picket duty. They relieved us of that duty after we had a full day of marching.

When on the march with no enemy to delay us and no obstructions to remove, we would take a lively step and about once an hour have a rest for ten or fifteen minutes. When these halts were made every knapsack dropped from our shoulders and unless it was wet, we with our knapsacks for a pillow would stretch out on the ground. Many would fall to sleep, if only for five minutes, be greatly rested, and would then march as though they had slept for hours.

Normally, during the march from Atlanta to Savannah the locations in the marching column of the three divisions of the Corps changed each day; this system was also carried out by the three brigades of each division. Every third day a division would have the advance, on the next day the rear, followed by a day at the center. As there were three brigades in each division they also used the same daily shift.

On our first day's march we stopped at the little town of Decatur which showed the dire effects of war for both Armies had occupied it during the campaign. Here we had our dinner and rested, our meal was entirely from government rations for we had not yet organized to get food from the country as we went along. We were the troops in the advance, so had a much longer time to rest than those that followed us. There is a tendency to string out on the march and when the head of the column halts, it waits for the rear to catch up. The 20th Corps had the reputation of keeping well closed up on the march and of having little straggling, with the waiting time not more than twenty minutes before we were in perfect formation. About three-thirty in the afternoon we were passing Stone Mountain. This excited the surprise and wonder of our boys whose homes were in the shadow of the Adirondacks; when home, they looked at mountains every day but they never saw a mountain like this. It is unique in that it looks like a big round stone as smooth as a paving block without, as far as we could see, any vegetation or trees on its surface. It stands alone and has no connection with any mountain range. I thought it was about eight hundred feet high;[2] it took quite a long time to pass by it. We had an easy day's march of eighteen miles this first day over excellent roads. It was six o'clock before our camp was formed.

[2] Bull is slightly in error. Stone Mountain thrusts upward only about 600 feet from the surrounding plateau.

We were in open country. The fields were all fenced and we had the rails to build fires. November nights in Georgia are not warm so we made our fires up close to our tents, with plenty of rails to keep the fires burning until morning. We sat around that night elated with the successful beginning of our march to an unknown somewhere and wondered when and where it would end. Before six that night the sun went down and as darkness came we looked toward the west where we saw the sky lighted by the flames of burning Atlanta. It was a grand but sorrowful sight; the homes of thousands of people, most of whom were innocent of any wrongdoing, were being destroyed. By eight we were ready for our beds; we had marched eighteen miles with a load of fifty pounds on our backs, so had to get some rest for the next day. Before bedtime we sat around our fires, smoked, played cards, sang, and talked; these were the normal ways we spent our time in camp. As this campaign developed the Negroes soon became our camp followers and they were a new source of almost constant fun when we were camped.

After the Negroes began to follow the Army these "contrabands" swarmed our camp at night; they could sing and dance and the boys kept them busy. They sang the plantation hymns and songs and it was as natural for them to dance as to breathe. They often had banjos which they thumbed for music; when they had no banjos our boys would beat time on their knees with their hands; then no young darkey could keep his feet quiet and would dance as long as any one beat time.

While on this campaign, the "Tattoo" would ring out early on the night air, then shortly afterwards "Taps": all lights out, all was quiet and the men and their faithful, loyal helpers, the animals, were at rest for the night. Our Cavalry, who were our guards on the picket line, had a sleepless night. The camp was quiet except when some braying mule gave forth his shout, or some courier with orders from headquarters rode close to the sleeping men. After midnight, the fires died down as the blaze from the burning rails grew less and less until only the bed of live coals remained which would be there when we needed them for our breakfast fire. But no matter how tired all were after our day's march, by three in the morning some men, throwing off their blankets, placed rails on the coals so that soon there would be blazing fires warming the camp. Sleeping on the ground, even though it was dry, chilled us to the bone; we woke with our teeth chattering as we stood around the early morning fires to warm ourselves. After the night was gone, our Brigade Bugler would sound the Reveille, followed by our Regimental drum corps beating morning call.

Immediately the Army awoke, men stiff from yesterday's march. Without waiting for roll call (we did not have it on the march) the men crowded around the fire for warmth before they began the work of preparing the morning meal and packing up. Then all was animation, the men laughed, played jokes and sang, even the animals, though it was still dark, seemed to understand that a new day had come, that new duties were before them and they whinnied and brayed for their food. Each group of men who had formed a mess began their labors; one took the canteens and went for water, another acted as cook and prepared breakfast, the remaining man pulled down the tent and packed up. As our tents only held three, that number was the limit of the mess, that was equipped with a hatchet, frying pan, and coffee pot; so each carried an extra article in addition to their plate, knife, and fork, and spoon. Our table furnishings were not extensive but were all we could carry and they answered our needs.

With this account of our first day's march, I have given a rather complete description of the routine duties required to meet the marching and campaigning conditions, that continued with little change all the way to Savannah. We started under ideal weather, good roads and only a small force of the enemy in our front who could oppose or harass us. This continued for the first twenty days. The worst foes the soldier had to contend with on such a campaign were rain and mud. As far as my diary records, we had only one day's rain until we were within seventy-five miles of Savannah. At one time it did get cold but it was not cold enough to cause any delay. It was hard to endure chilly weather when it was wet, but if the ground was dry let it be ever so cold we had little trouble keeping warm when marching; and at night we could build huge fires close to our tents, and get a good night's sleep for usually we had an ample supply of fuel.

The country over which we moved on our first day's march had during the siege of Atlanta been overrun by both Armies and was completely stripped of everything in the way of needed supplies. Beyond Stone Mountain we crossed the boundary of the devastated and entered and continued through the richest farming section of Georgia. This region was filled with food for man and beast that could be used by the Army if collected as we marched along. As the amount we could carry in our wagons was limited, the plans of General Sherman included obtaining, on a large scale, food and other supplies that we could use.

There could be no individual straggling for food, so foraging was organized and put in operation as soon as we were beyond Stone Mountain. An officer was appointed from each regiment to have charge of the men detailed as foragers and two or three men were taken from each company for that work. They were to start out early each morning and first report to the cavalry in our advance who would furnish them protection. Then they went to the plantations in the area covered by the day's march where they gathered such supplies as they found that were needed for food or would be useful to the command they represented. There were also details to do the work of destruction. Cotton gins and cotton in storage were burned and corn meal or fodder, not taken for use, was destroyed. Since most of the forage was in stacks often far from buildings, plantation improvements were usually not burned. Care was taken not to wreck residences and I do not remember to have seen more than half a dozen private houses burned during the campaign, and they caught fire from burning cotton or cotton gins.

As to the manner in which the work of our foragers was done, I have no personal knowledge; I was never on any detail for that work myself. While I saw the necessity of securing supplies from the country over which we had to pass, the gathering of them was not work I desired. There were those in the Company who were anxious for the detail and they would be more efficient and successful than those who had no heart in seizing the property of the plantation owners. The detail was given to those who volunteered and they did it successfully.

Various ways were taken by the inhabitants along our route to conceal their property. The usual manner was to pack the food in boxes which were buried in the fields; horses and mules were driven into the swamps. As the concealment was done almost entirely by Negroes and they knew where every box was buried and every horse and mule hid it did not take long to locate them. The Negroes were used, or I might say forced, to reveal the hiding places. There were instances where our foragers took property other than food and supplies but I do not think such action was common. I can say, I never saw during the march any evidence of such action on the part of any detail from our Regiment. The valuable thing for us and our foragers themselves was food and food was what they sought. We certainly had no desire or use for silver plate or bric-a-brac and could not have loaded ourselves with it if it had been piled in front of us. The boys would sometimes return to camp wearing some old absurdity of a coat or hat that would greatly amuse us. I once saw a "bummer"[3] dressed in an old military uniform that he said he found in a deserted mansion. It looked at least one hundred years old. He wore an old Andrew Jackson style[4] of military hat and had on a coat with immense epaulets and a big sword dragging on the ground behind him. He was an amusing sight, and for all the world looked like a comic

---

[3] Common name for foragers.
[4] Presumably Bull had in mind some form of cocked hat.

opera General. That any great amount of valuables belonging to noncombatants other than food and other supplies needed were taken during the march through Georgia I am sure did not apply to any force with which I was connected.

Our foraging detail first started on foot. The country over which they operated had so wide a frontage and the plantations were so scattered that when food was found the distance back to camp was so great they had to be provided with mules or horses. When they started out in the morning they looked like a company of mounted infantry. As the cavalry would take for their own use all the good horses, the foragers had to be satisfied with the discards; their appearance would defy description. However, they served the purpose of carrying the men and supplies they gathered. At times it was as late as midnight before they reached us, riding or leading the old animals that carried the food that we so anxiously awaited. Usually, they brought ham, bacon, meal, and sweet potatoes; often the carcass of a pig or razorback, which could only be captured by shooting for they could run like deer. They sometimes found sorghum, geese, and turkeys; but turkeys were the least wanted for we did not have time to cook them on the march. Fresh pork, ham and sweet potatoes could be easily cooked and surplus could be carried for use in an emergency. While in the rich farming country our "bummers" had no trouble coming in each night with more than enough rations; but when we reached the poor Piney country near Savannah there were bare pickings, and little but potatoes and cowpeas could be gathered. It was either a feast or a famine. The first fifteen days was our time of plenty, from that time on until Savannah was captured we were hungry for about all we had to eat came from our scant wagon supply.

On the morning of Wednesday the 16th, the second day of our march, we were up early and every preparation was made for an early start but it was a long time before our Regiment was on the way. We had yet to learn that the shift in position in the column determined the time of our morning movement. Our Division having the advance the first day was now in the rear, so we had to wait until the 2nd and 3rd Divisions and all the trains had passed us. This gave us an additional two hours' rest before we swung into line. It soon became evident that it was to be a slow march; everything dragged; it was go a short distance then halt; this continued until well after noon. During the first two days from Atlanta, we followed the railroad that runs to Augusta. This road had been previously destroyed as far as Stone Mountain; beyond there it had not been disturbed. We moved in a northeasterly direction a distance away from the railroad, while the 14th Corps followed it, destroying it as they advanced. This work delayed them so they could not cover much distance during the day. This was the cause of our slow progress for we could not be so far ahead at the end of the day that we were not in contact with them at the end of our march. We crossed the Yellow River, not a large stream. The bridge had not been destroyed which indicated that there were no enemy in our front. We camped near Rock Ridge Church, after an easy march of only ten miles. Here we received our first rations from foragers, some fresh meat and potatoes.

On the 17th we made a much longer march, still going away from the railroad. We surmised that we were going toward Augusta as we were all day on the main road leading toward that city. It was a very rich country in which there was plenty of food and forage. We covered fifteen miles and camped at Flat Creek.

On the 18th we were again in the lead; so to get an early start we were up before daybreak, were soon packed and had eaten our breakfast; and by six-thirty were on our way. Our Corps was now some twelve or fifteen miles from the railroad. Instead of continuing on the road that took us away from it, we turned south and headed for the town of Social Circle that was on the Augusta railroad. It was quite a pretty place but as far as we could discover it was misnamed for we found no evidence of the residents being either social or cordial with us. The white people kept very much by themselves and we saw little of them; but the darkeys were on hand as usual and made a great show of their ivories. The railroad depot and sheds, in which was stored a quantity of cotton, were burned, but no private property was destroyed.

The 20th Corps was directed to destroy the railroad from Social Circle to Madison, a distance of fifteen miles. As soon as the noon meal was over we began the work. The railroads in the South were poorly constructed; they were not only badly graded but the lightest possible material was used. The rail did not weigh more than thirty pounds to the yard, was soft iron, and the ends were pounded down flat from long-continued operation. They did not seem to have had any maintenance since the war began. The ties were spaced from three to four feet apart and the bridges were of southern pine, which when fired would burn like pitch. There were few sidings. It was a wonder that such a road could run and the cars be kept on the track. Had it been a road of modern construction it would have been an almost endless job to wreck it, but as it was built it was like child's play. All tools, axes, bars, clamps, etc., were supplied from the wagons. The way we did the work was to line our men along the track, then with bars made of wood or iron raise the track, with both rails and ties clinging together, push the rails over on the ties were they could then be separated by iron malls. The ties would be gathered and piled up crosswise to a height of four feet with the rails placed on top. When the ties were fired the rails would become red hot and could be twisted and destroyed. The rapidity with which this could be done was surprising. During the day two divisions of our Corps wrecked ten miles. The other division passed us and continued the work further on near Madison: before noon the next day they had destroyed the road through that town and continued on for some distance to the Little Oconee River where they burned the bridge. We kept on with the work until night and then camped at Burk's plantation. It was cold and Burk did not have many fences on his plantation when we left the next morning. It had been a hard day for we had gone fully twenty miles besides doing our work on the railroad. We were tired, hungry and dirty, however, we had been in a prosperous country and our "bummers" had found plenty of food.

On Saturday the 19th, we finished wrecking the road early in the morning and about ten o'clock took up our line of march toward Madison, which town we reached shortly after noon. It was quite a handsome place situated in the most productive part of Georgia. It was something of a resort for southern people who resided in that region. It was a county seat and there was evidently much business done there. The many fine residences were built in the same manner of all the better class of southern homes, extensive piazzas in front with tall fluted columns reaching almost to the top of the houses. The town boundaries were spread out with many of the residences surrounded by extensive grounds. There was much railroad property in which was stored cotton and supplies for the Confederate Army. After taking such things as we could use these buildings and the remaining supplies were burned. Like all towns we passed through, there was a great scarcity of white people; but there were as usual Negroes by the hundreds, who came on the streets to see us. They seemed happy to look at the "Yankees" whom they had been told were inhuman monsters. It was amusing to note their surprise, at first, as we marched along. They thought we were colored troops and it was no wonder they did for we were nearly as black as they were from the work of wrecking the railroad. The smoke from the burning ties covered our hands and faces with a black veneer that could only be removed by soap and water, and we had no soap. The houses were all closed and not a person was seen from window or porch but they sure heard the despised "Yankees" if they did not see them for we marched through the town with all our bands and drum corps playing and the troops shouting themselves hoarse. We felt that the people of these seemingly prosperous cities were more responsible for the war than those whose farms we had overrun since leaving Atlanta. We wanted to impress on them some idea of the power and magnitude of the Army they so hated and despised; so we made all the show we could when we went through Madison. After we left Madison we turned directly south and away from the Augusta railroad. This new direction showed us that Augusta was not our objective point. In going to Madison we went some twenty miles out of our way in order to destroy the railroad and permanently cut off all rail service from Augusta west. Since leaving Atlanta, more than fifty miles of that line had been destroyed. We camped that night about four miles beyond Madison.

On Sunday, the 20th, we made a good march; the day was pleasant but threatened rain. We were on the main road leading to Milledgeville by way of Eatonton.

The next day we had a severe rain, the first since we left Atlanta. The storm made the road slippery and soft and our trains were delayed so it was late at night when we were all in and the trains parked. During the day we passed through Eatonton, quite a good-sized town but without any railroad so there were no cotton or buildings to destroy. We gave no demonstration when we went through this village; the rain had dampened our enthusiasm. Our camp was within fourteen miles of Milledgeville; that night it cleared and became cold.

On the 22nd Reveille sounded early but we were not to march for some time as ours was the rear division, but everything was hurried that morning; the leading troops were soon out of the way and by eight o'clock we were marching. It was cold but fair weather; the roads were not bad and the nearer we came to the city the better they were. The country was covered with plantations and it was a red-letter day for our foragers. By noon the advance was in the vicinity of Milledgeville and then halted for the troops in the rear to close up. It was not known but there might be a defense made of the capital, as it had been evident there was a small force of the enemy on our front from Eatonton on toward Milledgeville. However, it was soon found that no resistance would be made and by two o'clock our advance occupied the city.

It was as quiet to all appearance as Madison had been; all the prominent people had fled. The Governor of Georgia, the Legislature that had been in session, the Judges, and all other state officials had left the capital. Not a hand had been raised to defend Milledgeville and the "Yankees" were in possession without firing a shot. We marched through the edge of the town, crossed a small river and camped on a hill south of the river and town. No part of our Division, so far as I knew, made a parade in the city but all proceeded to camp on the plantation of a prominent man who had disappeared, leaving his plantation and other property in the hands of his slaves. General Williams,[5] our Corps Commander, occupied the mansion as his headquarters. Our camp was just back of the Negro cabins in a large cultivated field where we found more than a thousand bushels of sweet potatoes were buried; every one was eaten before twenty-four hours had passed. That evening when we arrived, we were notified we were to remain here for a day's rest. Our right wing had met with some opposition and it would take a day for them to close up and get in line with us. The night of the 22nd was very cold, there was a bitter north wind and light snow; however, there were plenty of fence rails and much wood had been gathered so we kept warm with rousing fires. Our foragers had a great day: they brought in hens, geese, turkeys, and fresh pork; we had sweet potatoes from the field where we camped.

Thursday, November 24th, had been named Thanksgiving Day by the President so a party of us boys determined that we would celebrate the day on the 23rd while we were resting and had plenty of food for a feast. We thought we had much to be thankful for; the fact we were alive was ample cause, and had we not just covered one hundred miles of the enemy's country, with not a gun fired by our left wing,

---

[5] Williams relieved Slocum as commander of the XX Corps on November 11, 1864.

except to bring down razorback pigs; further, were we not in possession of the capital of Georgia. We had come from a community where Thanksgiving was regarded as a great day, not only for religious services but a day for family reunions, the day when great preparations were made for a Thanksgiving Dinner. Early in the morning ten of us bunched our food holdings for the dinner. We had several hens, a goose, some fresh pork, a bag of wheat flour and coffee. We went to the cabin of an old Negro aunty in the slave quarters; made her a Thanksgiving offer of two dollars and she went to work. There was no stove, just a big open fireplace where the cooking was done. Nothing could be roasted but she had kettles so our meat was fricasseed and all went into the pot together. It was cold outside, in fact there were little flurries of snow, and we fellows stuck close to the cabin that day enjoying the warmth of the big wood fire and by no means disliking the fragrance of the meal that was cooking. We did what we could to help the old aunty, who was big, fat, and black as tar; we picked the fowls, brought the water and kept the fire while she did the cooking. With the wheat flour she made biscuits, baked in an iron Dutch oven. All declared they had never eaten anything better than those biscuits and I don't think we ever had. The kettle she baked them in had an iron cover on which she placed live coals; they baked perfectly. By one o'clock the dinner was ready and while we had only a modest bill of fare we were satisfied. We had watched and waited so long we were nearly famished and to us the dinner was a feast. We had all we could eat. I do not believe there were many homes in the North who had their Thanksgiving Dinner on the 24th who were more thankful than we were in the Negro hut in Milledgeville. After our dinner that lasted two hours we lingered in the cabin as long as we dared; we would have slept in the cabin if we could have left camp for the night. At six in the evening we gathered our things together and after giving a good part of our uneaten food to Aunt Susan, as we called her, bid her goodby; but took with us food for the next day. We tried to sleep on the ground, but it was so cold and our cover so light it seemed as though we would perish before morning. The memory of that meal lingered long. We were soon to have a lean and hungry time and the boys would say there will be no Milledgeville dinner today.

On the morning of November 24th the Army was up early and the march was resumed. There would now be no delay that could be avoided, until we reached a place where a base could be established. About three days' journey from where we were, we would leave the fertile agricultural lands of Georgia and enter the Piney-Savannah region, where there was little farming and no large plantations, the country being largely populated by the "poor whites." There it would be impossible for our foragers to find and gather enough food, so the rations in our wagons would have to be used. We started with only eight days' supply so haste was imperative. It had taken eight days to come from Atlanta to Milledgeville, an average of sixteen miles per day. We were now some one hundred and seventy-five miles from Savannah. If we continued at the same rate it would take twelve days to reach that city. We could hardly expect to keep up that rate of progress as we were coming into a more difficult country; there were swamps, streams, and large rivers to cross, which would take time; besides we must expect to find some enemy in our front who, if they could not permanently halt us, would cause delay. Everything was being done to push forward rapidly. We were taking one of the main highways leading to Savannah.

Before the Army left Milledgeville all stores, factories, machine shops, and depots, as well as more than two thousand bales of cotton were burned, but no private property or state buildings were disturbed. Only such property was destroyed as could be of use to the Confederate government or Army. We went as far as June Creek, a distance of fifteen miles, and although our foragers were able to collect food sufficient for the day, the country was much poorer and their work was difficult.

On Friday the 25th, we again made an early start and were on the road by eight o'clock. After five miles a very familiar sound came to our ears, skirmishing at the front, the first we had heard in the campaign. Our Cavalry had run into a waiting enemy at Buffalo Creek. The bridge had been burned and an enemy cavalry and artillery force were there. There were so many of them that our advance waited for the infantry to come up. Our 1st and 2nd Brigades arrived first on the ground; we went to the right and they to the left, crossing the stream that was not so wide at different places. When we were over the creek, the enemy fell back, followed by our Cavalry for about two miles; then they turned and drove our men back in a hurry. Both of our Brigades were in line and we soon disposed of them, with the 2nd Brigade following after them for over two miles in a running fight. All told we had fifteen killed and wounded. A few prisoners were taken and from them we learned that Wheeler's Cavalry, several thousand strong, were in our front. They had come from Macon, had crossed the Oconee River and were now between us and Savannah, where the enemy was now as rapidly as possible concentrating their scattered Army. Up to this time they had been outwitted by General Sherman, who had made feints at both Augusta and Macon that had caused them to hold their forces in those two cities. They had discovered their mistake and General Wheeler had placed his Cavalry in our front to harrass and delay our advance as much as he could. After our skirmish, a bridge had to be built over Buffalo Creek for our trains and much delay was caused; however, during the afternoon they crossed and we moved on about four miles, making in all ten miles that day.

We had a lively time on Saturday the 26th. As usual we started early, taking the road to Sandersville. Soon Wheeler's men put up a fight at every convenient point where they could delay us; besides fighting they blocked the road by felling the large trees that lined it. Our Pioneers made short work of clearing the road of trees so they hardly halted our march. We skirmished up to the village of Sandersville driving the Johnnies ahead of us. This was quite a fine town of some eight hundred people. Like the other towns we passed through, the population that remained consisted mostly of old white people and children and Negroes, the Negroes our only friends. All were frightened for the firing was active as we drove through the streets. General Sherman was with our column and was close to the front when we went through Sandersville. At the outskirts our force was halted for the trains to come up in our rear. When they reached the village they were parked for the day, guarded by the 3rd Division, while the 1st and 2nd were to begin again to destroy the railroad. This would delay the march so the trains remained parked until we had finished our work. Our two Divisions wrecked about four miles of the road that day.

On the 27th our two Divisions made an early start; our objective point was Davisboro, twelve miles distant. We continued to destroy the railroad as we advanced, making a complete job of it for ten miles. When we camped that night near the town we were tired and dirty but fortunately our foragers were on hand with a good supply of food. They were in good form that day and had better success than we had expected, considering the country we were in.

From this time on there was much sameness in our daily progress so I will pass on rapidly, giving chiefly the brief record pencilled by me each day in my diary.

Monday the 28th, from near Davisboro we marched in an easterly direction about twelve miles and halted near the Ogeechee River, which we had to cross. We found the bridge destroyed and as the stream was quite large a bridge had to be built. We were surprised to find no enemy on the opposite side, we expected them to stand there since this was the last river of any size we had to cross before reaching Savannah. The Confederates seemed to have lost their old vigor; they could hardly be induced to make a stand at any place and when they did so it was in a very feeble way. As we advanced many Johnnies deserted and came into our lines. The rank and file of their Army seemed disheartened and those coming in said that they could not hold together much longer. We had to wait for the pontoon bridge, so we stacked our guns and rested in the nearby woods. Late in the afternoon the 14th Corps reached the river to make the crossing first.

Tuesday the 29th. The bridge was not finished until afternoon, then a part of the 14th went over. After four o'clock we followed them and started for a town called Louisville which we passed about sundown. We stopped four miles beyond for the night, not far from the railroad that we would begin destroying in the morning. The weather was fine and we had a short march and easy day. Our camp was in a pine forest and our fires made from pine knots lighted up the black forest.

Wednesday the 30th. The 1st and 2nd Divisions continued the destruction of the railroad which ran some distance from the right of our line of march. When we finished our work we returned to where our trains were located but did not get settled until late that night.

Thursday December 1st. At seven in the morning we were on the march, following the 2nd Division which had the advance that day. The roads were very bad and we made slow progress as the enemy had destroyed all the bridges and placed many obstructions in our way. We had a force of the 1st Michigan Engineers in our front who removed obstructions and built bridges rapidly. However, we had many delays and did not get into camp until eleven that night after marching about fifteen miles. As the Reveille had sounded at three that morning we had been in the harness more than twenty hours.

Friday the 2nd, notwithstanding the late hour the night before, Reveille sounded at three A.M.; it seemed as though we had hardly been asleep when we were called out. Our food now chiefly sweet potatoes, ham, and bacon (when our foragers could get them). Our breakfast that morning was not elaborate as our foragers came in with scant returns but we had some coffee and a half ration of hardtack from the wagons. Although we left camp by six in the morning we met with many delays and only made ten miles when we camped within six miles of Millen, where was located one of the prison pens[6] for captured Federal soldiers. The prisoners had been removed and taken to some place further north. This was a very warm day.

Saturday the 3rd. We destroyed several miles of railroad working toward Millen, which place we passed. In the afternoon I visited the prison stockade and saw something of the manner in which our men who were prisoners were treated as they were crowded into this pen. They must have nearly all lived underground for they seemingly had no tents or blankets and in order to have any cover from storms and any warmth for their bodies dug holes or caves in the earth, into which they were herded like beasts. The whole inclosure within the stockade was dug up and formed into these underground houses. Some were quite large where several men were together; others just large enough to crawl in and have protection from storm and cold. As I looked at these dens I did not wonder there were so many graves outside the stockade. I felt thankful that it was not my fate to be taken to one of these hells at the time I was wounded at Chancellorsville.

There were many who visited the pen and I heard them say they would never be taken prisoner; they would prefer to be shot than put in such a place. I wondered what could have been their condition during wet weather. They must have been driven out like rats from a sewer during a flood. Terrible stories were told of the cruelty suffered by these prisoners. We had hoped to release them but they were moved before we reached Millen. There was not a soul around the place when we arrived and the only things left were a few dirty, filthy-looking rags. Not a long distance from the prison I was amazed to see the largest spring I ever saw; from it gushed a stream that would be called a small river in the

[6] Camp Lawton, near Millen, had been established in the summer of 1864 to receive excess prisoners from Andersonville. It contained about 42 acres and housed as many as 10,200 Union soldiers, making it one of the largest military prisons in the world at the time.

North. The spring proper was forty feet wide and the water
came up with tremendous force from the bottom that was
twenty to thirty feet below the surface, rising up five or six
feet above the general level. The water was clear and cold,
and I believe would have been enough for a large city. The
stream from the spring ran near the stockade and I think
furnished water for the prison; if so, they had at least good
water. We early went into camp beyond Millen.

The remaining days of our march were uneventful until
we reached the vicinity of Savannah. The enemy seemed to
have abandoned all effort to halt us and such a stand as they
did make was feeble. We were marching on through the
immense piney region of Georgia; the roads were like tun-
nels through the great pine groves. These trees, standing
from eighty to one hundred feet high, were from two to
three feet in diameter at the butt and were all straight as an
arrow. The soil was sandy so we had little mud and marched
about fifteen miles a day. This was a very poor country from
which to gather supplies and our foragers came in with little
for our daily rations; but even under this condition not much
was taken from our wagons, and we were short of food.
There was little grumbling, for we knew that what we had
must hold out until we reached Savannah, or some other
place on the coast where food by sea was waiting us. In spite
of lack of food we continued to make good progress; Sunday,
December 4th, about fourteen miles; Monday, December
5th, about sixteen miles; and Tuesday, December 6th, about
fourteen miles.

Wednesday, the 7th. It rained all day and we had a disagreeable march. The trains were delayed and we stood for
hours waiting for them to move; it was late when we parked
and camped within a mile of Springfield. We were now
rapidly nearing Savannah and it was essential to keep the
Army well in hand and so place it that it would cover all
roads leading toward the city.

Thursday, the 8th. The 3rd Division was left with our train
at Springfield, while the 1st and 2nd went to the right in the

direction of the Ogeechee River. We advanced fifteen miles and camped for the night near the river. On the following morning we continued toward Savannah. We were in a region where we might at any time find trouble so we continued with caution. There was no trouble in the morning but early in the afternoon we came to a place called Mile Swamp and there ran into the enemy.[7] On the opposite side they had a redoubt manned with guns and something of a force of cavalry. As soon as our Division came up their battery opened on us, covering the road that crossed the swamp. The 1st and 2nd Brigades were at once deployed, skirmishers thrown out, and an advance ordered. The swamp proved to be passable and our 1st Brigade after crossing came down on the flank of the Johnnies and sent them running. They did not put up any kind of a fight and retreated in such a hurry as to leave one of their caissons which was taken along with a few prisoners. This was the last effort, as far as I know, made by the enemy to delay the left wing of our Army until we reached the fortifications at Savannah. We camped that night near the captured redoubt some ten miles from Savannah and six miles from their line of defense outside of the city.

Saturday December 10th. This was the last day of our March to the Sea. It was now twenty-six days since we left Atlanta. We actually marched twenty-five days as we had our day's rest at Milledgeville. Our longest march was twenty-one miles, our shortest six miles. Miles marched did not measure energy expended. In fact the day we only went six miles was the most fatiguing of all. We were with our train; it had rained all day in torrents, the roads were bad and the train delayed. We could only stand and wait, hour after hour, while the tired mules crept along with their heavily loaded wagons. It was after ten that night before we parked the train. Taken as a whole, however, we had not only been successful but it was an enjoyable march. Not a member of our Company had been on the sick list. Every man we started

---

[7]   Generally referred to as the skirmish at Ebenezer Creek.

with, except Nicholson,[8] a forager who was captured and made prisoner near Madison, finished the march. If only food could be had the march could continue, as far as we cared.

The prevailing feeling among the men was a desire to finish the job; they wanted to get back home. The mass of those in this Army were veterans, nearly all had served three years, many much longer, and all were tired of army life. They had faced the loss of home comforts and loss of business opportunity and endured privation and danger to maintain the integrity of their country. They were not in the service as soldiers of fortune, they were intelligent and could see that the Rebellion was nearing its end, so were willing and anxious to meet quickly any privation or danger that would bring a speedy end to the war.

Savannah was circled by swamps, lagoons, canals, and rivers; all bridges were destroyed. Beyond all these water hazards were the enemy fortifications, manned by such forces as had been gathered together. When we reached the vicinity of the swampy ground west of the city, we halted and the investment of Savannah was begun. The 14th Corps passed going to the right, their left connecting with us; beyond them the right wing, 15th and 17th Corps, arrived and deployed. When our position in the line was established we stacked arms and erected our tents. The land was low and damp so we gathered boughs from the pine trees and Spanish moss from the live oaks to make a foundation for our beds. There were many live oaks, beautiful to look at with their long veils of moss that trailed the ground, seeming for the world like the beards of the Old Testament prophets as seen in Bible pictures. The moss made a good foundation for our beds.

We were told we were to remain here for some time, how long we did not know, but Savannah of necessity must be taken in a few days unless connection at some other place was

[8]   Private (later Corporal) Charles Nicholson had enlisted from Ft. Ann. He had been wounded at Chancellorsville.

made with our fleet; we must have food soon. Our foragers were all in, there was no place to forage; all we had to eat was what could be taken from the wagons and that supply was nearly exhausted. We received a half ration of hardtack and some fresh meat. The animals that were taken during the march were now being slaughtered. The meat was thin and tough, we boiled it and boiled it but it was not possible to make much out of it. We longed for a piece of salt pork! However, we were well fixed for quarters and hoped to get a good rest.

We were no more than settled in our camp than we were directed to construct light breastworks. We were not near, so far as we could see, any large force of the enemy. However, it was thought advisable to build defenses as the enemy might, if there was danger of their being surrounded, make a break somewhere along our lines. Should they do that, they might mass all their force on some point so it would be well to have works for defense. We spent one day at this work; our breastworks were not elaborate but we felt that with them we could hold off any force that might be sent against us. After that we had little to do but await the results of the operations that we learned were to be made by the right wing.

On December 13th the 15th Corps assaulted and captured Fort McAllister and communications were open to the fleet with its ships loaded with supplies. This did not mean we would have the food at once for it had to be freighted by wagon in a roundabout way to reach us. It took at least a week to do the work of building roads and bridges and bring the supplies to where they could be distributed. Before we received any supplies from the fleet a new source of food was most luckily opened to us; it was like manna in the wilderness. Upon the banks of the Savannah and Ogeechee Rivers had been raised a fine crop of rice. It was ready for harvest and there were mills close by, so we put them at work threshing it. This rice was fresh and good and we could hardly get enough of it; we lived almost entirely on it for two weeks. It is hard to say what we would have done without it but we would have gone hungry. It is hard to understand why the enemy did not destroy this crop before we reached Savannah or why they did not harvest it. During the time we were waiting there was not much to do. In front of us was an impassable swamp, heavily timbered. Some distance to the right and left of us, where our batteries were located, there was a good deal of artillery action but there was no skirmishing in our front as the two forces could not get within a mile of each other.

By December 20th it was evident that we were to make an attack. At our left, near the Savannah River, was a place where the swamp narrowed and only a wide, dead stream was between our lines. Preparations were made to cross at that point and attack their redoubt and the works beyond. If the Confederates had remained, this assault would have been made within forty-eight hours by our 1st and 2nd Brigades. We were spared that action, which would have been bloody, for the enemy evacuated Savannah on December 20th.

On the 21st, General Geary's men who were located near the point that was to be assaulted discovered the absence of the Johnnies and crossed the stream on bales of cotton which had been gathered to use in the attack: advancing, they went into the city and took possession. General Hardee, fearing his last road of retreat would be cut off, had during the night withdrawn and crossed the Savannah River into South Carolina; and Savannah was left to the Terrible Sherman Yankees. Our troops moved to higher ground near the city where we remained until the Campaign of the Carolinas was begun about January 15th, 1865.

Before the New Year each Corps was marched through Broad Street, passing in review before General Sherman: first the 15th Corps, followed by the 14th, which was followed by the 17th; last but not least the 20th Corps whose marching was praised highly by all who saw the parade.

We remained in Savannah only long enough to have a short rest and to secure supplies necessary for the new campaign. Shoes were the chief article of wear we received; many of the men had to have them if they marched as their feet were nearly bare. The three weeks spent in Savannah were enjoyable, the weather was fine and the food good and plenty. No drilling was done. Our future campaign was in all probability march and march, and we needed no training for that.

GEORGIA

SOUTH CAROLINA

Saluda R.

Columbia

Lexington

Aiken

Atlanta

Social Circle

Madison

Little Oconee R.

Georgia RR

Augusta

Savannah R.

Davisboro

Milledgeville

Gordon

Sandersville

Central RR of Georgia

Millen

Macon

Ogeechee R.

Springfield

Hardeeville

Savannah

Greensboro

Carolina RR

RTH CAROLINA

Raleigh

Weldon

Roanoke R.

Tar R.

Goldsboro

Averasborough   Bentonville

ke

Neuse R.

Fayetteville

Little Pee Dee R.

Cheraw

Pee Dee R.

Wilmington

Ft. Fisher

gton and
ester RR

ATLANTIC OCEAN

Santee R.

N

Charleston

rt

Bull's approximate route of march

0   25   50

Miles

The Campaign of the Carolinas

CHAPTER SEVEN

The Campaign of the Carolinas

January 15th-March 24th, 1865

Talhe people of the North had hardly ceased their rejoicing over the real Christmas present[1] our Army had made them in the capture of Savannah, before General Sherman began preparations for the final chapter of the campaign, the March through the Carolinas. After we reached Savannah, and before we had been put on full rations, he secured and was having placed in wagons supplies for the next movement.

The men of our Army had a lean and hungry Christmas in Savannah. While the Armies nearer home in Virginia and Tennessee were having their turkey dinners, furnished and forwarded them by the people of the North, we at Savannah, were so far away we could not be reached. We had boiled

---

[1] On December 22, 1864, Sherman re-established communications with Washington by sending Lincoln a jaunty telegram: "I beg to present you as a Christmas gift, the city of Savannah, with one hundred and fifty guns and plenty of ammunition, also about twenty-five thousand bales of cotton." W. T. Sherman, *Memoirs of General William T. Sherman* (New York, 1875), II, 231.

rice, Georgia fresh beef that was left from those driven along
with us on our march through the state, and coffee.

Our camp was on the outskirts of the city, on a bluff about
fifty feet above the tide water. We were told that in all
probability we would only be there a short time and it would
not be necessary to build an elaborate camp. However, there
was plenty of material all around us, so in two or three days
we had a very comfortable place to stay in until we left
Savannah. We were not to use these quarters for long as
General Sherman was making the preparations for an immediate departure.

On January 10th the right wing was on the move, a large
part of it going by boat to some place[2] in South Carolina. The
remainder crossed the Savannah River and was advancing
up the coast to connect with the troops that had gone by
transports. We were to have started by January 10th but a
great storm struck us, and for three days the rain continued
and was heavy. All the vicinity of Savannah was afloat. The
river rose rapidly and overflowed its banks. The current was
so rapid that the pontoon bridge connecting the city with the
South Carolina side was in danger of breaking. Before we
could cross, the bridge had to be strengthened; it was not
safe until January 16th.

The 17th of January, 1865 was the date of the beginning
of the campaign, so far as the left wing of the Army, to which
we were connected, was concerned. During the morning of
January 17th we were busy packing and getting ready. By
noon everything was packed and we were awaiting the start.
At about one o'clock, marching orders came and we at once
started on our new campaign, our Regiment leading the 1st
Brigade, which had the advance in the Division. We marched
without show or parade, in fours, to the Savannah River,
breaking step as we crossed the pontoon bridge. The river
was high and the bridge swayed and seemed shaky, but we

---

[2] The troops of the XVII Corps came ashore at Beaufort on Port Royal Island,
S.C.

reached South Carolina safely. Then filing to the left, we marched in a northeasterly direction going about seven miles, and at six P.M. camped near the old camping ground of the 3rd Division of our Corps, that had recently moved from there. The day was pleasant, and we were not tired for we had only made a short march.

On Wednesday, January 18th, the weather was again pleasant, though not warm, and the road was quite good. We made a short march going only seven miles. The general direction of our march was up the Savannah River, though several miles north of it. The country through which we passed was badly wrecked, many of the houses were burned. We camped that night in pine woods near the highway where we found plenty of pine knots for our fires which were necessary, as it was quite cold. There was every indication of rain and we raised our tents. It was well we raised our tents as it began to rain at midnight and the storm continued all day. After a cheerless breakfast we started on the march at nine o'clock on the 19th; as usual on rainy days everything dragged. We made only eight miles and were on the road until eight that night. During the day we passed through Hardeeville, which at best could have been just a bad-looking place, now it can hardly be described as there was not much of it left standing. One of the boys said it looked warstruck and it certainly did. At Hardeeville we passed the 3rd Division which had camped there and went on to a town not far from the Savannah River called Purysburg where we went into camp back from the river lowlands. As it had rained all day we were pretty well drenched when we halted.

We reached Purysburg in a pouring rainstorm and learned we were to remain there for some time, awaiting the arrival of other units of the Army that had been delayed by bad weather. Also because the right wing had been held up for several days, by the enemy's strong defense. We were held back until the 24th and during that time, it rained almost constantly. The river rose rapidly and overflowed its banks with the low country back of the river submerged in many places. This of course halted everything as no movement could be safe except in boats. Finding on the 24th that if we remained longer where we were camped we might be drowned out as the water was constantly rising, we moved back about a mile to higher ground. It was said we might remain for a long time so we began building quite fine quarters; but did no more than get started, than marching orders were received.

We broke camp at seven in the morning Friday, January 27th, and were soon on the move, our Regiment leading the Brigade. The road was very wet but passably good as the soil was sandy. We made an easy march of twelve miles and at five o'clock camped where two roads crossed. The road we crossed led to Sisters Ferry, a landing on the Savannah River where supplies for the Army were arriving.

On Saturday, January 28th, instead of marching ahead that morning as we expected, we were held in camp until ten in the morning, then five Companies of our Regiment, our Company D among them, under command of Major Tanner,[3] were ordered to move down to Sisters Ferry to find what the condition of the road might be. We started at once and for a couple of miles found the road good but on reaching the lowland that borders the river for four miles, a great share of the road was inundated and impassable and the bridge over Cypress Creek had been carried away by the flood. When we reached the stream and found we could go no further, we returned to camp. Soon after we reached there the whole Brigade was ordered down as far as the swamp and an attempt was made to bridge the stream, but having no material to work with it was soon abandoned and we returned to the main road. We then moved in a westerly direction about three miles and at seven P.M. camped for the night. This had been a hard, wearisome day for all of us.

---

[3]   Adolphus H. Tanner (1833-1882) was a Whitehall, N.Y., lawyer who served as Captain of Company C before succeeding Rogers as Major, August 10, 1863, and Lieutenant Colonel, February 20, 1865.

We were up early on Sunday January 29th, the march going toward Robertville, eight miles from our starting point, and reached there about noon. We found just outside the town a small body of Rebel cavalry, who made a feeble stand but after a few shots they retreated in a hurry and barely delayed us a half hour. From Robertville we took a road leading to Sisters Ferry. After going a mile on the road the Brigade halted and our Regiment was sent forward on the road that leads to the causeway crossing the Great Black Swamp bordering Cypress Creek. The swamp was more than two miles wide and near the center ran a creek. The causeway was about fifteen feet wide, made of earth, and five feet higher than the swamp. We found it covered with water in many places and in some low places it was fully two feet or more deep. The only guide we had over the flooded road were the posts and railing on each side of the causeway. Upon reaching the creek we found the bridge all gone except one stringer. As it was impossible to cross on that, we were ordered back to the starting point one mile from Robertville. We reached our camping ground about dark looking much like a lot of drowned rats. We built rousing fires and dried our clothes as well as we could but our shoes were soaked inside as well as outside; it was with difficulty that we got them dry. The weather was cold and the water we waded in seemed cold as ice. We passed a very uncomfortable night.

Monday January 30th, we did not move, awaiting the completion of the bridge over Cypress Creek. As this was given to other troops to do we had an opportunity to stay in camp and get ourselves thoroughly dried out. We also had a chance to work at our shoes, which were so shrunk from water we could hardly get them on our feet.

At eight A.M. on Tuesday, January 31 we again started for Sisters Ferry, eight miles from our camp. When we reached the causeway we found there was no abatement of the flood so for two miles we had to wade; and found beyond the bridge it was deeper than the day before, one place three feet deep. As the weather was cold we suffered but the water and cold hastened our march. Notwithstanding, there was little grumbling, all trying to take it as good-naturedly as possible. We thought after reaching the Ferry we would have a chance to rest and dry our clothes but were immediately sent up the river on a reconnaissance in search of the enemy that were reported to be there. We marched several miles toward Lawtonville, saw no enemy and about dark were back at the Ferry, tired and dragged out. Then we learned that the Brigade was to remain a few days to guard the supplies being received and to help reload them in wagons which were to be refilled here. In addition we were to do other work, chiefly to corduroy the causeway. As good a camping place as could be found was given us but the rains had made the ground wet and when we dug our vaults[4] the water filled them within a foot of the surface. We then raised our tents and cut pine branches and laid them six inches deep in an attempt to keep out the dampness. This was better than lying on the ground; but the branches were quite large and not smooth, so it was not a downy bed.

We remained at the Ferry until February 4th, busily engaged in guard duty, helping unload supplies from barges, and reloading them in our wagons. We also built an additional dock at the landing so that more than one barge could be handled at a time. All the time we were there the weather was bad. It rained so much and was so cold that it was impossible for us to get any rest.

February 4th, during the afternoon we were relieved by a Brigade of the 14th Corps that came from Savannah along the south side of the river. When they arrived, we packed up at once and at three in the afternoon started for Robertville, returning by the road through the Black Swamp. We found the submerged part better than when we went to Sisters Ferry but at places the water was up to our knees. The remainder of the road was in terrible condition from being cut up by the wagons that carried supplies. At nine that night

[4] Latrines.

we finally reached a large plantation just ouside of Robertville where we camped on high ground. The plantation was a
fine one called the "Manor"[5] with the mansion still standing,
although the owner and his family had fled. Everything in
the house was in a deplorable condition; in fact completely
wrecked. The place was said to belong to a prominent secessionist; some troops stopped to give it bad treatment. The
grudge held against South Carolina and her people by many
soldiers was very intense; many times they ruthlessly destroyed property when they heard it belonged to an active
secessionist. They excused their actions by saying that they
wished such people to suffer for their responsibility in bringing upon our country the Civil War.

On Sunday, February 5th, we did not break camp until
nearly noon. Then we passed through Robertville, now consisting chiefly of standing chimneys and ash heaps. We then
took a road nearly northeast for about ten miles and halted
at a place called Johnson's Cross Roads where we camped in
the woods. Our Brigade was now marching with the 2nd
Division for our 1st Division with the exception of our Brigade had passed on ahead of us several days before. We were
to remain with the 2nd Division until we reached our own,
which was now several miles away on another road.

We made quite a long march on Monday, February 6th of
from twelve to fifteen miles, notwithstanding that it rained
all day. We went through another burned town, Loudenville;
only a part was now standing. It continued to rain all night
and we had anything but a comfortable time. Our camp was
near Beech Branch.

The next day, the wagon train was placed in our charge as
the Brigade did not start early; as we had to wait until the
2nd Division troops all passed us on the way to Duck Branch.
It rained and was stormy all day. The roads were next to

[5] Probably the plantation of the Robert family from whom the village took its
name. If so, the destruction was ironic for Captain Henry Martyn Robert, best
known as the author of *Robert's Rules of Order*, was a Union officer.

impassable with sticky mud; and it was with great difficulty the trains could be moved. We had to corduroy the road in many places and it took all day to reach Duck Creek, only five miles from where we started. This stream had the usual swamp margin and it was in flood and could not be crossed without bridging. A detail was made in the Brigade for two hundred and fifty men to build the bridge while the rest corduroyed the road over the swamp. The road was not completed until midnight along with the bridge. Then we raised our tents in the woods, wet to the skin, cold and hungry, to get such rest as we could until morning. It was one of the worst days of fatigue and discomfort we had experienced since leaving Savannah.

It was one P.M., Wednesday, February 8th, before all our train of about three hundred wagons was over the bridge we had constructed. Many of the wagons mired before we reached the corduroy road, and had to be pulled out of the mud by the men, as the mules and horses when they became nervous and discouraged would not pull a pound. After the wagons were all over the stream we followed them, wading in the water that covered the road. When we had left the swamp, we struck higher ground with quite a good road through better country. We made fast time that afternoon going fourteen miles to another swamp named Coosawhatchie, where we camped. Hardly had we broken ranks than a large detail was ordered to work on the road which had to be corduroyed across the swamp. I was thankful it was not my time for detail as I felt about done up as it was. They called on our Company for ten men and a sergeant. When the boys started for their night's work they were not cheerful.

Thursday, February 9th, we were called out early in the morning and not later than six o'clock crossed the swamp. There seemed to be a great similarity in swamps in this country, every stream had one lining its banks for from one-half to one mile wide on each side. During the wet season water covered the road leading to the bridge. The bridge was usually built two or three feet above the general level of the swamp and was not covered by water unless there was a very heavy freshet. The natives traveled by horseback or in wagons, so could cross without getting wet. At two or three places we found footbridges; they were about three feet above the ground, one plank wide with railing on one side. We used these footbridges on two occasions, but found they delayed our progress. It took a long time to cross single file and further, when once over, it required rapid marching to close up to proper distance. The Coosawhatchie was no exception to the general rule of swamps, further there was no footbridge so we had to wade across. When we reached dry ground our feet each seemed to weigh fifty pounds. Then we chugged along, our feet churning the water out of our shoes that were wet all day. We were told we would soon leave this low country and come to a region where there would be fewer swamps. We could not get there too soon.

It was early in the morning when we again joined the 2nd Division that was ahead of us. We then marched steadily all day, going seventeen miles. We camped a mile from Blackville which was situated on the railroad running from Charleston to Augusta. Much of this road had been destroyed by troops who were ahead of us. That day we went through a country that was higher and better than any we had covered since we left Savannah, but it looked desolate as many of the houses had been burned and much damage done.

At seven A.M. on Friday, February 10th our Brigade started on a reconnaissance in the direction of South Edisto River. At eight o'clock we passed through what might have been Blackville but there was not much left to show how much of a village it had been. We crossed the river about ten in the morning after marching seven miles. On the further side of the stream was a small body of Wheeler's Cavalry. After we threw out our skirmishers and a few shots were fired they retreated. The river at this point was not wide and with no great trouble a footbridge was built that we crossed marching by twos. It took a long time for the Brigade to cross that way. When we came to the open country we found earth-works had been built to prevent our crossing the swamp but they had been abandoned without being used. We camped that night near these works. At two places that day we had slight skirmishes, but without any loss to us.

Saturday, February 11th, as other troops were to follow on the road over which we had traveled the day before, we were held for their arrival, but we were not idle. A large part of the Brigade was sent back to the river to build a bridge to replace one that had been burned by the enemy and also to corduroy the entire road from the river to our camp. This was necessary for the use of the trains and artillery that were coming. There was timber in plenty along the road to furnish material for the work. During the day we joined our own 1st Division from which we had been so long separated. We were sure glad to be with them again. We felt lost when we were away from our own Red Star Division.[6] At six in the evening we returned to camp and found our foragers were in with an abundance of food. For the past week they had been success-ful so we were not suffering from hunger. When food was plentiful and of fair quality there was little grumbling, even though the men were tired, cold, and wet from almost con-stant rain and wading the swamps. That night we had fresh pork and it tasted fine.

On Sunday, February 12th, our Brigade acted as guard to the trains of both the 1st and 2nd Divisions. As we were in the rear we were late in starting and then went slowly toward the North Edisto River. The road was bad and many times we had to draw the wagons by hand from holes in which they sank to the wheel hubs. We made a march of ten to twelve miles, getting as far as the river. The train was not in and parked until midnight and it was one o'clock before we could spread our blankets to get what sleep we could.

---

[6] The divisions of the XX Corps wore the Corps's star badge in distinctive colors: 1st Division, red; 2nd Division, white; and 3rd Division, blue.

The next day, our Brigade still acted as guard to our train and as all the troops had to cross the river ahead of us and it took them all day, our wagons were not started until six in the evening and we crossed at nine-thirty. We went about five miles but as we had to stay with the wagons until all were parked, we did not make our beds until after midnight.

We pulled out at seven the following morning and marched slowly during the forenoon. The weather was cold and cloudy and by noon it began to rain. By one o'clock we had gone six miles, and greatly to our relief as it was raining hard, we halted and were ordered to make camp along the road which led to Lexington Court House. The rain continued all day and long after midnight it was beating on our tents, with big drops coming through on us as we tried to sleep.

Wednesday, February 15th, our Brigade was assigned to be rear guard to cover and protect our Corps train (troops, artillery, and the train). As they all had to pass us before we started, it was again one o'clock before we fell in and started. The rain had ceased but the road was wet and muddy and the wagons seemed to crawl. We would march a little way and then halt and wait. It was so wet we could not sit down and rest but had to stand with all our equipment on our shoulders. It seemed twice as heavy as when we were in motion. In the afternoon and evening we crossed two creeks, the Congaree[7] and Red Branch. These streams greatly delayed our progress; at the Congaree we were held up more than two hours waiting for the trains to cross. When it became dark we thought we might come to a halt but kept on the same old way, hour after hour, and did not get our knapsacks off our backs until one in the morning. We had gone only eleven miles and camped near Lexington Court House. I think we were as tired as if we had marched thirty miles over good roads. It was so near morning when we camped that many got no supper, saying they would have a "combination meal" in the morning.

[7] Actually the Scouter Branch of Congaree River.

When our foragers came in that night they brought little food. They either covered a poor country or one that had been already so thoroughly foraged there was nothing left for us. That day we had a "hunger" march as we were on half rations; fortunately it was not a long one. We were now approaching Columbia, the capital of the state, on a road of that name. After we marched on this road for a short time we left it and followed an unfinished railroad to the Congaree River where we camped only four miles from Columbia. This was an easy day, the road was good and we only went seven miles.

On Friday, February 17th, we camped so close to Columbia that we thought that we would march through the city so we were disappointed when at eight the next morning we went in a direction that took us three miles west of the town. After a short distance we reached Zion Church, located near a ferry over the Saluda River where we found a pontoon bridge had been laid. When we arrived some of our Cavalry were crossing and they were followed by the 14th Corps. It took them until night to cross; then our Division went over and after we marched two miles camped rather early. Our foragers came in with very little food. The country for the last three days had been a piney region with buildings and farms looking poverty-stricken; the people seemingly were poor whites who from what we saw of them in the South were poorer even than the slaves.

Saturday, February 18th, our Regiment was again detailed to be train guard and we did not get an early start. The wagons did not get clear use of the road until noon and we could not get underway until every wagon was on the road. Our progress was slow, the roads bad, and we had many hindrances, so we only made eight miles although we did not get to our camp until nine that night. Rations were a little better and more plentiful but not too much for our need.

On Sunday, we seemed to be making very slow progress but starting early we continued toward Broad River, five miles from our camp, and reached the ferry at noon. A pontoon bridge had been laid and the 14th Corps was crossing. As it would take them all day and into the night, we went into camp on the south side of the river. Our march was over poor country and poor roads. Our experience so far in this state led us to feel that South Carolina, as we when schoolboys learned in our geographies, was a well-watered state. We seemed to strike rivers, large streams, and great swamps nearly every day, separated by only a few miles.

We were called out early on Monday, February 20th, but did not get started until nearly nine o'clock. We crossed over our pontoon bridge and passed across a railroad that went up the north side of the river from Columbia. Then taking a road running north, we continued three miles to another stream called Little River. The enemy had burned all the bridges but the stream was not large or deep, so could be forded. Most of the men removed their shoes to keep them dry, and then waded. The water was only up to our knees but was cold and, one of the boys said, very wet. After crossing we stopped for a short time to squeeze the water out of our pants and put on our shoes. We continued on for five miles over good roads and through a better country than we had been in for a long time. The white people had nearly all deserted their homes and almost the only people we saw were Negroes. We passed many places where houses had been burned, perhaps accidentally. Everything in the way of supplies, cotton, grain, corn, etc. not taken for use by the Army was burned. This included cotton gins, outbuildings, sheds, and storehouses; many dwellings would accidentally catch fire, especially when the owners were not there to look after them. I hardly think our own men sympathized so greatly that they wasted any strength in any fire fighting for South Carolina secessionists. We camped early after a march of only eight miles.

Tuesday, February 21st, our Regiment was again with the Corps rear guard and so did not get started until ten o'clock; but this was early for that service. We took the road leading to Winnsboro, about ten miles away, and reached there at three in the afternoon. This was quite a large town, the business center of that part of the state. It was filled with all kinds of supplies. There were great quantities of cotton in storehouses and many bales around the railroad depot. Every building holding supplies and the depot were burned. I can hardly describe the appearance of Winnsboro when we left; it was deplorable. All the stores were completely gutted and many of the private houses were badly dealt with. The town had first been occupied by some of our western troops who did not seem to have any scruples or make any exceptions in their work of destruction. We made a halt in the town for a half hour but were not allowed to break ranks. We then camped two miles beyond the town. For the last two days our foragers had brought in great quantities of food, much more than we could use. Unfortunately we could not carry this extra food for use in lean times for our equipment loaded us to the limit of our strength.

Wednesday, February 22nd. The duty of guarding the trains was not much relished and, had we had any option in the matter, would never have chosen the job. It was not especially dangerous but disliked because of the hard hours of work that usually lasted into the night. Before the guard could move, the day was half spent and we had rather work days than nights. As the guard went to the front the next day it often happened they had no rest, as was the case with us this time. Our Regiment was rear guard for not only our own train but, in addition, for two hundred and fifty Cavalry wagons that were now with us. Although the column started on time, it was noon before we were underway and then the advance was slow as the road was badly cut up. It was three the next morning when we came to a halt, three miles behind our troops that had camped on the south bank of the Catawba River. We had made thirteen miles and it had taken us fifteen hours. It was four in the morning before we could spread our blankets for an hour or two of rest before starting the next day's march.

At night, a pontoon bridge was laid across the river not far from where we had camped. The river was not large but the rains had made it bank full. The country here was rocky and hilly, and the river different than others we had crossed as it ran through a narrow valley with high hills on each side. A road had to be made to and from the bridge that morning so it was late when the troops commenced to go over. At noon it started to rain and then trouble came. The trains had just started crossing and as soon as the wagons reached the clay hill on the north side of the stream they could get no farther; the mules would slip and slide and fall in the clay road. The column had to be halted two miles beyond the river to stay until the trains could be brought up. A very large detail was made to go and help the teams. From the river to the top of the hill the road was corduroyed and then the men went to work helping the mules pull the wagons up the hill. The effort was slow and exhausting, but at last it was done. The men were a mass of mud when they finished the job. General Sherman was there dismounted, giving orders and directions to help hasten the work. As we had been with the train the day before and most of the night, we escaped the detail. We moved on and went into camp two miles from the river. We made ourselves as comfortable as we could in the rain that continued all the afternoon and evening.

Friday, February 24th. By the work done the afternoon and the night before, the train was close up that morning and by six o'clock we pulled out for another day's march. It was still raining hard and the road was wet but after we left the hill at the river the soil was sandy and there was no mud to drag our feet through. After marching for two hours in the driving rain and going three miles, we came to a halt as we found the road filled with troops of the 17th Corps. As they were to go ahead of us and use the road all day, we put up our tents for that day and night. On as dry a place as we could find we cut pine boughs for a bed and were tired enough to get a night's rest.

No movement of our troops the next day, February 25th. General Sherman seemed to be concentrating the Army there, as his right wing, the 15th and 17th Corps, passed all day. The weather was damp and unpleasant but we enjoyed our day of rest. The bummers brought in large quantities of food and we had a feast day.

On Sunday, February 26th, our Brigade marched in the rear Division, guarding the train. Over such roads as we were now using this meant helping the train along rather than doing guard duty. Since we followed along the road that had been used by the 17th Corps many bad places had been repaired, so we were not delayed. Our march was a short one of only eight miles and at ten that night the train was up and parked near Hanging Rock Creek.

This was another bad place to cross with our trains and it took until five in the evening of Monday, February 27th. I was detailed with five men from our Company to assist at the crossing but did not have a hard time as the mules managed to drag the wagons. After the trains were over we joined our Company and went about two miles and camped. It was a stormy and unpleasant day.

Tuesday, February 28th, our Brigade was again rear guard but the entire Division had to work on the road; it might be said that all were train guards. We struck the worst roads we had had to use; fully five miles were corduroyed. After this was done the train made good progress. Without corduroy the ground was so wet and spongy that when a wagon cut through the upper crust it would have to be lifted bodily from the mud. During the day we made ten miles, crossing Lynch Creek on a bridge that had in some way escaped destruction. We had our train in by ten that night, which was remarkable time considering the work done on the road. Our foragers had good fortune that day and we had plenty of food.

Our Brigade had been with the train nearly all of the last ten days and we rejoiced the next morning to know we were to be in the advance. As our Brigade led the Corps our

Regiment marched all day, close to the escort of General Williams, who was in command. At an early hour we started, first crossing Lynch Creek. We then followed a highway leading northeast traveling at a fast pace as the road was good and we had no detentions of any kind. Although it rained all day we covered fifteen miles by two in the afternoon when we halted and camped. We had had so much rain and wetting from swamps and rivers the past month that an ordinary rain did not bother us much any more. We seemed to be getting used to it but it put our clothes in bad condition. They had been wet and dry so many times they had shrunk out of shape and were worn out; our shoes were nearly gone. If we did not get to some base soon we would have no pants or shoes.

On Thursday, March 2nd, we were surprised to find we would be again in the lead. The reason was that the 2nd and 3rd Divisions,[8] which the day before had guarded the trains, had not yet reported because of the condition of the roads. There seemed to be reason for haste so we did not wait for them but went forward at once. We were called very early and by five-thirty had packed and eaten our breakfast, and at six were in line and on our way. Ours was the third Regiment, following the 141st New York and 5th Connecticut, with the 46th Pennsylvania in our rear. We advanced rapidly over the road on which we had been marching toward Chesterfield; when within two miles of that town we halted, there was trouble ahead.

Soon we heard a few shots from the front a half mile away, where an enemy line of skirmishers was located. Colonel Selfridge,[9] Commander of the Brigade, at the front with his Staff, dropped back to where we were to direct operations.

---

[8] The 3rd Division was commanded by Brigadier General William T. Ward. Its brigades were led by Colonels Henry Case, Daniel Dustin, and William Cogswell.

[9] James L. Selfridge was Lieutenant Colonel and, after May 10, 1863 Colonel, of the 46th Pennsylvania. He was breveted a Brigadier General in March 1865.

The 141st and 5th were at once deployed as skirmishers and the 46th and our 123rd were spread out behind in company columns so we could quickly form a line of battle. Within fifteen minutes we were ready and an advance ordered. As soon as we started the Johnnies fell back. They did not seem to have a very large force, and we had them on the run, firing wildly as they retreated. We followed fast after them, driving them through a large open field surrounding a village. Then they opened on us with a battery near the town. By that time one of our 1st Division batteries that had been close up with us unlimbered and opened on them; then their battery limbered up and ran away. We followed them at double-quick and did not stop until we had chased them over a creek a mile beyond. They had fired the bridge after they crossed and then placed their battery so as to command it and then opened up. Our battery was in position by this time and soon drove them away. The 5th Connecticut in the advance rushed the bridge and put out the fire before much damage was done. This ended the skirmish, only a small affair. While not very dangerous, it was exhausting for when we reached the creek we had been on the run for over three miles. We had ten casualties all told. It was nearly evening and we halted in the valley near the creek where it was just a mudhole and a place impossible to make camp. We gathered rails and pine knots and made fires, expecting to stand around all night. At nine o'clock to our relief we moved back toward the village on high ground where we made camp. It was a hard day and we were tired boys.

Friday, March 3rd, we had ample time to get breakfast before our work began. This we did not always have as it took much longer to prepare the food when we got it from foragers than when we had army rations. Now in place of hardtack we usually had corn meal which must be boiled and made into pudding; that took time. It was eight o'clock before we were called into line. We marched to the creek and in the vicinity of the bridge our Regiment was halted and divided; one wing of which our Company was a part was to corduroy all the road over swampy ground, the rest were to strengthen the bridge that had been partly burned. The road building was a nasty job as for a half mile from the creek the ground on each side was just mud. We went at it and by three in the afternoon both the bridge and road crews were finished. Those who worked on the bridge were lucky, their work was clean and easy; ours was a mess and we were mud from head to foot. At four that afternoon we crossed the creek and marched two miles beyond, then turned back nearly to the bridge, much disgusted.

At the usual hour the following morning the troops were in motion but as our Division was to bring up the rear we were not called at an early hour. The 2nd and 3rd Divisions with all their trains as well as the Cavalry train had to pass before we could start. By noon all but the trains had passed and their slowness was due to the condition of the road. It was not until dark that we filed into the road behind the trains. This meant a night's march for us as orders required that all trains be brought up close to the troops in the lead each night. We followed on after them as they moved on slowly hour after hour. The night was starless and dark, and the road muddy when not covered with corduroy. It was worth ones life, almost, to walk on the uneven timbers of the corduroy when it was so dark they could not be seen. After trying it once we kept off the timbers and plowed through the mud. It was about four in the morning when we reached the encamped troops. We had come eight miles but it seemed twenty. There is nothing so tiresome as dragging along behind a train at night. The troops we had followed had made camp near the Great Peedee River. Each day we seemed to cover the distance from one river to another.

Sunday, March 5th was lucky for us as we could not march as the 14th Corps had the road with their train; it took them all day to cross the river. This gave us the morning for a good rest after our all-night tramp. We had hoped to remain quiet until the next morning and everything looked favorable until five in the afternoon, when there came a very distressing order. Five Companies of our Regiment, under Major Gray,[10] were called for road building; our Company was one of them. Shortly after five in the afternoon we started across the river, which was a rather large stream, on a pontoon bridge and began our work on the low ground along the river. This road had already been used by part of our trains and was so badly cut up it was almost impassable. A large force was at work and the road had been already repaired for two miles. We were given a place and then began to corduroy our section. We built fires of pine knots for light; at the same time we were so smoked up we looked like the darkies that followed us. We had one-half the food ration that day; the country seemed poor and foraging difficult.

The 2nd Division had the advance the next day, we followed them. As they did not start until eight o'clock it was nearly nine before we were on our way. We did not cross the pontoon bridge as we filed right and went in the direction of Cheraw, marching on what was called the Plank Road. This was somewhat smoother than our army-made corduroy roads but was still pretty rough as many of the planks were either broken or gone; but the day was bright and there was no mud, so we went at a fast pace. It was nine miles to Cheraw from where we started. We reached there at two in the afternoon and came to a halt in the outskirts. It was not a large place but was a business center in this part of the state. A good many supplies like cotton were burned and the smoke from the slow-burning cotton filled the air. We were to cross the river here on a pontoon bridge that had been laid by the right wing, but found that a Division of the 15th Corps was crossing and we would have to wait until the entire Corps with its trains had gone past. We stacked our guns and waited; it seemed to us there was no end to the Corps. It was six in the evening before the troops were over and it was nine when the trains were moving and they were still going at

---

[10]   Henry C. Gray of North Whitecreek, N.Y., served as Captain of Company G until succeeding Tanner as Major on February 20, 1865.

midnight. In the meantime we spread our blankets and were sleeping on the ground. About three in the morning the cry of "fall in, fall in" sounded and with a good deal of smothered "bad talk," blankets were rolled up, guns seized, and we were ready to start on our way. We crossed the bridge and then marched two miles and at four in the morning halted and were told we would start again at seven o'clock. We dropped to the ground for another hour's sleep which was all we could get if we had any breakfast before the next day's march.

Our march was finished so late that morning that we did not make camp. Most of the men just dropped down on their ponchos for an hour's rest before eating breakfast. Our foragers were having a hard duty, they could gather only a little food; and as we could get nothing from our wagons but sugar and coffee, we were about famished at times. We started as planned, our Division having the lead. It was a good day's march of not less than fifteen miles. We must be near the North Carolina line, as the town of Cheraw, which we had passed, was only twenty miles from the line. Our camp was at a place called Middletown Station, but I could not discover any railroad or village worthy of a name. The country we moved through that day was poor with plenty of sand and pine trees. However, our foragers had better luck and for supper, and a late supper it was at ten that night, we had ham and sweet potatoes. Nothing ever better.

At six A.M. on Wednesday, March 8th, we were on the road, our Brigade leading the Division. The road was through a great pine forest of mammoth trees; it seemed as though we were passing through a tunnel. The trees were so close to the road they only left a pathway. We had reached the tar and resin producing country. The large trees were all tapped for their gum which was then taken to factories and converted into tar and resin. We passed one of these black looking factories but it was in flames. It made a great fire and dense black smoke. After going five miles we ran into the 14th Corps who were ahead of us on the road. If we were to go on without delay, and haste seemed to be required, we

would have to take another road. There was one two miles
away but in order to reach it we had to make a connecting
road. This was started at once, cutting the underbrush and
trees to make a road ten feet wide but avoiding large trees as
much as possible. While it was crooked it could be used by
our Division and its train. It had been raining since before
noon, but after reaching our new road we marched on for
several miles. However, the rain kept getting worse and
worse every mile we went, until finally at six in the evening
we halted for the night after a day's march of twelve miles.
We were short of rations again that night. I can hardly
wonder at that; it was such a wretched country with few
houses. The people we saw were a starved-looking lot; it was
a crime to take their food from them.

On Thursday, March 9th, the rains again put everything
under water. The greater part of the day was spent by our
Division in building bridges and corduroy roads. Ahead of
us were two streams we had to cross, Mill Creek and an
unnamed creek, both swollen to the size of rivers. At daybreak we were called out to go to work. It had rained so hard
during the night that not many men stayed under their tents;
the ground was so soaked with water it was more comfortable
to stand by the fires. By six we were off and on reaching Mill
Creek, which ordinarily was a small stream, found it had
overflowed its banks and we had to wade through the water
for a long distance; much of the time with water up to our
knees. The road to the next creek, a distance of several miles,
had to be repaired; and our whole Division was put to work
with the Engineers sent to the unnamed creek to build a long
bridge. It was not a pleasant job in our wet clothes with water
up to our knees but we had the work done by three in the
afternoon, including the bridge that was one hundred feet
long. Then the Division crossed and we camped three miles
beyond. In the afternoon it again began to rain and continued into the evening. However, we were so thoroughly wet
from wading the streams that the rain did not add much to
our discomfort. Our foragers did not come in and all we had

to eat was the little left over from the day before. At night we made great fires and dried our clothes as well as we could. It was a miserable night.

The weather conditions were so bad on the 10th and the roads so in need of repairs that the rotations of Divisions did not follow in the usual way. Our 1st had the lead again. We started at six o'clock in the advance of all the trains and found the roads in horrible condition. Every small stream, and we crossed several, was in flood with water running over the road so we had to wade. Many places the road had to be corduroyed. All this delayed us but by three-thirty we came to Rock Creek, nine miles from where we started. Here we halted for it was necessary to place a pontoon bridge. This creek was like a large river and we did not feel unhappy that it was so wide and deep that we could not wade it. Our foragers came in with small returns, chiefly cowpeas with a few potatoes. Cowpeas would never be eaten by a human being unless he was in a starving condition. The only way they can be eaten is to boil them and make a thick soup; when cooled the mess looks like yellow mud and does not have much more taste. We boiled ours that night and, as we were nearly starved, ate them with satisfaction. After such days of privation we all had visions of our mother's pantry and the loaded supper table at home. We would be more than thankful for the broken pieces and crumbs that were gathered to be given to the chickens and pigs.

The pontoon train came up late in the evening, so the bridge and approaches were not ready to cross until nearly noon the next day. This gave us a chance to rest, and fitted us for the hard afternoon march that was coming. That morning we each were issued three hardtacks which with the cowpeas was supposed to sustain us for twenty-four hours. During the forenoon we had time to cook our soup and that with one cracker and coffee constituted our meal. At noon hurried orders were received for the 1st and 2nd Divisions to make a forced march to Fayetteville to connect with the 14th Corps who were ahead of us on another road. It was understood that the enemy were at Fayetteville in force and we might be needed in case of attack. At noon we crossed the bridge and as rapidly as we could started toward that town. Within five miles of our start, we struck two creeks, one of which we had to wade. It was Puppy Creek, and when the boys were crossing they barked like dogs. It seemed to relieve them to make a joke of their discomfort. After we had gone ten miles we reached a plank road running to Fayetteville. It was not much of an improvement over the dirt road we had been on for it was badly worn and the planks broken and loose. All the afternoon we rushed forward as fast as we could go and at nine-thirty that night camped after marching twenty miles since noon. We were then only two miles from the town. While eating our soup that night, Jed Backus,[11] one of our mess, said to me, "If I had the contents of my mother's swill pail tonight, you can bet that I would rob the pigs of their supper." We had that day about reached the limit, a little more and we would be starving.

Our forced march seemed to have been useless as the 14th Corps occupied the town that night after only a slight skirmish. There was said to be quite a large force of the enemy there but they retired without making a fight. The next day we stayed in camp, as we were to wait the rest of the Corps with the trains. That morning we had little to eat but at night our foragers came in with a lot and we had a meal of ham, bacon, corn meal, etc. I saw some of our men eating corn they said they stole from the mules. They browned it in their spiders. It did not pop, and was hard, but tasted good to hungry men. The weather was clear and warm and we had nothing to do, so had a good rest.

Monday morning, March 13th, we were told that we were to march through Fayetteville during the day and were to be reviewed by General Sherman. Orders were given to clean up as well as we could but about all we could do was to scrape

[11]   Private Jarius D. Backus enlisted from Putnam, N.Y.

the mud off our uniforms. When that was done it did not much improve our looks, it only showed more clearly our ragged condition. Many had little below the knees in the way of pants; some were so far gone they hung down in strings to their feet. Our shoes were so worn it was a problem how to make them last until the end of the campaign. We made ourselves as presentable as we could, and the review started at noon. We marched through the principal street of the city, that had all the earmarks of a southern town, with its rather attractive homes for the gentry, its whitewashed cabins for the Negroes, and with its marketplace in the center of the widest street. General Sherman reviewed us beyond the marketplace. We did not make a handsome show but I think "Uncle Billy" was well pleased with us. After the review we passed over one of the pontoon bridges that spanned the Cape Fear River and went into camp four miles from the city near a plank road that ran to the north.

Had a fine rest in camp Tuesday, no guard duty, no picketing, no work of any kind. We were waiting for our trains and the rest of the Army to cross to the north side of the river. The day was fine, our rations were plenty, and we enjoyed every minute of our rest.

On Wednesday March 15th, by six o'clock we had our breakfast, packed our knapsacks, and were ready to fall into line; but it was eight-thirty before the order to move was given. We then entered a road, which was called the Raleigh Plank Road, which ran to that city in a northerly direction. As soon as we started it began to rain. Our greatest enemy in this campaign was rain, not alone in the discomfort it brought us but from its flooding the roads and streams, causing labor and delay. We advanced rather slowly and it was evident the enemy might be in our front not far ahead. This delayed our Cavalry advance. We heard slight but distant cannonading at our left. At two in the afternoon we halted and camped along the plank road; it was raining and it continued all night.

When I woke on Thursday, March 16th, the rain was beating hard on our tent and the ground was wet under our blankets. This forced us out early but it was eight o'clock before we were on the march. Our Brigade was in the rear guard; and the 3rd Division and the other Brigades of our own had to move ahead of us. The rain had made the road soft and our progress was slow as the teams could hardly move the wagons. We dragged along in a tiresome way until noon and had gone about four miles. Then we heard artillery firing ahead of us and soon after an orderly from our Corps Headquarters arrived in haste. The Brigade was to leave the train at once and go to the front, where our men were in line, as a large force of the enemy had been encountered. The Regiments were in different places along the train, but they were assembled and went forward at a swift gait. It was three miles to the front where active musketry firing was heard.[12]

Our Cavalry had run into the enemy early in the day and had attacked them in their usual impetuous manner, thinking to drive them without much trouble. They soon found they had a force to contend with that could not be forced back by Cavalry alone. The 3rd Division and the other two Brigades of the 1st Division, when they reached the Cavalry, formed in line of battle and then attacked the Johnnies and the fighting was becoming quite heavy.

When we reached the front we formed two lines of battle; the 5th Connecticut and 123rd New York were in the first line. We advanced through the pine woods at the right of the road. Our formation had hardly been completed, when from our right and front a body of Kilpatrick's[13] Cavalry that had been located on our right flank to guard against attack from that quarter, came down on us in retreat, the yelling Rebels close behind them. We got there just in time to prevent a flanking force getting in the rear of our line. As soon as the Cavalry had moved from our front we opened fire and had little trouble stopping their advance. The enemy seemed to

---

[12]   Battle of Averasborough, N.C., sometimes called the Battle of Taylor's Hole.
[13]   3rd Cavalry division commanded by Brigadier General Judson Kilpatrick.

have lost their vim. After halting this flanking movement we found our line was quite a distance in front of the 3rd Division at our left and fell back to connect with them. Then the whole line advanced and the enemy was driven back into entrenchments they had constructed before they advanced to engage our troops. It was nearly dark and our line was halted and we began to build breastworks; by midnight we had a strong line. The contest of that afternoon was a small affair as far as we were concerned; we had only four men wounded but farther to our left the fighting was severe, our Corps lost in killed and wounded fully five hundred men.[14] The Johnnies were now in strong entrenchments and, unless they could be flanked out, might give us trouble.

That night the skirmishing all along the line was heavy. Our troops were coming up in large numbers, many of the 14th Corps were now in our rear. The fighting had no effect on the weather as it continued to rain all the afternoon and continued that night. The enemy seemed to have a large force in our front and from then on we might expect hard fighting.

Friday, March 17th, early in the morning our skirmishers found the enemy had silently departed and none of us felt sorry. If we must fight them we preferred not to do it in a swamp with mud and water halfway up to our knees. We stood around in our now useless trenches until noon and were then moved to a drier place until we could continue the march which was delayed by the 14th Corps that had the road. At four in the afternoon we started toward the Black River but we made slow work of it. The road was cut up by wagons and artillery and in places was impassable. On the surface of the road the mud looked smooth and like varnish; but when the mules and wagons moved along, they found holes two feet deep. The wagons would sink to the wheel hubs and the mules would be helpless. The whole Brigade

---

[14] The actual Union casualties were 95 killed, 533 wounded, and 54 missing while those of the Confederates totalled 865 men.

was set at the job of getting the wagons through the slough. In many cases the mules had to be taken from the wagons, logs had to be brought and placed across the road, the wheels pried up with long levers, ropes hitched to the wagons, and then a hundred men pulling and pushing, yelling and swearing would after a while get the wagon out of the mire and on higher ground. After that the place would be corduroyed so as not to let another wagon into the hole. We kept at this work until ten-thirty that night, and made in six and one-half hours time a march of one and one-half miles. Then we stopped for the night. The name of the place where we had the battle was Averasborough.

While working on one of the worst jobs of wagon moving that we had that day, Dan O'Connor, one of the Irish members of our Company, had the misfortune of slipping down in the mud. He was a sight to behold and had to stand a lot of chaffing from the boys. After digging himself out and scraping off as much mud as he could, he came to where I was standing, and said, "R.C. do you know what day this is?" "Why yes, Dan," I said, "it is Friday." He said, "Yes, I know it is Friday, but more than that, it is St. Patrick's Day, and I wish I was in Old Ireland this minute!" There were others of us who wished we were in some better place than Averasborough pulling wagons out of the mud.

On Saturday, March 18th, we ate very sparingly for the reason there was little to eat. The foragers on account of the rain were as much hampered in their work as we were in getting the trains over the road. The slower we advanced the less new country they had in which to search for food. We were out early in the morning as usual and soon found it was to be another day of work with the wagons and road. First our Regiment was to go back two miles and rescue ten wagons that had mired and been abandoned by the rest of the train that had in some way, miraculously I think, escaped the same fate. It took until noon to get the wagons out of the mud and started on the corduroy road, that had been built up to near where they had stalled. They needed no further help from us, so we returned to camp. Then we went forward toward Black River where another job was waiting that was just as disagreeable as moving the wagons.

The storm had caused a great flood that covered with water all the lowlands adjacent to the river. There was no way of reaching the bridges except by wading. These conditions became so normal that we would go through an inundated piece of road without a halt and any extra profanity; the men came to take these things philosophically. But this crossing was the worst we had met for depth of water; it was up to my cartridge box and many of the shorter men had to remove their belts to keep their cartridges dry. We halted for a half hour when we crossed to drain out our clothing. It was eleven that night before we reached the Brigade camp. It was in a "tapped" pine forest, lighted by setting fire to the gum on the trees that would burn and smoke for hours. All of us were pretty well done up after the eight-mile march in our water-soaked clothes but were able to stand around the fires to dry out. We were a sight to behold as the black pitchy smoke had added one more coat of coal-black to our faces and hands; we were like Negroes.

We slept with our shoes on; we did not dare take them off for fear they would shrink so much we could not get them on in the morning. They were good and tight when we awoke. Our foragers came in with a good supply of food and on Sunday we had our first real meal in a week. At seven in the morning we were in line but as we were to guard the train did not start until eight-thirty. It was a large train, our entire Corps baggage and ordnance and also the ambulance wagons. In them were the men wounded at Averasborough, four hundred of them, besides there were many sick men. My heart bled for the wounded who were being dragged over the rough road; for I knew from experience what they were suffering. The road was better that day and up to noon we made good headway.

Then we heard heavy cannonading to our right[15] far ahead of us and within an hour's time we were ordered to leave the train and march at once to the front. We made a lively march and in an hour reached the left of our troops who were actively engaged. When we had nearly reached the firing, we were filed to the right into the woods and formed in line of battle. Our 3rd Brigade had reached the front just ahead of us, was deployed and formed the first line while our Brigade was in the second line. Without delay we advanced. The enemy had attempted a flank movement on the left of the 14th Corps while we were forming and the left Regiments of that Corps had fallen back because they were overlapped by the Johnnies. We had advanced but a short distance when meeting this enemy flanking force brisk firing was begun by the 3rd Brigade which continued for some time. When they found that they had run into a new line the enemy abandoned the flanking movement and fell back a half mile. We advanced through the woods and coming to an open field on quite an elevation halted and were ordered to entrench, and before night had a good line of works. A number of our batteries were located on the hill near us and opened fire on the enemy's line but when night came they ceased fire.

The greater part of the battle was far to our right and continued until night; skirmishing was active all night. The 14th Corps was severely engaged all day; having the advance they were the first to contact the enemy. They met them about ten in the morning and thinking that they were only a small Cavalry force attempted to brush them aside. They found that they were up against an Army and before they could form a line, Johnston attacked them and then during the day forced them back at least two miles. After our Corps reached them there was no further retreat. That night the whole left wing was in line and well entrenched; so we had no fears of the morrow. We slept on the ground back of our

[15]   Battle of Bentonville, N.C.

works, with our guns at our side so that at a moment's warning we would be ready for action. I often wondered why so many of our battles were fought on Sunday.

Monday, March 20th, upon our part of the line comparative quiet prevailed. There had been, however, a good deal of skirmishing at our right and our artillery had been active. At noon our Regiment marched forward about a mile to near the picket line, and after remaining a few minutes was ordered back to our old position. I could not imagine what we went for. No attack had been made on our flank since we reached here. We did not look for a fight that day unless General Johnston forced one as our Corps were scattered and General Sherman surely would not risk making an attack until the right wing was up with us. Our Army was concentrating here as many troops came in and our wagons were now up with us. It was a beautiful spring day, I might say a summer day, and we enjoyed our rest. I was detailed for picket duty that afternoon, for me the first detail in a long time as until now the work had been done by the Cavalry who had been constantly in the advance. We went on duty at six.

That night our picket detail reported at the front to relieve a picket force that had been on duty for twenty-four hours. The line was about one-half mile in front of our works, and the men who had preceded us had dug pits and we were well protected in case of attack. The enemy's picket line did not seem very close, and there was no skirmishing during the night.

The next afternoon on our way to the picket line I saw fifteen unburied Confederate soldiers lying where they had fallen. It was not a pleasant sight to me, even though these men had been our enemies. I thought when I saw them, of the sorrow and grief there would be in fifteen homes somewhere; and for what had these young lives been sacrificed? I hoped if I survived the war never to witness or take part in another. There should be some way to settle political differences without slaughtering human beings and wearing out the bodies and sapping the strength of those who may be fortunate enough to escape the death penalty. After posting the pickets I was at the reserve post until morning.

We passed a quiet night, no skirmishing or any trouble on our front, and so far as I could judge it was quiet along the entire line. It was a fair warm night, and the service was easy for all the men had to do was keep awake and watch the front. About six in the morning Uncle Joe Young[16] of our Company who was on picket duty came to the reserve post bringing in two Johnnies, fully armed and equipped. While on post Joe had seen them in the woods beyond and as they did not seem unfriendly he shouted to them to come in and he would not shoot. They seemed to have had all the war they wanted and willingly came in and surrendered to old Joe. When he brought them in I said, "Uncle Joe how did you do it?" He said, "Why I surrounded them." Joe is the oldest man in our Company and about the only one of middle age who had been able to stand the hardships of army life and still be with us. I was glad that Uncle Joe, as the boys called him and treated him as though he was their uncle, got the Johnnies; it made him feel so good. The Johnnies brought us news. They said the enemy had retreated that night and their excuse for being caught was that they had been left behind; but we thought they seemed very happy to have been captured. An advance was made by our picket line; we went for some distance but finding no enemy returned. Before seven in the morning we returned to our Regiment which was prepared to march. We had to be satisfied with a breakfast of cowpea porridge. By nine o'clock we started, taking a road leading to Goldsboro. The road was good and we went about fifteen miles and camped near a creek misnamed Falling Water, for the waters were not falling now; the stream was bank full, and still rising. This creek emptied into the Neuse River not far below us which was the last we had to cross in this campaign. That afternoon to our

[16]   Private Joseph Young enlisted from Dresden, N.Y. He was 43 years old.

great satisfaction we drew army rations. The hardtack, so despised when we first began soldiering, seemed like a luxury.

On Thursday, March 23rd, our Division marched in the rear so we did not get started until ten o'clock. We were not much detained at any place, and before one in the afternoon crossed the Neuse River at Cox's Bridge. From there we continued several miles on a road running parallel and north of the river, much of the way through a great pine forest where the trees had been fired and were still burning. The forest was filled with stifling, black smoke and in places the heat from the greasy burning trees was so intense that it was almost impossible to march on the road. The smoke added another coat of tar to our already blackened faces, hands, and hair.

At Cox's Bridge we came in contact again with the outside world from which we had been separated for more than two months. There we found lined up to welcome us a Brigade of General Terry's 10th Corps, who recently came from Wilmington to meet us and to cooperate with us in the final roundup which we believed would come soon. The troops at the bridge were colored men and they made the mistake of thinking when they first saw us that we were also Negroes. This was not surprising as we were certainly as black as they were. We had had no soap for weeks and were completely covered with greasy black that could not be removed by water alone. While in the matter of our complexion we might resemble our colored comrades, in other ways we presented a strange contrast. Their uniforms were new and well fitted, bright and clean, their shoes were new, black, and shining; their guns were the Springfield latest model and almost sparkled with brightness. The men looked fat and sleek, showing the good care and food they had received. Their officers were splendidly dressed, with buttons shining and wearing new unfaded sashes. What a contrast did they present to Sherman's veterans, some of those passing them had followed that great leader for four years.

They were campaigns that had for toil, hardship, privation, and endurance few equals. These men of Sherman's
Army as they passed by that day looked thin and gaunt, their
hair had not been cut for three months; it was long and
ragged. The faces of these young soldiers, most of them
hardly more than boys, were covered with the unshaven
beards of youth. Uniforms, worn threadbare and in rags,
from head to foot were covered wtih mud. Their shoes were
in the last stage of existence, many being held together with
strings tied around them. Yet these men were hard as iron,
toughened by an active campaign of more than three years.
This is a feeble description of them as they marched with no
attempt to make a show. They knew the work they started
nearly four years ago would soon be finished and then, God
willing, it would be "Home Sweet Home" again. In making
this contrast between our veterans and the new troops we
saw I did not criticize or belittle them. I had no doubt that
they would become good soldiers and if they remained long
in the service would lose their fresh appearance. We camped
within seven miles of Goldsboro, our goal in the campaign.

Friday, March 24th, everyone was anxious to get to Goldsboro, the termination of our sixty-six day campaign from
Savannah through the Carolinas. The Reveille sounded long
before five o'clock and after a light breakfast which it did not
take long to prepare and still shorter time to eat, at six we
started on our march. The road was sandy and dry and
dusty, so the march was not pleasant but we made good
headway and about nine the big square Court House in the
middle of the town came in sight. We were to be reviewed by
General Sherman as we marched through the city. Our drum
corps was at the head of the Regiment, and we passed the
reviewing stand in as good form as we could. We had a
chance to show "Uncle Billy" our ragged clothes. Some of the
boys took off the shoes that had been lashed to their feet and
walked barefoot. Goldsboro was a small place and it did not
take long to reach the suburbs after we reached the reviewing stand. We continued on to a village called Scottsville lo-

cated on a railroad about two miles from the city. It was said
we were to remain here for a few days to get a short rest and
draw supplies of clothing that we would need before continuing north. When we were dismissed, our knapsacks came off
in a hurry and I gave a sigh of relief from the burden. I am
sure that every man in our Company felt much as I did; to
know that for a few days we were not each morning to
shoulder our load, nor were we to build corduroy roads, pull
wagons out of the mud, or wade swamps and rivers. We
would have a short vacation, then what?

We had finished a sixty-six day march that covered five
hundred miles, fought two quite severe battles, and accomplished what we set out to do. We gave the State of South
Carolina, especially, and North Carolina, in part, a taste of
warfare, and had placed them in such condition they could
do nothing more to help the cause of the Confederacy. But
the miles traveled and battles fought counted for little in the
balance sheet of energy expended; it was the rains and the
floods, and the swamps and the rivers, and the roads that
counted big. None but those who took part in this campaign
through the Carolinas and who endured the hardships of the
march can measure the effort made.

We had a good camping ground assigned us which we laid
out in the usual way, pitched our tents so as to make a
company street; then there was a great cry for soap. That
night I did not think we would be taken for colored men.

CHAPTER EIGHT

The Last Campaign

March 24th-June 8th, 1865

In continuing my record of the Carolina Campaign, I will write very briefly of our experience in this last movement of Sherman's Army. The march from Goldsboro on to Raleigh was really a continuation of the campaign that started from Savannah on January 17th and had been temporarily halted March 24th to give the men a rest and to secure needed supplies if we were to continue the march.

We remained in camp at Scottsville seventeen days, and during that time had a good rest. The weather was warm and pleasant. We had a fine camping ground but spent no time working on it, other than put up our tents and ditch them. It was understood that as soon as we received our clothing and supplies the Army would be on the move. Almost every one of our Company had to have a blouse, pants, and shoes. After we had new clothing, had cast off the bespattered rags, and donned the new uniforms we looked like different men. Our outfit then compared with that of the troops we met at Cox's Bridge.

Orders were received on April 9th to make all preparations to start on the 10th. During the time we were in Goldsboro all our mail that had accumulated for more than three
months was delivered and a good share of our time was
taken reading and answering letters. I wrote home that we
would soon be off again but hoped not for another sixty day
march. It was even more than that for it was seventy days and
ended in Washington. Earlier than four in the morning of
the 10th all was stirring in the camp. Tents were taken down,
knapsacks packed, breakfast eaten, and at five o'clock all
were ready to fall-in. Then the Regiment was formed and at
five-thirty the "Forward" was sounded. The 1st Brigade of
the 1st Division led the Corps and our Regiment led the
brigade. We passed through Goldsboro, and headed west.
About nine o'clock, after we had gone about six miles, we
heard firing ahead of us. A halt was made and soon the small
advance escort that preceded our column came galloping
back with the information that a large body of the enemy's
Cavalry was in our front and they refused to depart as usual
after our men were sighted. After a few shots were fired,
finding themselves outnumbered they returned for infantry
help. Our Regiment being in the lead was ordered forward
to brush them away. We advanced to the front about a half
mile where the enemy was sighted. They had lined up back
of a cleared field a half mile from us. Our Company D and
Company K were deployed as skirmishers, and at once went
forward with the Johnnies firing at us. As there was no halt
on our part they began to fall back, keeping about gun-shot
away. When we had driven them some two miles we halted
and the whole Regiment was deployed as skirmishers, with
the 141st New York in our rear as support. Then the whole
line was ordered forward, the firing became sharp with the
retiring enemy firing briskly.

By noon the air had become hot and sultry, and while we
had several early April showers that had somewhat cooled us
off, we had advanced so fast, almost on a run, we were wet
not only from the rain but from the violent exercise. We

were carrying all our equipment and baggage which was load enough when we were marching on good roads; but when we were running through fields, through forests, and climbing rail fences, the heat was almost unbearable. A few of our men were so overheated they had to go to the rear.

We continued to push the enemy back until one in the afternoon when we came to one of those detestable swamps. This one was the border of Moccasin Creek, which we found later had two channels, both of which were bridged. The Johnnies had hurriedly crossed and removed most of the planking; then waited for our advance. We found the swamp covered with water, but our officers, thinking it might be shallow enough to ford, ordered us to cross. A hundred yards from the edge the water was up to my belt and we had to halt as the first branch of the creek was just ahead and too deep to ford. We were ordered back and a few planks were found and hurriedly put over the bridge timbers that the Johnnies had left in place. We went over single file; deployed again in the swamp and advanced with the water above our knees and very cold. Again it became deeper and soon we saw the unexpected second channel and halted. The enemy in the meantime kept firing away, but they could not see us so the singing bullets went over our heads. One of our batteries began to shell them on the far side of the swamp and after an hour they fell back from the earthwork they had built. The second bridge was soon repaired and we were out again on dry ground, again deployed as skirmishers. Wet and dripping, we followed the retreating enemy who though falling back continued a musketry firing that was harmless since they were so far away. When we had advanced something more than a mile we halted. It was getting dark and we camped in a pine grove.

While our day's skirmishing had been more exciting and exhausting than it was dangerous, there had been some loss. In our Regiment one was killed[1] and four were wounded.

---

[1] William H. Toohey, Private, Company K.

We saw two of the enemy dead and at a house beyond the swamp they left eight of their wounded. A few Johnnies were captured. They belonged in either the 1st South Carolina or 6th North Carolina Regiments; both these Cavalry commands were in our front that day. I have written at some length about this little fight for the reason that it was the last time our Regiment met Southern troops as enemies. The young man killed that day was probably the last infantry soldier of Sherman's Army to give up his life in battle. It was sad and pathetic that this young soldier who had been in all the campaigns of the 123rd New York Infantry had escaped all harm until the war was really over. General Lee had surrendered his Army at Appomattox the day before our skirmish at Moccasin Creek.

The morning of the 11th, we continued our march, now in the rear of the Division. There was no opposition by the enemy so we made a good distance and camped early in the evening a short distance from Smithfield.

The morning of the 12th of April 1865 proved to be a time that would never be forgotten by us. We were out early, soon after breakfast had been eaten, and we were waiting orders to fall in; a courier riding in great haste came and left orders at the Headquarters of every Regiment. Then the Regiments were ordered into line; as our Division was camped in an open field it looked as though we were forming a line of battle to make ready for an advance. After the formation was completed Colonel Rogers rode to the center, remained sitting on his horse and then taking a paper in his hand read loudly so all could hear a short order from General Sherman. It announced that on April 9th General Lee had surrendered the Army of Northern Virginia to General Grant at Appomattox Court House.

It would be impossible for me to describe the scene that followed. The men went wild, ranks were broken, and shouting and crying, the men in their joy hugged and kissed each other. Never have I witnessed such happiness. The news seemed too good to be true. We felt that the great hour that for three years we had looked for, fought for and prayed for, had come. We could see the end for a certainty, as we knew that after the surrender of General Lee there could be no effective opposition by General Johnston. The shouting did not cease until we had to stop from sheer exhaustion. Then we reformed and took up the march. A happier one was never made by the 123rd New York Infantry than the one on April 12th as we hastened on toward Raleigh.

Early on the 13th, we reached Raleigh, capital of North Carolina. There was no opposition made by the enemy. The city as we found it was not large, but it was a fine town with outstanding buildings and churches. It showed none of the effects of war as most of the southern towns we had passed enroute for the reason that Raleigh had been far removed from any zone of strife. After we went through the town we made our camp near the State Lunatic Asylum. It was filled with demented people who rejoiced to see us, thinking that we would let them out. They filled the windows shouting for us to set them free. One of the inmates made a great plea, saying he was sane and had been placed in the asylum by the secessionists because he was a Union man. Our officers who looked into the matter found he was one of the most violent inmates in the institution. We left him there but he did make a good plea.

As negotiations were going on with General Johnston for the surrender of his Army, we were held at Raleigh until they could be completed. While waiting we had little to do but rest. On April 22nd we were reviewed by General Sherman after we had marched through the streets of Raleigh. April 25th, negotiations having come to a halt because of some misunderstanding, the Army was ordered forward to compel by force what had failed by peaceful methods. At seven in the morning we marched and at night halted near the town of Hillsboro, which was not far from Johnston's Army which was in entrenchments. We remained here until April 28th, during which time Johnston surrendered. Then we started on our return to Raleigh.

When we were halfway there, we were halted so another announcement could be made. This told us of the assassination of President Lincoln. The sorrow of our men was as great as had been their joy when we heard of the surrender of General Lee. President Lincoln was the idol of the men in the service, everyone reverenced him and they could not have felt greater grief had they heard of the death of some near relative. The remainder of the march to Raleigh was made in almost complete silence. When remarks were made they were curses against the murderers of the President.

It was days before the Army recovered from the sorrow it felt at the death of Lincoln but time rolled on and then came the word that we were soon to begin our Homeward March. We remained in Raleigh until April 30th, only two days but they were busy days, as during that time all preparations had to be made for the march on to Washington. As no transportation could be had, the long journey was to be made on foot. This was no hardship to us who had already marched so many miles in the face of the enemy. Now home was in sight, a march of only three hundred miles through a peaceful land would be just a pleasure trip.

April 30th, 1865, we began the "Homeward March" from Raleigh, N.C. the last, and to me, I can truly say, the happiest made by Sherman's Army. It was to differ greatly from any made by us that preceded it. As in our other marches we were to carry our usual load of goods and equipment but our cartridge boxes were emptied of all but five cartridges. We were to go through the country from Raleigh to Washington in an orderly manner, no straggling would be allowed; there were to be no foragers to gather food from the area through which we passed and no destruction of property of any kind would be permitted.

Every consideration was to be given to the people we met on our line of march who were to be no longer regarded as enemies but as friends. It was to be, indeed, a peaceful march through a peaceful country. All were cautioned to conduct themselves in as friendly a way as though they were march-

ing through Pennsylvania or New York. The usual army
ration was to be issued us; food other than that, when needed, was to be paid for when acquired. Everything connected
with the Army, as when on a war basis, was to accompany us.
Our trains, our ambulances, our pontoons, our artillery were
all to go with us. Happily on this march not many guards
were required to protect the property. We were to take the
most direct route, first to Richmond and from there to Washington.

Our march to Richmond was made in eleven days. Some
days we went as far as twenty miles; on others, when we were
delayed by bad roads or had to lay our pontoons across
rivers, not more than ten miles. The bridges over many
streams had been destroyed during the war. It seemed to be
a land of rivers. I noted in my diary that May 1st we crossed
the Tar River; May 2nd, Flat Creek; May 3rd, Roanoke; May
4th, Meherrin; May 5th, Nottoway; May 6th, Little Nottoway; May 7th, Appomattox; and May 11th, the James River.
A river was crossed nearly every day until we reached Richmond.

The country from Raleigh to Richmond did not appeal
strongly to us northern people. It was mostly wooded, and
where farms were cultivated, they did not look prosperous.
Nearly all buildings were poor and ill-kept. On the way to
Richmond we saw many ex-Confederates who had returned
to their homes; and they were at work in their fields, plowing
and preparing for spring planting. We could honestly con-
fess and acknowledge to them, and to ourselves, that we
would much rather meet them under these peaceful conditions than face them in the line of battle. Upon reaching
Manchester, on the south side of the James River opposite
Richmond, we found a division of Union troops lined up to
receive us. We braced up, got into step, and made as good a
showing as we could when we passed them. At Richmond we
paraded through the principal streets, past Libby Prison and
the Capitol Building on the hill. On the 11th we camped
north of the city.

Three days later we reached Spotsylvania and there the
column halted for a time to allow the men to visit the famous
battlefield. I went to the Bloody Angle where just a year
before the fierce engagement had taken place. Hardly anything had apparently been changed or disturbed. The dou-
blefaced entrenchments that had been occupied on one side
by Union troops and six feet away on the other side by the
Confederates still stood as at the time of the battle. I saw the
famous tree that had been shot down by bullets fired in the
action. It lay lengthwise of the trench on the Confederate
side. The tree had been not more than ten feet from the
Union line; it was nearly eighteen inches in diameter and was
cut down by Minié bullets.[2] Around the foot of the tree were
many chips, and I placed several in my knapsack. On the
south side of the trench the Confederate dead had been
given scant burial; as many as one hundred skeletons were
counted in a distance of not more than two hundred feet. On
the northern side the dead were buried behind and facing
the trench. There were very many graves, each marked with
a wooden headboard. On many parts of the field the dead
had not been buried; and as we looked over the ground
where the charges had been made by our forces, we saw
many places where there were growths of grass in the almost
barren field. They marked the remains of Union soldiers,
only a skeleton, encased in a mouldy uniform of blue with
rusty gun and equipment at the side. It was a gruesome sight
and made us all the more thankful that the war was at last
ended. That night our column camped on Brook Road, a
memorable place in the Great Wilderness Battle.

About noon, May 15th, we reached Chancellorsville. The
column halted for three hours to give the 20th Corps men a
chance to visit the battlefield where two years before they
fought and suffered so severely. I was glad to see the field

[2] The cylindro-conoidal Minié bullet normally fired from the muzzle-loading
rifles commonly used by both armies.

again, which to me had been a place of trial, and to renew my
acquaintance with its familiar surroundings. But what a contrast it presented to what was there two years before. Then it
was the scene of fiercest battle, the air filled with smoke, with
shrieking, bursting shells and hissing Miniés that were bringing wounds and death to thousands. But now what a change!
Everything was quiet and peaceful. The day was bright and
beautiful, with no powder fumes filling the air. Almost the
only sound, other than our excited words, was the singing of
the birds, perhaps a requiem to the dead, who in thousands
all around us lay in unmarked and many in unmade graves.
In the natural surroundings there seemed to be little change
since two years ago. The low hill with our earthworks where
our batteries had stood during the battle looked very natural to me. Back of where our guns had stood during the
action was still the old graveyard with its whitewashed fence,
now showing signs of neglect for it did not look so white.
The Chancellor House had evidently not been touched since
it was burned on that memorable 3rd of May 1863.

We marched to the place we had formed our line that fatal
morning where many laid down their lives. There was little
change there. The trees we had cut and felled in our front as
protection still lay as they had fallen, but were now dead and
leafless. I could locate the exact spot in our line where I had
been wounded and the place by the little run in the rear
where I had been carried. I went to the old log house around
which hundreds of us wounded had been gathered after the
retreat of our Army. I lived over again in my memory the
awful eleven days spent there where such suffering was
endured. I felt a great sense of gratitude to God that I had
not only survived my wounds at Chancellorsville but during
the two years of active service since that time I had escaped
unscathed, and rejoiced that I was alive and homeward
bound. After three hours on the battlefield we resumed our
march and camped about two miles from the Chancellor
House on the road leading to United States Ford.

On May 16th we crossed the Rappahannock at the Ford and marched toward Aquia Creek and Dumfries. On the 18th we crossed Bull Run near the old battleground and camped near Fairfax. On the 19th, the last day of our journey, we reached Alexandria, and passed on toward Washington and camped that night within a mile of our old Arlington Heights Camp where we received our first training of September 1862.

When we halted on the Heights with Washington almost at our feet, we knew that our Homeward March was not only finished but that, except for the coming Grand Review, our marching days were over. I know a sigh of relief and feeling of satisfaction came to all our boys. The work they had started out to do was done, the Rebellion over and the Union saved. The men of our Regiment who had survived had completed a circuit through an enemy's country and were back again to the spot from whence they started. What had we not experienced in that record-making time. When we marched away from Arlington, raw recruits, in 1862, hardly an inroad had been made by our armies into the Confederate States. Now, upon our return, every part of the South had been recovered by our forces. In accomplishing this work, without reflecting on the campaigns of other Armies, all of whom did their share, it may be said that no Army conquered more territory, suffered greater hardships, fought harder battles, or marched more miles, than the Army of General Sherman that looked down on Washington from Arlington Heights.

Our war service was to end with the Grand Review in Washington May 24th. When we reached Arlington after our long march from Raleigh we were very weary, but we were so well satisfied with what we had done and there were such bright prospects ahead of us that we gave little heed to any feeling of fatigue. We knew then that to us an end of future marches had come; that our weary shoulders would no longer be burdened by our heavy knapsacks, our guns would be racked, and we would be freed from the routine of military life. Hardly any of us were soldiers from choice. We did not like the discipline required by the duties called for by military action. For three long years we had been in the Army from a sense of obligation to our country; now the war was over we longed to return to civil life. Certainly we had reason to rejoice that our lives had been spared and we had been able to endure the hardships and privations of the service to the end.

We remained at Arlington until May 23rd and during the time had nothing to do but prepare for the Grand Review. We had only our old uniforms that had lasted through our long marches so we could not hope to make a dress parade, but we brushed and cleaned them, burnished our buttons, blackened our old worn shoes as much as we could, for they were the color of the mud through which we had tramped. We cleaned our muskets until they shone. Our guns, which were our pride, could not have looked better.

No one slept the night of the 23rd. We were to break camp at midnight and everything was to be packed and carried as we were not to return to Arlington. We took great pains in packing our knapsacks to make them look as uniform as possible, so they would not disfigure us as we paraded. At midnight we had our breakfast as there would be no opportunity after we started to prepare a meal.

About two in the morning we were called into line and soon after, our Division leading the Corps, our Brigade leading the Division, and our own Regiment leading the Brigade, started slowly on the march to Washington. We had been camped some three miles from the Long Bridge spanning the Potomac River. There were many halts as the whole Corps behind us was forming for the parade and we were not to cross the bridge until every organization was in its proper place. It was nearly daybreak when we reached and crossed the Long Bridge for the last time. How much shorter our regimental line was than it had been on September 29th, 1862 when we crossed on our way to Harpers Ferry to join and become a part of the old 12th Corps. At that time there were a thousand men in line, now only a scant four hundred. The dead from disease and those killed in action, the wounded and incapacitated told the story of the missing six hundred. It was only the remnant left that crossed the bridge to take part in the Review.

A description of the Review cannot be made by me. I was only a participant and able to see only a small part of the Army that followed us. I know that we leading the 20th Corps were given great applause by the hundreds of thousands of spectators who lined the streets of Washington for miles. We marched in company front the whole distance and I am sure our marching was good. There were thousands of soldiers of the Army of the Potomac who had marched the day before on the streets; they shouted themselves hoarse in welcoming our return, as the old 12th Corps of which we had been a part before going west had for two years been with them in the great campaigns of the Army of the Potomac. It was a proud day for all of us, and the Review was a fitting ending of our long service.

At the conclusion of the Review, we were marched to the north of the city, just outside of the fortified line, there to camp until we were discharged and transportation and service papers prepared for us to return home. We were in this camp until June 8th 1865, and that day received our discharges. Within a few days we were taken by rail to Albany, New York, and there encamped in the fields about two miles north of the city.

We marched to the little hillside where we were to make our last camp; where we halted we came to a front, then the order "stack arms" was given. Our guns, that we had carried for so many miles in attack and defense and by most of the boys so carefully handled and so lovingly regarded, were stacked for the last time. Their deadly work in our hands was over, they were ready for the ordnance to take them over.

Within a week all matters pertaining to our discharge and pay had been settled, our camp was to be broken up, and we were at liberty to return to our homes, there to take up the active duties of civil life, that would of necessity come to us all. Looking back now[3] I realize, far more than I did then, how unprepared we were to meet the life conditions that faced us, not alone from wounds or broken health but from the greater reason that our long absence during the years of life when we would have fitted ourselves by education and experience for a successful effort were years gone. Many faced the future with the handicap of physical weakness, ignorance and lost opportunities.

I shall never forget the last meeting our Company had before we separated to go home. Our tents had been taken down, our knapsacks packed, and we were breaking camp for the last time. When we were finished, our greatly respected and much loved Company Commander, Captain Anderson, gave his last "fall in" command to his men. Without arms or equipment and some in civilian clothes that had replaced their faded uniforms we formed in line. The Captain in a broken voice, for he could not control his emotions, bid us farewell and Godspeed. When he had finished, we men crowded about him to shake his hand and each others.

Surely we all rejoiced that the end had come, that victory was ours and that home was near. But there was after all a sadness deep down in our hearts in this parting hour. We boys had been together for three years; we had formed close friendships; we had slept under the same blanket; we had faced the enemy shoulder to shoulder on the firing line; we had marched side by side; we had borne danger, hardship, and privation alike; thus a comradeship had grown as only such conditions could form. So it was hard to separate and say goodby, one with the other; but we shook hands all around, and laughed and seemed to make merry, while our hearts were heavy and our eyes ready to shed tears.

[3] Written in 1913.

BIBLIOGRAPHY

Note. This listing is not intended to be a guide to additional reading upon the campaigns in which Sergeant Bull served but as an indication of the works consulted in preparing the annotation.

A Record of the Commissioned Officers, Non-Commissioned Officers and Privates of the Regiments Which Were Organized in the State of New York. 8 vols. Albany: Weed, Parsons & Co., 1865-66.

Bartlett, A. W. *History of the Twelfth Regiment New Hampshire Volunteers In The War of the Rebellion.* Concord: Ira C. Evans, 1897.

Boatner, Mark Mayo, III. *The Civil War Dictionary.* New York: David McKay Co., Inc., 1959.

Bowen, James L. *History of the Twenty-seventh Regiment, Massachusetts Volunteers, in the Civil War of 1861-1865.* Holyoke: 1884.

Cox, Jacob D. *Atlanta.* New York: Thomas Yoseloff, 1963.

————. *The March to the Sea - Franklin and Nashville.* New York: Thomas Yoseloff, 1963.

Dictionary of American Biography. 20 vols. New York: Charles Scribner's Sons, 1928-1936.

Dyer, Frederick H. *A Compendium of the War of the Rebellion.* 3 vols. New York: Thomas Yoseloff, 1959.

Glazier, Willard Worcester. *The Capture, The Prison-Pen, and The Escape.* New York: R. H. Ferguson & Co., 1870.

Heitman, Francis B. *Historical Register and Dictionary of the United States Army.* 2 vols. Washington: Government Printing Office, 1903.

History and Biography of Washington County and the Town of Queensbury, N.Y. Richmond, Ind.: Gresham Publishing Co., 1894.

[Johnson, Crisfield]. *History of Washington County, New York.* Philadelphia: Everts & Ensign, 1871.

Johnson, Robert U., and Clarence C. Buel. *Battles and Leaders of the Civil War.* 4 vols. New York: The Century Co., 1888.

Leech, Margaret. *Reveille in Washington, 1860-1865.* New York: Harper & Bros., 1941.

Morhous, Henry C. *Reminiscences of the 123d Regiment, N.Y.S.V., Giving a Complete History of Its Three Years Service in the War.* Greenwich: People's Journal Book and Job Office, 1879.

Phisterer, Frederick. *New York in the War of the Rebellion, 1861-1865.* 6 vols. Albany: J. B. Lyon Co., 1912.

———. *Statistical Record of the Armies of the United States.* New York: Thomas Yoseloff, 1963.

Scott, Henry L. *Military Dictionary.* New York: D. Van Nostrand Co., 1862.

Sherman, William T. *Memoirs of General William T. Sherman.* 2 vols. New York: D. Appleton & Co., 1875.

Stone, William L. (Ed.) *Washington County New York: Its History to the Close of the Nineteenth Century.* New York: New York History Co., 1901.

War of the Rebellion. A Compilation of the Official Records of the Union and Confederate Armies. 128 vols. Washington: Government Printing Office, 1880-1901.

INDEX

Black River, N.C., 227, 229
Blackville, S.C., 209
Blair, Maj. Gen. Frank P., 99n
Blanchard, Mr., 58, 63
Blanchard, Pvt. Edward, 141
Bolivar Heights, Va., 21-22
Bridgeport, Ala., 95, 97, 99
Bridges, Pontoon, 39, 40, 84, 108, 113,
    143-44, 202, 212-13, 215, 220, 223,
    225, 243; Temporary, 40, 115, 144-
    45, 190, 192, 205-6, 208, 222
Brigades: 1st, 1st Div., VI Corps, 56n;
    2nd, 1st Div., XII Corps, 21n; 1st,
    1st Div., XX Corps, 104, 119, 126,
    145-46, 165-66, 171, 190, 195, 198,
    202, 205, 209-11, 216-18, 221, 226-
    27, 238, 247; 2nd, 1st. Div., XX
    Corps, 105-6, 190, 195, 198; 3rd,
    1st Div., XX Corps, 105, 150, 230;
    Jersey, 56
Broad River, S.C., 212-13
Brough, Gov. John, 93
Brown, Col. Henry W., 56n
Buffalo, N.Y., 100
Buffalo Creek, Ga., 190
Bull, Sgt. Rice C.: reasons for enlist-
    ment, 1; enlistment, 3-4; elected
    corporal, 4; wounded, 57-58; pris-
    oner, 60-83; befriended by Con-
    federate soldier, 68-70, 72-73, 77-
    78, 82-83; leave, 87, 89; return to
    unit, 89-95; meets Confederate
    friend again, 97-98; recruiting duty,
    100; Atlanta Campaign, 101-71;
    March to the Sea, 173-99; in the
    Carolinas, 203-41; march to Wash-
    ington, 242-48; discharged, 248-49
Bull Run, Va., 20n, 42n, 98n, 246
Bummers, see Foraging
Burials, 20, 22, 47, 149, 152
Burk's plantation, 184
Burnside, Maj. Gen. Ambrose E., 27,
    29n, 32
Buschbeck, Col. Adolphus, 116n
Butterfield, Maj. Gen. Daniel, 128n

Camp Chase, D.C., 9-10
Camp Lawton Prison, Ga., 193-94

Candy, Col. Charles, 116n
Cape Fear River, N.C., 225
Carman, Col. Ezra A., 156n
Carolinas, Campaign in, 132n, 203-41
Case, Col. Henry, 217n
Casey, Maj. Gen. Silas, 13, 15
Cassville, Ga., 109, 111-13, 143
Casualties, 47, 66-67, 94, 104n, 106, 119,
    134, 136, 151, 190, 218, 227
Catawba River, S.C., 214-15
Cavalry, Confederate, 40-41, 63, 95,
    190, 205, 209, 238, 240; Union, 39-
    41, 84, 109, 164, 169, 176, 180, 190,
    212, 225-26
Cedar Creek, Va., 66n
Chancellor House, 42, 46, 52-53, 59-61,
    69, 84, 245
Chancellorsville, Va., 42, 62, 70, 82, 84;
    Battle of, 12n, 20n, 39-63, 66-67n,
    70, 86, 89, 90n, 95, 97-98, 152, 193,
    196n, 244-45
Charleston, S.C., 209
Chattahoochee River, Ga., 137, 139,
    143, 150, 163, 165, 170-71
Chattanooga, Tenn., 95, 96n, 97, 99n,
    100, 103, 114, 151n, 171
Cheraw, S.C., 220-21
Chesterfield, S.C., 217
Chickahominy River, Va., 23
Chickamauga, Ga., 95n, 96n, 97, 135n
Christmas, 27-28, 201-2
Cincinnati, Ohio, 93
Cleveland, Ohio, 24, 100
Clothing, issued, 32, 198-99, 237; car-
    ried on march, 112
Coburn, Col. John, 167
Coffee, 11-12, 16, 72, 76-77, 91, 102,
    104, 107, 109, 115, 145, 166, 192,
    223
Cogswell, Col. William, 166, 217n
Colgrove, Col. Silas, 55
Columbia, S.C., 212-13
Columbus, Ohio, 92
Congaree River, S.C., 211-12
Connecticut Regiments, 5th, 49n, 104n,
    145, 147, 159, 166, 217-18, 226;
    20th, 21n
Connolly, Surgeon Richard S., 31